Flexible Exchange Rates
for a Stable World Economy

Joseph E. Gagnon
with Marc Hinterschweiger

PETERSON INSTITUTE FOR INTERNATIONAL ECONOMICS
Washington, DC
September 2011

Joseph E. Gagnon, senior fellow since September 2009, was visiting associate director, Division of Monetary Affairs (2008–09) at the US Federal Reserve Board. Previously he served at the US Federal Reserve Board as associate director, Division of International Finance (1999–2008), and senior economist (1987–97). He has also served at the US Treasury Department (1994–95 and 1997–99) and has taught at the University of California's Haas School of Business (1990–91). He has published numerous articles in economics journals, including the *Journal of International Economics*, the *Journal of Monetary Economics*, the *Quarterly Journal of Economics*, and the *Journal of International Money and Finance*, and has contributed to several edited volumes. He received a BA from Harvard University in 1981 and a PhD in economics from Stanford University in 1987.

Marc Hinterschweiger has been a research analyst with the Peterson Institute since 2008. He is also a PhD candidate in economics at Ludwig-Maximilians University (LMU) in Munich, Germany. His research focuses on the transmission mechanism of monetary policy, asset prices, and financial crises. He previously worked at the Rhenish-Westfalian Institute for Economic Research (RWI) in Essen, Germany. He holds a BA in economics (2005) and a BA in international affairs (2006) from the University of St. Gallen, Switzerland. He earned a master's degree in public policy from Harvard University's Kennedy School of Government (2008), where he was a McCloy scholar, specializing in international trade and finance. He has been a member of the German National Academic Foundation (Studienstiftung des deutschen Volkes) since 2002.

PETER G. PETERSON INSTITUTE FOR INTERNATIONAL ECONOMICS
1750 Massachusetts Avenue, NW
Washington, DC 20036-1903
(202) 328-9000   FAX: (202) 659-3225
www.piie.com

C. Fred Bergsten, *Director*
Edward A. Tureen, *Director of Publications, Marketing, and Web Development*

Graphics typesetted by BMWW
Printing by United Book Press, Inc.
Cover design by Sese-Paul Design
Cover photo: © Adrian Pingstone; B.S.P.I.—Corbis; Danausi; Leigh Thelmadatter; goodstock—Fotolia; and Skyhobo—ISTOCKPHOTO

Printed in the United States of America
13 12 11   5 4 3 2 1

Library of Congress Cataloging-in-Publication Data
Gagnon, Joseph E.
 Flexible exchange rates for a stable world economy / Joseph E. Gagnon; with Marc Hinterschweiger.
    p. cm.
 Includes bibliographical references and index.
 ISBN 978-0-88132-627-7
 1. Foreign exchange rates. 2. Monetary policy. I. Hinterschweiger, Marc. II. Title.
 HG3851.G334 2011
 332.4'562—dc23

                              2011032670

To Paul

❧

To Leah

Contents

Preface

Exchange rate policy is always on the agenda when finance ministers and central bankers meet and the Peterson Institute for International Economics has addressed these issues extensively throughout its 30-year history. In just the past four years, the Institute has published *The Euro at Ten: The Next Global Currency?* edited by Jean Pisani-Ferry and Adam Posen (2009); *The Future of China's Exchange Rate Policy* by Morris Goldstein and Nicholas Lardy (2009); *Debating China's Exchange Rate Policy* edited by Morris Goldstein and Nicholas Lardy (2008); *Accountability and Oversight of US Exchange Rate Policy* by C. Randall Henning (2008); and *Reference Rates and the International Monetary System* by John Williamson (2007).

This book examines the broad parameters of exchange rate policy in light of both theory and real-world experience. What are the costs and benefits of flexible versus fixed rates? How much of a role should the exchange rate play in monetary policy? The focus is on the advanced economies and the leading emerging markets but some attention is devoted to the low-income developing economies as well.

When they are allowed to float freely, exchange rates are much more volatile than would be implied by economic fundamentals. This conclusion will not be surprising to many readers though it remains contested within the halls of academia. But the principal finding of this book is that using monetary policy to fight exchange rate volatility, including through the adoption of a fixed rate regime, leads to greater volatility of employment, output, and inflation. Thus the "cure" for exchange rate volatility is usually worse than the disease. This finding is demonstrated in economic models, in historical case studies and in statistical analysis.

The book devotes considerable attention to understanding why volatile exchange rates do not destabilize inflation and output. The most important factor appears to be that goods and services produced abroad are not very close substitutes for goods and services produced at home. This imperfect substitutability means that exchange rate fluctuations have very little effect on inflation and only a moderate effect on output.

In the advanced economies, currency intervention is widely viewed as a weak policy tool because financial markets are deep and liquid enough to absorb the associated portfolio shifts. In many developing economies however, financial markets are subject to legal and functional restrictions that enhance the potency of foreign exchange intervention. In recent years, a number of developing economies have chosen to use massive intervention to hold down their currencies and generate current account surpluses while deploying tight monetary policy to avoid domestic overheating and inflation. China is the leading example. The accompanying rise in foreign exchange reserves of developing economies is clearly unsustainable and may be the biggest problem in the international monetary system today. This development strategy gives rise to a net drain on aggregate demand in the rest of the world that many economies are finding hard to offset through conventional monetary and fiscal policies. The result has been a woefully subpar economic recovery in Europe, Japan, and the United States. The book concludes with a discussion of new "rules of the game" for foreign exchange intervention to prevent excessive buildups of reserves and to help damp exchange rate fluctuations modestly.

Joseph Gagnon served for 25 years as a researcher and policy advisor at the Federal Reserve Board and the US Treasury Department. He has been a senior fellow with the Institute since September 2009. This book pulls together results from his own research and policy experience as well as from a comprehensive survey of academic research over the past two decades on exchange rates and their effects on the global economy. Marc Hinterschweiger is a research analyst at the Institute and is working on his doctoral dissertation at the Ludwig Maximilians University of Munich.

The Peter G. Peterson Institute for International Economics is a private, nonprofit institution for the study and discussion of international economic policy. Its purpose is to analyze important issues in that area and to develop and communicate practical new approaches for dealing with them. The Institute is completely nonpartisan.

The Institute is funded by a highly diversified group of philanthropic foundations, private corporations, and interested individuals. About 35 percent of the Institute's resources in our latest fiscal year was provided by contributors outside the United States.

The Institute's Board of Directors bears overall responsibilities for the Institute and gives general guidance and approval to its research program, including the identification of topics that are likely to become important over the medium run (one to three years) and that should be addressed by the Institute. The director, working closely with the staff and outside Advisory

Committee, is responsible for the development of particular projects and makes the final decision to publish an individual study.

The Institute hopes that its studies and other activities will contribute to building a stronger foundation for international economic policy around the world. We invite readers of these publications to let us know how they think we can best accomplish this objective.

C. FRED BERGSTEN
Director
August 2011

Acknowledgments

This book began as an exploration of a puzzle that was attracting attention among economists and policymakers: Many countries had conquered inflation and yet exchange rates continued to be highly volatile. Most economists and policymakers had believed that price stability and exchange rate stability were closely linked.

My own research on the low pass-through of exchange rates into import prices and consumer prices formed the initial basis for the book. But I felt compelled to expand my work to tackle the issues of what drives exchange rate volatility, what effects exchange rates have on real economic activity, how these results differ between advanced and developing economies, and what all these results imply for economic policy. I realized that other research of mine had a direct bearing on some of these questions. I also realized that there was an opening for a book that would put all these pieces together and that would survey the relevant literature since the early 1990s.

The book is designed to be accessible to readers with different backgrounds and interests. For the busy policymaker, an overview of the book's findings is contained in chapter 1, and each chapter starts with a short summary. The main body of each chapter develops the book's thesis while keeping technical jargon and mathematics to a minimum. It is assumed that the reader has taken an introductory course in economics, but a specialized degree is not required. For those who have the technical background and who want to dig deeper into the academic literature, the boxes and appendices provide detailed surveys.

I have benefited enormously from the advice and support of the following professional colleagues, here at the Institute and at the Federal Reserve, the Treasury, and academia: Anders Åslund, Fred Bergsten, Menzie Chinn, William Cline, Mac Destler, Etienne Gagnon, Morris Goldstein, Joseph Gruber, Jane

Haltmaier, Randall Henning, Gary Hufbauer, Olivier Jeanne, Karen Johnson, Steven Kamin, Mohsin Khan, Jacob Kirkegaard, Michael Klein, Jaewoo Lee, Michael Lind, Catherine Mann, Michael Mussa, Yasuo Noda, Adam Posen, Michael Prell, Carmen Reinhart, Andrew Rose, Howard Rosen, Bradley Setser, Mark Sobel, Arvind Subramanian, Edwin Truman, Angel Ubide, Nicolas Veron, Robert Vigfusson, Steven Weisman, and John Williamson. I thank Jonathan Ostry, Atish Ghosh, and Charalambos Tsangarides for sharing their data on historical exchange rate regimes.

The Institute's publications staff has done everything in their power to smooth the process and to ensure a high-quality product. I thank, in particular, Madona Devasahayam, Susann Luetjen, and Edward Tureen.

Most importantly, I thank my research analyst and coauthor, Marc Hinterschweiger, for his incredible proficiency with all the figures, simulations, and statistics, as well as his considerable input in the drafting of the text.

JOSEPH E. GAGNON
August 2011

1

Introduction and Overview

When I was young I thought that money was the most important thing in life.
Now that I am old, I know it is.

—Oscar Wilde

More and more of the world's currencies have floated freely against each other since the early 1970s. In the 1950s and 1960s most currency values were held fixed with only rare realignments. This era of floating exchange rates has been marked by high volatility and large swings in currency values. For example, the US dollar was worth 84 Japanese yen in April 1995, 145 yen in August 1998, and 103 yen in December 1999.

These large swings have caught the attention of economists, politicians, and civil servants. For example, both French President Nicolas Sarkozy[1] and Nobel Prize–winning economist Robert Mundell (2011) recently called for a return to fixed exchange rates. And, in January 2011, an informal group of former finance ministers, central bank governors, and other high-level policymakers declared that governments had to address volatile exchange rates and the global trade imbalances caused in part by "large, lasting swings in currency values" in order to improve the international monetary system (Palais-Royal Initiative 2011). Manufacturers in countries with strong currencies have regularly denounced their loss of global competitiveness, which they consider a result of unfair and opaque currency manipulations by foreigners. Tourists from countries with weak currencies bemoan the expense of foreign travel. And everyone who exports, imports, and invests across borders faces tremendous uncertainty about future revenues, expenses, and returns. Is the current system (or nonsystem, as some consider it) the best way to manage the world's major currencies?

---

1. See "The Euro Decade and Its Lessons," *Wall Street Journal*, January 2, 2009. Sarkozy later backed away from his call for fixed exchange rates, saying only that he wanted to "avoid excessive volatility of currencies" (Angela Doland, "Sarkozy Looks to Limit Exchange Rate Swings," Associated Press, August 25, 2010).

Figure 1.1   Euro-dollar exchange rate

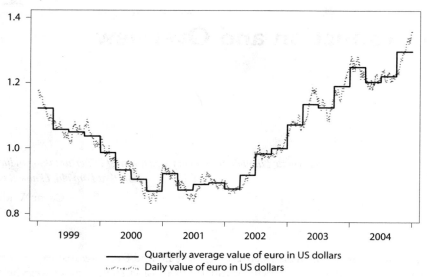

dollars per euro

Quarterly average value of euro in US dollars

Daily value of euro in US dollars

Sources: Datastream.

This book argues that a return to fixed or tightly managed exchange rates would not serve the best interests of households or businesses or governments. Instead, a return to fixed exchange rates would reverse the progress made during the past 25 years toward more stable inflation and economic output in many countries and might lead to more frequent financial crises. This is true for the major economies of the euro area, Japan, and the United States, and also for many smaller economies, including many that are relatively open to international trade and investment. However, floating rates may not be advantageous for (1) countries that seek deep political and economic integration with their neighbors and (2) very small and/or poor countries that lack the institutional resources to prudently manage an independent monetary policy; for these countries, an exchange rate firmly anchored to the currency of a major trading partner (or a currency union) may be more appropriate. Even so, some very small and very poor countries have had good economic outcomes over the past decade with floating exchange rates.

Exchange Rate Volatility Does Not Impede Steady Growth with Low Inflation

Figure 1.1 shows the impressive volatility of the euro-dollar exchange rate between 1999 and 2004. On a quarterly-average basis, the euro depreciated against the dollar by about 25 percent from the beginning of 1999 through

Figure 1.2   Real GDP in the euro area and the United States

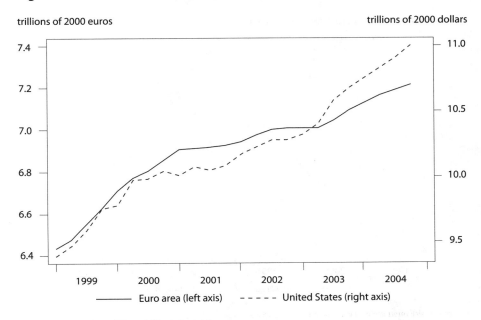

trillions of 2000 euros   trillions of 2000 dollars

Euro area (left axis)   – – – – United States (right axis)

Source: IMF *International Financial Statistics* database.

the end of 2000, remained roughly steady through the first part of 2002, and then appreciated by more than 45 percent by the end of 2004. During the latter period, as the euro appreciated sharply, the euro-area economy grew by 15 percent and the US economy grew by 19 percent, when each economy is measured in terms of its own currency. When measured in terms of euros, however, the US economy shrank by 18 percent, and when measured in terms of dollars, the euro-area economy grew by 67 percent! This represents an enormous swing in the relative market value of economic output in these two economies. However, this swing in market valuation does not correspond to actual trends in the quantity of goods and services produced, and thereby profoundly challenges our understanding of the world economy.

The best measure of an economy's actual output of goods and services is real gross domestic product (GDP).[2] Figure 1.2 shows that real GDP in the euro area and the United States grew reasonably steadily during 1999–2004, the period of high exchange rate volatility. Both economies suffered a mild

---

2. Economists use the term real GDP to refer to the quantity of goods and services—that is, the number of cars and haircuts purchased. In order to add together cars, haircuts, etc., real GDP is expressed in terms of the prices that prevailed in a given base year. In figure 1.2, that base year is 2000 and so the lines show the total volume of economic output at each point in time valued at the prices that existed in 2000. In contrast, economists use the term nominal GDP to refer to the value of goods and services in terms of each year's prices.

Figure 1.3   Inflation rates in the euro area and the United States

four-quarter changes of GDP deflator (percent)

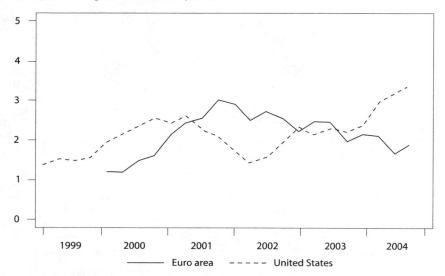

Source: IMF *International Financial Statistics* database.

slowdown in 2001, followed by a gradual recovery. The exchange rate fluctuations played no role in causing the shared slowdown; in fact, if the exchange rate had played a role, it would have had opposing effects, with growth accelerating in one economy and slowing in the other. The slowdown started earlier and ended earlier in the United States. It is possible that the relative lag in US growth during 2001 and 2002 was caused in part by dollar appreciation during 1999 and 2000, and that the relative surge in US growth that started in 2003 may have been related to the dollar depreciation that began in 2002. But the ratio between euro-area GDP and US GDP stayed within a range of 3 percentage points, many times smaller than the swing in the exchange rate. (Note that the scale of figure 1.2 is magnified relative to that of figure 1.1.)

The exchange rate fluctuations also do not appear to have influenced inflation rates in the two economies. Figure 1.3 shows that the average inflation rate during this period was close to 2 percent in both economies and that differences in their inflation rates never exceeded about 1 percentage point. US inflation rose somewhat in 2004, but it peaked at about 3 percent and remained there during 2005 (not shown). Both economies exhibited very low and stable rates of inflation in a global and historical context.

Overview of this Book

This book addresses the following questions:

- What causes large changes in currency values?
- Should globalization have prevented such large swings in the relative market values of the output of major economies?
- Does currency volatility make economic growth and inflation less stable? Why, or why not?
- Does exchange rate volatility have important long-run economic implications?
- What harm, if any, may be caused by stabilizing the value of one currency in terms of another?
- What is the best policy response to currency volatility? What would be the benefits and costs of returning to a system of fixed exchange rates or adopting a common global currency?

Chapter 2 explores the origins of national currencies and describes the various regimes for managing exchange rates, which lie along a spectrum from firmly fixed to freely floating. It examines the advantages and disadvantages of fixed versus floating exchange rates in terms of the ultimate objectives of economic policy. A fixed exchange rate reduces transaction costs in international business and also reduces uncertainty about the future value of the exchange rate, which may increase international trade, investment, and output in the long run. A floating exchange rate allows the central bank to better stabilize inflation and economic output, but only when there is a sound framework for monetary policy. Stabilizing inflation and output reduces two important elements of economic uncertainty, which may lead to higher long-run output.

Chapter 3 discusses the standard economic model linking exchange rates with financial markets and international trade. This model shows that, in the long run, exchange rates tend to equalize the prices of goods and services across economies, while in the short run, they respond to differences in interest rates across economies. However, the model fails to explain why floating exchange rates are so volatile. The excess volatility arises from financial-market behavior that is not well understood and may be harmful.

Chapter 4 shows that exchange rate regimes have little effect on countries' long-run economic growth or output. Currency stability does appear to boost international trade, although other factors are more important.

Chapter 5 shows that large fluctuations in a country's exchange rate do not necessarily lead to large swings in its inflation or growth rates, including for relatively small open economies. In particular, there is no close link between currency depreciation and inflation, despite widespread popular opinion to the contrary. Floating exchange rate regimes are associated with more stable rates of economic growth. The Great Recession of 2009 was caused by factors that had little to do with exchange rate regimes and struck economies with both fixed and floating exchange rates. The chapter explores the features of economic policy, international trade, and consumer markets that can insulate national economies from the negative effects of currency volatility. The most important policy feature is that the central bank must be willing and able to stabilize inflation and output. The most important economic features are that goods and services produced in different countries are not close substitutes and that consumers have a preference for goods and services produced at home. Trade barriers and the costs of trade are also important.

Chapter 6 uses a new mathematical model to confirm the standard textbook argument that monetary policy can stabilize an economy better under a floating exchange rate than under a fixed exchange rate. Chapter 6 also explores historical episodes in which policymakers responded well or poorly to currency volatility. Policymakers who focused on stabilizing the exchange rate often ended up destabilizing their economies, whereas policymakers who focused on stabilizing inflation and economic output often had to tolerate large swings in the exchange rate.

Chapter 7 briefly discusses fiscal policy. Monetary policy has proven to be better suited than fiscal policy for stabilizing inflation and output. In most circumstances, fiscal policy should not be used for stabilization except for automatic stabilizers such as progressive tax rates and unemployment benefits. Unsustainably high fiscal deficits eventually lead to fiscal crises, which are more abrupt in economies with firmly fixed exchange rates, including those within a currency union.

Chapter 8 examines the unique features of developing economies that mitigate some of the costs of a fixed exchange rate. Many developing economies have a history of weak institutions and governance. In these economies, a fixed exchange rate may deliver more stable inflation and output than a floating rate, and a fixed exchange rate regime may provide a natural transition toward improving the quality and credibility of policymaking institutions. However, the chapter points out some successful examples of floating exchange rate regimes among even the smallest and least developed economies. Many developing economies have either innate or policy-based barriers to private capital flows that enable the central bank to pursue stabilization of the exchange rate as well as inflation and output. But there are limits to this policy freedom, and policymakers are likely to find these limits ever more binding as their economies become more advanced and sophisticated. Attempts by policymakers in many developing economies to keep their currencies undervalued generated a flood of capital into the advanced economies, which increased the severity of the global financial crisis of 2008; these policies appear to have resumed in 2010 and 2011. Finally, fixed exchange rate regimes in developing economies are associated with a greater risk of financial crisis.

Chapter 9 draws a series of policy conclusions. The main conclusion is that a floating exchange rate regime is preferable, except for countries that seek deep economic and political integration with their neighbors or that do not have the institutional capacity to conduct stable monetary policy. The chapter ends with a speculative discussion on how central banks may be able to damp exchange rate volatility to a modest degree without giving up either the stabilization of inflation and output or the mobility of private capital.

This book makes a number of original contributions to the theory and data analysis of exchange rates and the economy, including

- direct measures of long-term risk premiums in exchange rates making use of inflation-indexed bond yields and long-run purchasing power parity (PPP) in order to eliminate unobserved expectations variables;

- regression tests of long-term real interest rate parity;

- an estimate of the transaction costs for the global economy of multiple exchange rates;

- a case study of the effect of exchange rates on retail prices of automobiles in Germany, the United Kingdom, and the United States;

- a modern calibrated model of a small open economy to explore the channels through which monetary policy and exchange rates influence the economy;

- historical case studies of productive and unproductive policy responses to large exchange rate fluctuations; and

- evidence that developing economies with flexible exchange rates have had superior economic outcomes over the past 10 years, even in some of the smallest and poorest economies.

2

A World of Multiple Monies

When one has thoroughly mastered the principles of Bimetallism[1]
one has the right to lead an introspective life.
—Miss Prism in Oscar Wilde's *The Importance of Being Earnest*

For most of human history, money was defined in terms of a precious commodity, typically gold or silver. The coining and standardization of money typically has been controlled at the national level, giving rise to different national currencies. For a long time before World War I and after World War II, most currencies were linked to gold, and thus the exchange rates between currencies were fixed. In 1973, the link to gold was abandoned, and the world's major currencies have floated against each other ever since. Many minor currencies also have floated, but others are linked to the currencies of their neighbors. In practice, there is a wide spectrum of exchange rate regimes, ranging from currency unions to freely floating exchange rates, with various degrees of limited flexibility in between.

Exchange rate policy is one aspect of monetary policy. The overall objectives of monetary policy are price stability, output stability, and the maximization of economic growth over the long run. Each type of exchange rate regime offers advantages and disadvantages in achieving these objectives. Broadly speaking, a fixed exchange rate regime reduces the risks associated with future exchange rate movements (provided that the regime is long-lasting) by reducing the volatility of exchange rates. This may reduce transaction costs, stabilize inflation, encourage international trade and cross-border investment, and promote long-run economic growth. On the other hand, a floating exchange rate regime grants the central bank freedom to pursue its objectives more directly. Many central banks with floating exchange rates have been directed by their governments to stabilize inflation and economic output, which may, in turn, encourage investment and long-run economic growth.

---

1. Bimetallism is a system in which money is defined in terms of two metals.

The Invention of Money

Money has several roles, and here we refer specifically to money as currency—in other words, as something widely accepted as payment for goods and services rendered.[2] Money is quite obviously one of humanity's greatest inventions. In his seminal treatise on money, William Stanley Jevons (1875, 3) declared, "Modern society could not exist in its present complex form without the means which money constitutes of valuing, distributing, and contracting for commodities of various kinds."

Before money, trade and employment were conducted through barter. Bartering requires each person in a transaction to possess a commodity or labor skill that the other desires, a condition described by Jevons (1875, 5) as the "double coincidence" of wants. Money greatly increases the opportunities for trade because it breaks the need for a double coincidence: A person can buy what he or she wants even if the seller does not want the buyer's skills or products. Widespread adoption of money enabled the specialization of labor, which is the fundamental building block of modern economies. The invention of money was no less important to economic development than the invention of agriculture, fire, or the wheel.

For money to work its magic, it is essential that many people share the same definition of what is money (or currency). The seller of a commodity or service is more willing to accept a given currency when there are more options available for spending that currency, which requires that sellers of other commodities and services also are willing to accept the currency.

The first currencies were basic commodities with intrinsic value, such as gold or seashells. With the rise of the nation-state, governments established standard measures and units for currencies in use in their jurisdictions, and most governments made the provision of currency a public monopoly. Over time, the links grew weaker between valuable commodities (such as gold) and currency. At first, banks issued paper receipts, or bills, for deposited valuables. Gradually, people realized that it was more convenient to use these receipts for transactions than to use actual gold or silver. Governments began to regulate banks' issuance of such bills to prevent bank failures from causing economic and commercial disruptions. In almost all countries, governments eventually took over the issuance of paper money.[3]

---

2. This is money's role as a medium of exchange. The other two important roles of money are as a unit of account and as a store of value. It is convenient and nearly universal to keep accounts of financial transactions and balance sheets in units of currency, and therefore, the role of money as a medium of exchange and as a unit of account are closely and uniquely linked. Money is not the only store of value, however. Others include real estate, durable goods, and various financial instruments that are claims on the future income of businesses, governments, and households. As a store of value, the word "money" often is used to mean wealth, despite the fact that money represents only a small share of total wealth.

3. Private banks still are allowed to issue paper currency under government supervision in Hong Kong, Macau, Northern Ireland, and Scotland.

For a long time, paper money was convertible, or redeemable, for gold or silver on demand. Initially, governments held large stocks of gold or silver to honor the promise of convertibility. Over time, governments learned that they were able to maintain the value of convertible paper money by reducing its supply when demand fell (relative to demand for gold) and increasing its supply when demand rose. The supply of paper money was adjusted using central bank purchases and sales of government or private-sector bonds, which also have the effect of lowering and raising interest rates. This allowed governments to reduce their large stocks of gold sitting idly in vaults, and it also gave rise to monetary policy as we currently know it—that is, the manipulation of the money supply to raise and lower interest rates.

Eventually, it became clear that paper money could remain valuable without being redeemable for a fixed amount of gold or silver. At first, convertibility was suspended only during wars and other emergencies. Nowadays, all countries use such "fiat" currencies, in which physical money has little intrinsic value and no fixed link to a particular commodity.[4] Instead, the value of a currency arises from the combination of government control (with limited issuance) and social custom, including laws that mandate the acceptance of currency as payment, or legal tender, for debts and taxes.

Currencies and Borders

In general, only one currency serves as legal tender in a given country.[5] But why stop at national borders? Wouldn't money be even more useful in greasing the wheels of commerce if all countries shared a common currency?

In some cases, currencies do transcend national boundaries, most notably the euro shared by the 17 members of the European Economic and Monetary Union (EMU). Other examples include the CFA franc, shared by predominantly francophone countries in central and western Africa,[6] and the US dollar, shared by the United States as well as Ecuador, El Salvador, Panama, and some other countries and territories. But these exceptions prove the rule: Most countries have a unique currency.

The remainder of this chapter discusses the nature of various exchange rate regimes and explores the costs and benefits of sharing a currency across borders. It also describes how some of the benefits from a common currency may be obtained by maintaining a firmly fixed exchange rate between two or more countries.

---

4. According to the International Monetary Fund (IMF 2010), none of the IMF's 187 members has a currency linked to gold or any other commodity.

5. The People's Republic of China is an exception, with separate currencies for the Hong Kong and Macau special administrative regions, which were reunited with China during the 1990s.

6. Technically, there are two CFA francs, one for central Africa and one for west Africa, but they have been fixed at the same value for decades.

Figure 2.1   The spectrum of exchange rate regimes

| Currency union | Hard peg | Adjustable peg | Soft peg | Managed float | Free float |

Source: Authors' illustration.

Exchange Rate Regimes

From the 1870s until the start of World War I, the major currencies were defined in terms of gold, and thus the exchange rates among them were fixed. The period between World War I and World War II brought the Great Depression and turbulence in foreign exchange markets as countries went on and off the gold standard. After World War II, policymakers sought to avoid the chaos of the interwar years by returning to a new regime of fixed exchange rates. Under the Bretton Woods system—named after the resort in New Hampshire where 44 Allied nations agreed to the regime—most currencies were pegged to the US dollar, and the dollar was linked to gold, although the link to gold was not as strict as under the prewar gold standard (private individuals could not convert currency freely for gold at the stated parity). During the 1960s, as the global economy grew faster than the supply of gold and the United States allowed inflation to creep up, a gap opened between the official price of gold and the market price. When this gap grew too great, the US government refused to sell gold for dollars at the official parity, even to other governments. The Bretton Woods system collapsed in 1973, after governments failed to agree on a realignment of currencies and gold parities, and the world entered the modern era of floating exchange rates.

Two striking features of the modern era are the broad spectrum of exchange rate arrangements and countries' occasional transitions between different regimes, both orderly and disorderly. These regimes can be grouped into six categories (figure 2.1):[7]

- *Currency union.* Two or more countries use the same currency, which is managed by a single monetary authority. The member countries of the currency union may share responsibility for operating the monetary authority or it may be run solely by one member country. The latter is referred to as dollarization, reflecting the use on these terms of the US dollar in countries such as Ecuador, El Salvador, and Panama.

- *Hard peg.* The currency is fixed within a narrow band to another currency or basket of currencies. The monetary authority is configured to enhance

---

7. These categories are broadly similar to those in table 4.1 of Ghosh, Gulde, and Wolf (2002). Note that the terms fixed exchange rate and pegged exchange rate are used synonymously in this book, as are flexible exchange rate and floating exchange rate.

the credibility of the peg, for example, by enshrining the peg's value in law or by requiring that the domestic money supply be backed 100 percent by foreign exchange reserves in the target currency.

- *Adjustable peg.* Like a hard peg, the currency is fixed within a narrow band to another currency or basket of currencies, but the central bank or the government is free to change the peg value at any time.

- *Soft peg.* This term is used to describe regimes that allow a wide range of movement against the reference currency (or basket) around a constant central parity and regimes in which the target exchange rate moves over time, either smoothly or in discrete steps. The latter is sometimes called a crawling peg.

- *Managed float.* Authorities devote substantial efforts to stabilizing the exchange rate but do not have any specific target or bands.

- *Free float.* Authorities allow the exchange rate to be set by the markets and do not try to stabilize its level, although they may try to smooth disorderly movements. The central bank also may take into consideration the economic effects of exchange rate movements in setting monetary policy that feeds back to the exchange rate.

Table 2.1 lists countries in each of these regimes as of April 2010 according to the International Monetary Fund (IMF 2010, table 1). The top section of the table lists four currency unions: in Europe, eastern Caribbean, central Africa, and west Africa. The external exchange rate regimes of these supranational currencies are listed under the appropriate category in the remainder of the table: The Caribbean currency has a hard peg to the US dollar; the two African currencies have an adjustable peg to the euro; and the euro floats freely.

The IMF has changed its classification scheme over time in response to changes in country practices. In addition, the IMF categories do not correspond exactly to the six broad regimes described above. Box 2.1 describes the evolution of the IMF's classification of exchange rate regimes, it explains how the IMF classification differs from the definitions used in this book, and it describes three other prominent classifications.

Tools for Managing Exchange Rates

Central banks have two main tools to fix the value of their currency. The primary tool is monetary policy—namely, the short-term interest rate, which is determined by money creation. As described in chapter 3, raising the interest rate increases a currency's value, and lowering the interest rate decreases a currency's value. A secondary tool is the purchase or sale of foreign exchange reserves, also called foreign exchange intervention. If market demand for a currency declines, the central bank can prop up its value by selling foreign exchange reserves and buying its own currency. In other words, the central bank steps in to support demand.

Table 2.1   The IMF's 2010 de facto classification of exchange rate arrangements

Currency unions	Hard peg (currency board)	Adjustable peg[b]	Soft peg[c]	Managed float[d]	Free float[e]
European Economic and Monetary Union (EMU): Austria, Belgium, Cyprus, Finland, France, Germany, Greece, Ireland, Italy, Luxembourg, Malta, Netherlands, Portugal, Slovak Republic, Slovenia, and Spain[a]	ECCU Bosnia and Herzegovina, Brunei Darussalam, Bulgaria, Djibouti, Estonia,[a] Hong Kong, and Lithuania	CAEMC WAEMU Aruba, Azerbaijan, Bahamas, Bahrain, Bangladesh, Barbados, Belarus, Belize, Bhutan, Bolivia, Burundi, Cambodia, Cape Verde, China, Comoros, Croatia, Denmark, Dominican Republic, Eritrea, Fiji, Guyana, Honduras, Iran, Iraq, Jamaica, Jordan, Kuwait, Lao, Latvia, Lebanon, Lesotho, Libya, Macedonia, Maldives, Morocco, Namibia, Nepal, Netherlands Antilles, Oman, Qatar, Rwanda, Samoa,	Algeria, Angola, Botswana, Costa Rica, Egypt, Ethiopia, Georgia, Guinea, Haiti, Kazakhstan, Kyrgyz Republic, Liberia, Malawi, Malaysia, Mauritania, Myanmar, Nicaragua, Nigeria, Paraguay, Russia, Singapore, Solomon Islands, Ukraine, Uzbekistan, Vanuatu, and Yemen	Afghanistan, Albania, Argentina, Armenia, Brazil, Colombia, Democratic Republic of Congo, The Gambia, Ghana, Guatemala, Hungary, Iceland, India, Indonesia, Israel, Kenya, Korea, Madagascar, Mexico, Moldova, Mongolia, Mozambique, Pakistan, Papua New Guinea, Peru, Philippines, Romania, Serbia, Seychelles, Sierra Leone, South Africa, Sudan, Switzerland, Tanzania, Thailand, Uganda, Uruguay, and Zambia	EMU Australia, Canada, Chile, Czech Republic, Japan, Mauritius, New Zealand, Norway, Poland, Somalia, Sweden, Turkey, United Kingdom, and United States
Eastern Caribbean Currency Union (ECCU): Antigua and Barbuda, Dominica, Grenada, St. Kitts and Nevis, St. Lucia, and St. Vincent and the Grenadines					
Central African Economic and Monetary Community (CAEMC): Cameroon, Central African Republic, Chad, Republic of Congo, Equatorial Guinea, and Gabon					
West African Economic and Monetary Union (WAEMU):					

Benin, Burkina Faso, Côte d'Ivoire, Guinea-Bissau, Mali, Niger, Senegal, and Togo

Unilateral adopters of a foreign currency (dollarization):
US dollar: Ecuador, El Salvador, Marshall Islands, Federated States of Micronesia, Palau, Panama, Timor-Leste, and Zimbabwe
Euro: Kosovo, Montenegro, and San Marino
Australian dollar: Kiribati

São Tomé and Príncipe, Saudi Arabia, Sri Lanka, Suriname, Swaziland, Syria, Tajikistan, Tonga, Trinidad and Tobago, Tunisia, Turkmenistan, United Arab Emirates, Venezuela, and Vietnam

a. Estonia joined EMU in January 2011.
b. This category includes the IMF categories conventional peg, stabilized arrangement, and pegged exchange rate within horizontal bands. In 2010, countries in the stabilized arrangement category were all pegged to another currency or currency basket. The horizontal bands in the third category were fairly narrow, at ±5 percent.
c. This category includes the IMF categories crawling peg, crawl-like arrangement, and other managed arrangement.
d. This category is the IMF category floating. These countries do not have any specific target for the exchange rate but engage in occasional or frequent policy actions to damp exchange rate movements, primarily through intervention in the foreign exchange market.
e. This category is the IMF category free floating.

Source: IMF (2010, table 1).

Box 2.1 Classifying exchange rate regimes[1]

The International Monetary Fund (IMF) has published its *Annual Report on Exchange Rate Arrangements and Exchange Restrictions* continuously since 1950. The regime categories have changed over time as the global monetary system has evolved.[2] Initially, the IMF reported simply whether a country had a fixed or a floating exchange rate. Later, information was added concerning the reference currency and the width of the band for countries with fixed rates. In recent years, the IMF has added considerable information regarding regimes that lie between simple pegs and free floats (see table 2.1).

The IMF formerly based its classifications entirely on what country authorities reported to the IMF staff. However, exchange rates did not always behave in a manner consistent with this "de jure" exchange rate regime. An influential paper by Maurice Obstfeld and Kenneth Rogoff (1995) found that many supposedly pegged exchange rates moved considerably over time. A subsequent paper by Guillermo Calvo and Carmen Reinhart (2002) showed that many supposedly floating exchange rates were actually being stabilized heavily by their respective authorities. Beginning in 1999, the IMF added its own assessment of the behavior of each member's monetary authorities, which eventually led to the publication of both de jure and "de facto" classifications.

The published IMF categories do not correspond exactly to the six broad groupings described in this book, mainly because the IMF relies on purely observable criteria. For example, some exchange rate regimes classified by the IMF as adjustable pegs are better described as hard pegs because of implicit commitments that are widely viewed as credible. Denmark and Latvia are examples of relatively hard but nominally adjustable pegs. Some regimes classified as soft pegs may be better described as managed floats if the authorities routinely adjust their exchange rate target in response to economic and market conditions; Singapore is an example of such a flexible approach. Finally, the difference between managed floating and free floating is not clear-cut. The IMF bases these categories on the frequency of foreign exchange intervention (described in the next section of the text), but frequent intervention is not necessarily effective nor does it indicate the importance authorities place on the level of the exchange rate. The IMF's procedures also ignore the use of monetary policy (through the short-term interest rate) to stabilize the exchange rate. In this book, a managed float is defined as a regime in which the central bank balances an exchange rate objective against other objectives—such as stable inflation and output—without defending any fixed value of the exchange rate. We define a free float as a regime in which the central

(box continues next page)

Box 2.1 Classifying exchange rate regimes *(continued)*

bank does not place any direct value on an exchange rate objective, although it may take into consideration the effects of the exchange rate on its other objectives.

Instead of relying on the IMF's assessment, some researchers characterize exchange rate regimes according to the actual behavior of exchange rates and, in some cases, use other data. Three prominent classifications are those of Eduardo Levy-Yeyati and Federico Sturzenegger (2003), Carmen Reinhart and Kenneth Rogoff (2004), and Jay Shambaugh (2004). These classifications are based on an annual analysis using daily or monthly data for each year.

- Levy-Yeyati and Sturzenegger (2003) classify currencies as pegged, intermediate, and floating based on cluster analysis of the change in the exchange rate, the volatility of the change in the exchange rate, and the change in foreign exchange reserves relative to a monetary aggregate. The principle is that the combination of a stable exchange rate and volatile reserves is an indicator of a fixed exchange rate, whereas the combination of a volatile exchange rate and stable reserves is an indicator of a floating exchange rate.
- Reinhart and Rogoff (2004) classify currencies based on their volatility relative to a band calculated over a five-year rolling window. The rolling band allows a currency to have a one-time devaluation even within a pegged regime.[3] An important innovation of this classification is that it uses only market-determined exchange rates. For countries and years in which the officially reported exchange rate deviates from a parallel or black-market rate, Reinhart and Rogoff base their classification on the parallel rate. Exchange rates are assigned across 14 categories, which are also aggregated into a coarser grouping of five categories.
- Shambaugh (2004) assigns currencies to only two categories: pegged or nonpegged. A currency is pegged if the official exchange rate stays within a ±2 percent band of the reference currency within the year, subject to the further condition that the peg lasts at least two years.

Klein and Shambaugh (2010, 47) show that if these three schemes and the IMF's classification are collapsed into only two categories—pegged and nonpegged—over the period 1973–2004, a pairwise comparison of the schemes are in agreement for 73 percent to 86 percent of the observations.

---

1. This box draws heavily on chapter 3 of Klein and Shambaugh (2010).
2. In the early years, much attention was focused on whether countries applied multiple currency practices, including applying different exchange rates to various types of transactions (imports versus exports, or goods and services versus financial flows). Few countries continue to maintain such multiple exchange rates.
3. The term devaluation is used to refer to an officially administered depreciation.

In a currency union, there are no internal exchange rates to manage, but the currency area as a whole must adopt an exchange rate regime for its relationships with its trading partners. Under a floating exchange rate, the monetary authority is free to use both monetary policy and foreign exchange intervention to pursue other goals.

In some countries, finance ministries play an important role in exchange rate policy, including through foreign exchange intervention. In addition, fiscal policy has an important influence on interest rates, especially long-term interest rates (chapter 7 briefly discusses fiscal policy). Nevertheless, exchange rates are primarily determined by monetary policy, and this book focuses on the role of monetary policy in the advanced economies and the relatively more advanced developing economies.

Financial Markets and the Impossible Trinity

Advanced economies have sophisticated financial markets with few restrictions on the international flow of capital. The foreign exchange markets in these economies are very large, and central banks would have to buy and sell impractically large quantities of foreign exchange in order to peg their exchange rates entirely through such intervention. In practice, these central banks rarely intervene in the foreign exchange markets. When they do, their purchases and sales have been small relative to various measures of money stocks, and these interventions have been widely considered to have had only limited effects (Truman 2003a).

A generally accepted principle of international finance is the impossible trinity, also known as the monetary policy trilemma (Frankel 1999; Obstfeld, Shambaugh, and Taylor 2004; Aizenman, Chinn, and Ito 2008). According to the principle of the impossible trinity, policymakers can choose only two of three desirable features of a policy regime: (1) monetary policy independence—the freedom to set the short-term interest rate; (2) exchange rate policy independence—the freedom to set (and thus stabilize) the exchange rate; and (3) free and open capital markets. For most of this book, the choice of free and open capital markets is taken for granted. Thus, the policy choice is between monetary independence and exchange rate independence. The choice is not all or nothing; it is possible to give up some monetary independence to gain some exchange rate independence, as in a managed float regime. However, the more tightly the exchange rate is controlled, the less freedom there is to set the interest rate.

Many developing economies have less sophisticated and more restricted financial markets that impede the flow of capital across borders. In these economies, the central bank has some scope to use the purchase and sale of foreign exchange reserves to stabilize the exchange rate while maintaining independent control of the short-term interest rate. (Chapter 8 examines issues relevant to these economies.)

Another difference between advanced economies and developing economies is the level of foreign-currency borrowing. There is relatively little foreign-currency borrowing in advanced economies by governments or households, and business foreign-currency borrowing is mainly limited to exporters. In contrast, such borrowing is extensive in many developing economies. (Chapters 7 and 8 explore the issue of foreign-currency borrowing.)

The Vanishing Middle

One implication of the impossible trinity for economies with highly mobile capital is that pegged exchange rates can be subjected to speculative attacks whenever the peg appears to conflict with other policy objectives, such as stable inflation and output. Speculative attacks occur when financial market participants perceive a one-way bet. For example, if there is a significant chance that the government will devalue its currency to fight an economic slowdown, then market participants will sell that currency, because if the currency is devalued, they can buy it back more cheaply and make a profit, and if the currency is not devalued, they can buy it back at the same price and suffer no loss. This feature of a pegged exchange rate under pressure—"heads I win, tails I break even"— makes it irresistible to financial market speculators. A classic example is the attack that drove the UK pound out of the Exchange Rate Mechanism (ERM) in 1992 (this example is discussed in chapter 6).

Central banks can use foreign exchange intervention and monetary policy to fight speculative attacks, but both tools have drawbacks. Raising interest rates reduces the one-way nature of the speculative bet because it gives investors an extra return to holding the domestic currency. But, if a sharp depreciation seems imminent, it takes an astronomical interest rate to offset the potential gains from selling the domestic currency. In 1992, the Swedish central bank offered banks an overnight rate of 500 percent to deter speculation, and monthly interest rates soared to more than 30 percent.[8] The drawback is that such high interest rates may be exactly the wrong medicine for a weak economy, as it was for Sweden in 1992. The alternative tool is foreign exchange intervention, but in economies with high capital mobility, the size of the necessary intervention can be enormous, and if the central bank or the government ultimately does devalue, the losses on the intervention can be very large.

As reported in two IMF studies (Rogoff et al. 2003; Ghosh, Ostry, and Tsangarides 2010), over the past two decades the dangers of speculative attack have led advanced economies and the more advanced developing economies to move away from adjustable pegs and soft pegs and toward more firmly fixed or floating regimes.[9] Managed floats are not subject to speculative attack because no specific value of the currency is defended, and hence there is no one-way bet.

---

8. See Tom Redburn, "But Don't Rush Out to Buy Kronor: Sweden's 500% Gamble," *New York Times*, September 17, 1992.

9. Denmark and Singapore are the only advanced economies in the middle regimes of table 2.1. As noted in box 2.1, these economies are more appropriately characterized as having a hard peg and a managed float, respectively.

At the other extreme, hard pegs are designed to convince market participants that there will never be a change in the value of the peg. However, the collapse of Argentina's hard peg in 2002 suggests that a true hard peg regime can be difficult to maintain. Perhaps for this reason, currency union and dollarization are considerably more common than hard pegs, and many countries that currently have hard pegs plan to join a currency union in the future.

Economic Objectives

Governments have many economic objectives and use many policy instruments to achieve them. For monetary policy and the choice of exchange rate regime, the most important objectives are:

- maximize total economic output (or national income) and employment;[10]
- stabilize output, employment, and prices; and
- maintain a sound and smoothly functioning financial system.

Economists generally agree that price stability is the most important objective for monetary policy for several reasons: (1) Monetary policy has a more lasting effect on prices than on output. (2) There are only rough estimates of the maximum sustainable levels of output and employment. (3) There are more suitable policy tools for promoting financial stability than short-term interest rates. Moreover, it is widely believed that reducing the volatility of prices is the most important action a central bank can take to enable the economy to reach its maximum sustainable level of output. In the words of Federal Reserve Chairman Ben Bernanke (2006):

> Stable prices are desirable in themselves and thus are an important goal of monetary policy. But stable prices are also a prerequisite to the achievement of the Federal Reserve's other mandated objectives, high employment and moderate long-term interest rates. In particular, low and stable inflation and inflation expectations enhance both economic growth and economic stability.

Nowadays, there are few economists who would disagree with this assertion, though some might add the stability of the financial system to the list of a central bank's core objectives.

There is less agreement among economists about what action central banks should take to stabilize economic output or employment beyond measures

---

10. Economic output is the total of goods and services produced in an economy. It is commonly measured by the gross domestic product, or GDP. National income equals GDP plus the income from a country's foreign investments and workers based abroad minus the income earned on domestic assets held by foreigners and by foreign workers in the domestic economy. Because the effects of cross-border investment and expatriate workers are small for most economies, output and income are nearly equal in most cases. Both output and income typically are measured in gross terms, meaning that the depreciation of fixed capital is not netted out, but this distinction is not important for the purposes of this book.

directly aimed at ensuring price stability. Many believe that central banks inherently seek to stabilize output at too high a level, generating unwanted inflation and ultimately destabilizing output. Others believe that central banks can, and indeed have, overcome this destructive tendency in recent decades. This book presents evidence to support the latter view. This book also refers to central banks' output and employment objectives interchangeably, because from the point of view of a central bank, stabilizing output is tantamount to stabilizing employment, and maximizing output is tantamount to maximizing employment. To have a different effect on output than on employment would require microeconomic policies that are not in the central bank toolkit.

Fiscal policy is another tool that governments can use to stabilize output, but for reasons discussed in chapter 7, its role is rather limited. Therefore, in most of this book, monetary policy is assumed to be the only useful tool for macroeconomic stabilization.

The view that monetary policy also should be used to stabilize the financial system, in addition to inflation and output, is controversial. In particular, some economists argue that interest rates should be adjusted in response to asset prices and measures of credit creation in order to reduce the risk of asset price bubbles and to damp financial excesses (Borio and White 2003, BIS 2009). To the extent that bubbles and financial exuberance tend to cause unsustainably high economic growth and excessive inflation, this view is fully consistent with stabilizing output and inflation. The more complicated question is whether interest rates should be raised to prick a bubble even when output and inflation are near their targets and are expected to remain there. Most economists likely would say no (Kohn 2008; Posen 2009; Blanchard, Dell'Ariccia, and Mauro 2010). The main reason is that asset bubbles are not very responsive to interest rates, so that the central bank might have to raise rates high enough to cause a recession in order to have any meaningful effect on a bubble. For example, US house prices continued to rise at rates higher than inflation during the period in 2004–05 that the Federal Reserve was steadily raising the short-term interest rate.

More broadly, monetary policy is not well-suited to dealing with problems related to the functioning of financial markets; regulatory policies appear more appropriate to this task. Even before the global financial crisis of 2008, most major central banks pursued the goal of maintaining stable payments and financial systems, but the tools they used to achieve this were supervision, regulation, and emergency lending, not monetary policy. Much of the global policy response to the financial crisis has been aimed at making regulatory and supervisory policies more reflective of the links in both directions between the financial system and the broader economy. It appears likely that monetary policy will continue to be focused on stabilizing inflation and output, and other tools will be used to pursue financial stability.

As shown in table 2.2, governments in many economies have assigned to monetary policy the task of stabilizing prices. In 12 of these 19 economies, price stability is the principal goal of monetary policy, and only Hong Kong and Russia have not set price stability as an explicit goal. The most common

Table 2.2 Monetary policy mandates in selected economies

Economy	Prices	Stabilize Exchange rate	Stabilize GDP/ employment	Maximize GDP/employment	Other
Australia	P[a]	s		s	
Brazil	P				
Canada	P	s	s	s	
China	P[b]	s		s	s[b]
Denmark	s	P			
Euro area	P			s	s[c]
Hong Kong		P			s[d]
India	o			o	
Japan	P		s	s	
Korea	P				s[e]
Mexico	P				
Russia		P			
Saudi Arabia	o	o			
Singapore	o		o	o	o[d]
Sweden	P				
Thailand	P	s			
Turkey	P	s		s[f]	
United Kingdom	P	s[g]			
United States	o			o	o[h]

P = principal objective; s = subsidiary objective; o = objectives not explicitly ranked

a. The Reserve Bank of Australia interprets its legal mandate of stabilizing the currency to mean stabilizing domestic prices. Furthermore, it states that achieving price stability is its principal means of attaining its other mandated goals of maintaining full employment and contributing to "the economic prosperity and welfare of the people of Australia."
b. According to the website of the People's Bank of China, "[t]he objective of the monetary policy is to maintain the stability of the value of the currency and thereby promote economic growth." However, a recent speech by Deputy Governor Hu Xiaolin suggests that currency stability may be interpreted primarily as price stability, as in Australia. Deputy Governor Hu also lists achieving a balanced current account as a goal of monetary policy (Exchange Rate Regime Reform and Monetary Policy Effectiveness, speech by Hu Xiaolin, July 26, 2010).
c. There is an objective of promoting European financial integration.
d. Hong Kong and Singapore also have objectives of promoting their international financial centers.
e. The Bank of Korea is required to carry out its policies "in harmony with the economic policy of the Government as long as this does not impede the price stabilization."
f. The Central Bank of the Republic of Turkey is directed to "support the growth and employment policies of the Government" to the extent that these are not in conflict with maintaining price stability.
g. One of the objectives of the Bank of England is to maintain "confidence in the currency," but this is pursued via price stability.
h. The Federal Reserve's third objective is "moderate long-term interest rates," but it is implicitly understood that achievement of the first two objectives is the best way to attain the third.

Notes: Most central banks also have objectives related to stability of the payments and/or financial systems, but these objectives are not listed in this table because achieving these objectives is generally assigned to the supervisory and regulatory functions of the bank as well as to the bank's direct lending to financial institutions.

Sources: Information on monetary policy mandates is taken from the websites of the respective central banks and it refers both to legislated objectives and to self-defined objectives.

additional goals are to stabilize the exchange rate and to maximize GDP and/or employment.

Most central banks tasked with stabilizing prices have a numerical target (or range) for inflation, set either elsewhere within the government or within the central bank itself.[11] The targeted annual rates of inflation (or central points of the associated ranges) vary from 1 percent in Japan to 5 percent in Turkey, but there is a pronounced cluster around 2 percent, especially in the advanced economies. In the developing economies, inflation goals typically are a little higher. It may seem surprising that price stability does not mean zero inflation, but there are several reasons for choosing a positive rate of inflation, which are discussed in box 2.2.

Research indicates that central banks often behave as if they are trying to stabilize economic output in addition to inflation, even in countries where stabilizing economic output is either not an explicit goal or is given less weight (Clarida, Galí, and Gertler 1998).

Relative Advantages of a Currency Union or a Free Float

Broadly speaking, the exchange rate regimes at each end of the spectrum are associated with the following tradeoffs:

- Moving toward a free float increases national economic sovereignty.
  - If accompanied by monetary policy oriented toward domestic economic stabilization, moving toward a free float reduces the volatility and uncertainty of inflation and output.

- Moving toward a currency union reduces economic transaction costs, facilitates greater economic and political integration, and reduces the volatility and uncertainty of exchange rates.
  - If monetary policy is not capable of stabilizing the domestic economy, moving toward a currency union may reduce the volatility and uncertainty of inflation and output, provided that monetary policy is stable for the union as a whole.
  - A country cannot peg its exchange rate to all other countries at the same time. Any benefit from a pegged exchange rate or currency union is partial at best.

What determines the relative benefits of these two exchange rate regimes?

- *Monetary policy.* The case for a floating exchange rate rests mainly on the ability of monetary policy to stabilize the domestic economy. For a country

---

11. Central banks in several of these countries are self-professed inflation targeters. According to Truman (2003b, 6), inflation targeting has four key elements: (1) Price stability is the principal goal of monetary policy. (2) There is a numerical target for price stability. (3) There is a time horizon for achieving this target. And (4) there is an ongoing process for evaluating success in achieving the target.

Box 2.2 Price stability does not require zero inflation

All countries that specify a numerical target for price stability have chosen to target a low but positive rate of inflation. Why not choose to target a constant price level or a zero rate of inflation? Below are four arguments for a low but positive rate of inflation.

Errors in Measuring Prices

There is an upward bias in the measurement of prices over time, primarily because of inadequate adjustment for quality improvements and the introduction of new goods. In principle, the price level captures the average movement over time in the prices of the goods and services that consumers buy, but because these goods and services change over time, statisticians must compensate for the effects of such changes on actual prices. For example, automobiles have changed enormously over time, with the addition of many new features (such as air conditioning, air bags, power windows, and antilock brakes) and increases in horsepower, reliability, and safety. Correspondingly, the price of an automobile has risen substantially over time. What matters for the measurement of inflation is what consumers would have spent on an automobile with the same quality and features in the previous year, but frequently there was no comparable auto in the previous year.

Quantifying the value of quality improvements in consumer goods and services is difficult, and most experts agree that statistical agencies tend to understate them. If quality improvements are understated, then inflation is overstated. This problem is particularly severe when new products are introduced. Overall, the consumer price index (CPI) in the United States probably overstates inflation by between $\frac{1}{2}$ and 1 percent per year.[1] Inflation is likely to be overstated by at least as much in other countries because many foreign statistical agencies do not go as far as the US Bureau of Labor Statistics in controlling for substitution bias and quality improvement.

Resistance to Price and Wage Cuts

In a modern market economy, the prices of various goods and services constantly change in response to changes in supply and demand. Changes that affect the price of one good relative to the price of another good are an essential feature of how the market directs consumers to buy the goods that are most abundant and producers to supply the goods that are most scarce. These market signals encourage efficiency and reduce waste.

(box continues next page)

Box 2.2   Price stability does not require zero inflation (continued)

An overall zero inflation rate would imply that the prices of some goods are rising while the prices of other goods are falling. Many economists believe that businesses and workers are particularly reluctant to accept decreases in prices and wages, and such downward rigidity in prices and wages means that achieving a zero average rate of inflation would require persistently high unemployment and excess capacity.[2] Targeting instead a low but positive average inflation rate means that even those businesses and workers receiving lower-than-average price and wage increases do not have to accept outright price and wage cuts.

Substitution between Currency and Productive Capital

The rate of return on currency is zero. In normal times, people hold the minimum amount of currency needed to conduct their transactions because they can earn a much higher return on other assets. However, as the rate of inflation declines toward zero, interest rates and other nominal rates of return also decline, reducing the penalty for holding currency. Because currency is very safe and convenient, with low inflation and low interest rates people will prefer to hold currency than more risky but more productive capital. Therefore, low inflation rates crowd out capital in much the same way that high interest rates on government debt crowd out capital. A lower stock of productive capital implies a lower long-run level of economic output.

The Zero Bound on Interest Rates

Central banks traditionally use short-term interest rates to stabilize economic activity and inflation around their target levels. The effect of interest rates on the economy depends critically on the level of inflation: What matters is the difference between the interest rate and the inflation rate, known as the "real interest rate." At times, central banks find it desirable to set the real interest rate below zero to stimulate economic activity, particularly during a recession. However, the real interest rate can be negative only when the inflation rate is positive because nominal interest rates cannot go below zero. Thus, it may be desirable to have a positive rate of inflation to give central banks running room to conduct stimulative monetary policy during bad times.

The vice chairman of the Federal Reserve Board, Janet Yellen (2011) has stated that a "modest positive rate of inflation over time allows for a slightly higher average level of nominal interest rates, thereby creating more scope for the [central

(box continues next page)

bank] to respond to adverse shocks. A modest positive inflation rate also reduces the risk that such shocks could result in deflation, which can be associated with poor macroeconomic performance."

According to research at the Federal Reserve Board, the risk of hitting the zero bound on nominal interest rates and the risk of falling into harmful deflation are considerably higher than most economists believed a few years ago (Chung et al. 2011).

---

1. The Boskin Commission (1996) reported an overstatement of ¾ to 1½ percent. Abraham (1997, 1998) identifies one ongoing revision to the construction of the CPI that would reduce this bias by about 0.2 percentage point and she describes other planned changes that would have unspecified effects. Abraham admits, however, that bias from quality adjustment and from the introduction of new goods would persist.

2. Akerlof, Dickens, and Perry (1996) present evidence of downward wage rigidity in the United States. Holden and Wulfsberg (2008) find that downward wage rigidity is important both at the individual level and at the industry level in most countries in the Organization for Economic Cooperation and Development (OECD).

in which independent monetary policy is a source of stability, a floating exchange rate may be preferable. For a country in which monetary policy is not a source of stability, pegging the exchange rate or joining a currency union may be preferable.

- *Trade.* More trade links with other members of a currency union increase the benefits of a common currency (McKinnon 1963).

- *Labor and capital mobility.* Greater mobility of labor and capital between members of a currency union reduces the cost of giving up monetary policy independence (Mundell 1961).

- *Economic structure.* Countries with a similar mix of industries are likely to face similar economic shocks and thus have less need for an independent monetary policy (Mundell 1961, Kenen 1969). For example, commodity-producing economies often have different expansion and contraction cycles than other economies.

- *Economic flexibility.* Countries with more competitive markets and flexible prices and wages suffer less from the loss of an independent monetary policy (Mundell 1961).

- *Fiscal policy.* Fiscal policy becomes more important as a stabilizing mechanism in a currency union (Kenen 1969). Automatic transfers from countries with growing economies to those with contracting economies help to reduce the cost of currency union. Fiscal crises are more sudden in a currency union because the loss of an independent monetary policy increases the risk of default, as demonstrated in the euro area during 2010–11 (De Grauwe 2011).

- *Exchange rate volatility.* When a floating exchange rate is excessively volatile, joining a currency union or pegging the exchange rate damps this volatility and thus may reduce any destabilizing effects on the economy (Flood and Rose 1995).

The effects of these factors may change over time. In particular, a currency union may encourage trade, cross-border investment, and labor mobility among the member countries and also may be accompanied by moves toward automatic fiscal transfers. Rose (2008) argues that the formation of the euro area has led to changes over time in member countries that have increased the benefits to them of currency stability.

In addition to the economic costs and benefits, exchange rate regimes also involve political costs and benefits. The formation of the euro area was driven as much by a political desire for greater integration as by any perceived economic benefits. In other cases, political considerations may outweigh the economic factors. Denmark retains its own currency at some cost (in terms of higher government bond yields) even though it is highly unlikely that the government will seek to exercise significant monetary policy autonomy from the European Central Bank.

Relative Advantages of Other Exchange Rate Regimes

Although much of the economic analysis of the costs and benefits of various exchange rate regimes focuses on the polar cases of a currency union and a free float, the optimal regime for a particular country does not have to be one of these extremes, especially if political constraints are taken seriously. The rest of this chapter considers the tradeoffs between each of the six exchange rate regimes.

Currency Union versus Hard Peg. On purely economic grounds, a jointly administered currency union is preferable to a hard peg because it reduces transaction costs without any further limits on monetary policy autonomy. In fact, smaller members of a currency union have a greater voice in monetary policy than they would under a hard peg. The case against a currency union relies on political considerations, namely the symbolic importance of having a national currency (again, Denmark is an example).

Some countries choose to unilaterally adopt another country's currency (dollarization) rather than a hard peg, even though this sacrifices seigniorage revenues and precludes any voice in monetary policy.[12] Some countries dollarize because there are no partner countries willing to form a currency union or because of the difficulty of establishing a truly credible hard peg. The demise

---

12. Seigniorage refers to the fiscal revenues from printing currency and minting coins.

of Argentina's currency board in 2002 shows that even apparently strong institutional features can not necessarily deliver a durable hard peg.

Hard Peg versus Adjustable Peg. An adjustable peg provides an element of independent monetary policy through the ability to change the peg value after a large economic shock. But this freedom to change the peg also creates uncertainty about the future value of the currency and thus raises transaction costs and may reduce trade and cross-border investment compared with a credible hard peg. As discussed above, adjustable peg regimes have proven to be untenable for countries with open capital markets, because any hint that the peg may change causes a speculative attack. For countries with low capital mobility, adjustable pegs remain a viable option. (Chapter 8 discusses options for these countries.)

Adjustable Peg versus Soft Peg. The choice between an adjustable peg and a soft peg is relevant only for countries with restrictions on international capital mobility.

Soft Peg versus Managed Float. A soft peg places some limits on the value of the exchange rate whereas a managed float does not. Neither regime differs much in terms of transaction costs. The difference lies mainly in the tradeoff between exchange rate stability and other economic objectives. A managed float is the only one of these two regimes that is tenable for an economy with a high degree of capital mobility because of the lack of any specified limit for the exchange rate.

Managed Float versus Free Float. The essential difference between a managed float and a free float is the weight the central bank places on stabilizing the exchange rate versus other goals, such as stabilizing the domestic economy. In a free float, stabilizing the exchange rate is given no weight, and other goals guide monetary policy. The choice between these regimes ultimately depends on the balance of economic gains from stabilizing the exchange rate and the economic costs of sacrificing other objectives to at least some extent. Neither regime reduces transaction costs. Both require the central bank to be fairly capable and sophisticated.

An economy with limited private capital mobility may find it possible to use a managed float to stabilize the exchange rate without sacrificing stability of inflation and output. But there are limits to this policy freedom, as discussed in chapter 8.

3

Are Floating Exchange Rates Too Volatile?

The chapter on the Fall of the Rupee you may omit. It is somewhat too sensational.
—Miss Prism in Oscar Wilde's *The Importance of Being Earnest*

Volatile exchange rates raise transaction costs and increase uncertainty for consumers, businesses, and governments. This chapter explores why exchange rates are much more volatile under a floating regime than under a fixed exchange rate regime, by examining the behavior of exchange rates both in economic theory and in the real world.

A key concept is the real exchange rate (RER), which is the ratio of average prices in the home market to average prices in the foreign market after converting foreign prices into the home currency. (The nominal exchange rate—or, more simply, the exchange rate—is the rate at which prices in foreign currency are converted into the home currency.) Arbitrage through international trade is a continual force tending to equate prices across markets and thus moving the RER toward 1, but this force operates slowly—it takes between two and five years to move the RER halfway back to 1 from any other value.

In standard economic theory, financial market participants move the exchange rate in response to differences between interest rates at home and abroad. But market participants are forward-looking, and they know that the exchange rate also must move over time to equalize prices across countries—in other words, to return the RER to 1. Markets set today's exchange rate value so that the future adjustment toward the long-run level offsets any difference in risk-adjusted interest rates between the two currencies. The currency with the higher interest rate is expected to depreciate against the currency with the lower interest rate—the loss from the depreciation offsets the gain from the higher interest rate.

However, the standard model implies that exchange rates should be much less volatile than they are in reality. An important factor appears to be missing from the standard model. Because this factor is related, at least in part, to changing perceptions of risk, it is generally called the risk premium. There is strong evidence that movements in risk premiums are the dominant force behind exchange rate volatility. It is hard to see what useful economic purpose the risk premium serves, and so there is a presumption that exchange rate volatility is excessive, but this is not yet fully supported by our rudimentary understanding of currency volatility.

The Theory of Exchange Rates with Mobile Private Capital

The starting point for determining whether exchange rate volatility is excessive is the economic theory of how exchange rates should behave.

Some Definitions

An exchange rate is the price of one currency in terms of another. A currency appreciates when it becomes more valuable relative to another currency; a currency depreciates when it becomes less valuable. The exchange rate between currency A and currency B can be quoted either as the number of units of currency A needed to buy one unit of currency B (this is the B – A exchange rate) or as the number of units of currency B needed to buy one unit of currency A (the A – B exchange rate). The two are reciprocals. In this book, the exchange rate is defined so that an appreciation of the home currency is an increase in the exchange rate. Thus, the exchange rate is expressed as units of foreign currency needed to buy one unit of home currency. When naming the exchange rate of two currencies the home currency is named first—for example, the dollar-yen exchange rate is the number of yen needed to buy one dollar. When the dollar appreciates against the yen, the dollar-yen exchange rate is said to rise.

Link to Sovereign Bonds

The exchange rate translates the prices of assets in one country into the currency of another. The function of financial markets, including the foreign exchange market, is to set the prices of various assets at levels that make investors satisfied to hold the amounts supplied of each asset. In general, investors are satisfied to hold an asset when the return they expect, adjusted for its riskiness, is no lower than the return on any other asset.

It can be difficult to compare the expected returns on various assets, especially when they are in different countries. Equity and real estate, in particular, embody unique attributes of the underlying companies and locations that give rise to widely differing views on the expected rates of return. Bonds are generally easier to compare, although they too are affected by unique characteristics associated with the liquidity and depth of the markets in which they trade and the possibility of default by the issuing entity. Bonds issued or guaranteed by the most secure entities, such as advanced-economy governments, have essentially no risk of default and generally trade in deep and liquid markets.[1] Differences in the liquidity and risk of default on such assets are so small that they can be (and generally are) ignored by most investors. The low levels of default and liquidity risk make sovereign bonds the most comparable financial assets across currencies.[2] The standard approach to modeling the exchange rate thus focuses on interest rates for sovereign bonds in the two currencies whose exchange rate is in question.

The rate of interest, or yield, on a bond is determined by its current price, its future redemption value, and any coupons remaining to be paid. For example, if a bond promising to pay $100 a year from today sells for $95, and there are no further coupon payments, the implied yield is 5.26 percent.[3] Bond market participants, including investors, brokers, and dealers, continually seek to buy bonds at the lowest possible price (and thus the highest yield) and to sell bonds at the highest possible price (and thus the lowest yield) for issues of a given quality. This arbitrage activity ensures that yields on bonds of the same maturity and quality are generally equal.[4]

Market participants also arbitrage between bonds denominated in different currencies. In general, investors buy bonds that have a higher return and sell bonds that have a lower return. This arbitrage pushes up the prices of bonds with higher returns, thereby lowering their rates of return, and does the opposite to bonds with initially lower returns. In addition to affecting the prices of bonds, arbitrage between bonds in different currencies works through the current and expected future values of the exchange rate. In the absence of default risk or exchange rate risk, arbitrage activity should keep equal the expected returns on bonds in different currencies, leading to the relationship known as uncovered interest rate parity (UIRP).[5]

UIRP should hold whenever capital is free to flow between countries. Under a fixed exchange rate regime, UIRP works entirely through changes in bond yields in the two countries. Under a floating exchange rate regime, UIRP works through bond yields and exchange rates. For convenience, the remainder of this chapter focuses on UIRP in the context of a floating exchange rate in

1. The sovereign debt crisis in the euro area in 2010–11 revealed that even advanced-economy governments may risk default if they borrow in a currency they do not control. Because Greece and Ireland are not free to print euros to pay off their debts, there is a significant risk of default on their bonds. This analysis focuses on bonds without any default risk.

2. Bank deposits, particularly those guaranteed by governments, are similar in many respects to sovereign bonds.

3. The interest rate in percentage points is $(100/95 - 1) \times 100$.

4. Differences in the liquidity of bonds, which may arise from differences in the volume issued, can also affect yields.

5. The word uncovered here refers to the fact that it is based on expectations of the future exchange rate that are not hedged, or covered, using the forward exchange rate. Covered interest rate parity is discussed later in this chapter. Appendix 3A reviews economic research on UIRP.

which the exchange rate responds to the interest rates in the two countries and not vice versa. Although there are many circumstances in which this assumption is roughly correct, this is nonetheless a convenient simplification for expositional purposes.

It's All about the Future

To understand UIRP, consider the problem of an investor based in the United States who is trying to decide whether to invest $100 in one-year US dollar bonds or one-year UK pound bonds. An investment is a commitment to forgo access to one's wealth for a specific period of time—in this case, a year.[6] In making this decision, it is absolutely critical to consider where the exchange rate will be one year from now.

The interest rate on one-year US bonds is $I1_D$, where I is the interest rate, 1 represents one year, and the subscript D indicates that the investment is domestic because the investor is in the United States. (The interest rate on a five-year US bond would thus be $I5_D$.) The interest rate on one-year UK bonds is $I1_F$, where F stands for foreign. If the investor buys the US bonds, the investment will be worth $100 plus the interest earned at the end of the year, as shown in equation 3.1(note that the interest rate is expressed in decimal form).

$$\text{Expected future value of } \$100 \text{ invested in US bonds} = \$100 \times (1+I1_D) \quad (3.1)$$

To buy the UK bonds, the investor first needs to convert $100 into pounds at today's exchange rate (E) and then buy $100 \times E$ pounds worth of UK bonds. The investment earns interest at rate $I1_F$, and at year end is worth $100 \times E \times (1+I1_F)$. The expected outcome of this investment is shown in equation 3.2. Because the UK bond receipts must be converted back into dollars at the exchange rate prevailing in one year, E^{e1} denotes the expected value of the exchange rate a year in the future. (Converting from pounds to dollars involves dividing by the exchange rate.) Note that equation 3.2 is expressed in terms of what the investor expects to happen to the exchange rate, which may be different from what actually happens.

$$\text{Expected future value of } \$100 \text{ invested in UK bonds} = \$100 \times E \times (1+I1_F) / E^{e1} \quad (3.2)$$

Investors direct their money to the bond that yields the highest expected return. This investment pressure increases demand for the currency of any country whose bonds have higher returns and reduces demand for the currency of any country whose bonds have lower returns. For example, if the United States initially had the higher return in the example above, investors would

---

6. Because bonds are marketable instruments (unlike bank deposits), investors have the option of selling them before maturity. But selling a bond means finding another investor willing to commit his money until the bond matures.

bid up the value of the dollar, E. Assuming that the future value of the dollar, E^{e1}, and interest rates in both countries remain unchanged, the net effect of a higher dollar is to raise the expected future value of investing in UK bonds, as implied by equation 3.2.[7] The arbitrage pressure raises the dollar, E, to the point at which the future value of investing in UK bonds (equation 3.2) equals the future value of investing in US bonds (equation 3.1).

The UIRP relationship, equation 3.3, is defined by setting the right-hand side of equation 3.1 equal to the right-hand side of equation 3.2 and dividing both sides by $100. This equation can be rewritten, putting E on the left, as in equation 3.4.

$$1 + I1_D = (1 + I1_F) \times (E / E^{e1}) \tag{3.3}$$

$$E / E^{e1} = (1 + I1_D) / (1 + I1_F) \tag{3.4}$$

UIRP, as shown in equation 3.4, is an arbitrage relationship between the exchange rate and the interest rate in each country. In principle, each of these variables affects the others. However, as discussed above, it is convenient for expository purposes to assume that interest rates do not respond to the exchange rate. Under that assumption, equation 3.4 tells us that movements in the ratio of gross interest rates between the two countries have a direct effect on the ratio between today's exchange rate and next year's expected exchange rate.[8] Equation 3.4, however, does not determine the level of the exchange rate based on today's interest rates alone. For given values of $I1_D$ and $I1_F$, there exist an infinite number of current exchange rates, E, and future exchange rates, E^{e1}, that satisfy UIRP. Thus, the UIRP model determines only the rate of change of the exchange rate that is expected in the future. When US interest rates are higher than UK interest rates, UIRP requires that the dollar be expected to depreciate against the pound ($E^{e1} < E$). When US interest rates are lower than UK interest rates, UIRP requires that the dollar be expected to appreciate against the pound ($E^{e1} > E$).

Figure 3.1 displays this property of UIRP. In this example, the one-year US interest rate is 1 percentage point higher than the one-year UK interest rate in year 0. For each value of the exchange rate, E, in year 0, the difference between the US and UK interest rates requires that the expected value of E in year 1, E^{e1}, be 1 percent lower than E. In geometric terms, the US-UK interest rate differential determines the slope of the expected future path of the exchange rate but not its level at any point in time. Thus, all the paths for the exchange rate shown in figure 3.1 are consistent with UIRP.

---

7. More generally, arbitrage might put downward pressure on the US bond yield and upward pressure on the UK bond yield. As discussed below, for maturities of less than five or ten years, the expected future value of the exchange rate also is likely to rise.

8. The gross interest rate equals one plus the (net) interest rate in decimal terms. A 5 percent net interest rate implies a gross interest rate of 1.05. It is also the ratio of final proceeds to initial principal on a bond investment.

Figure 3.1   Expected exchange rate paths with UIRP for one-year bonds

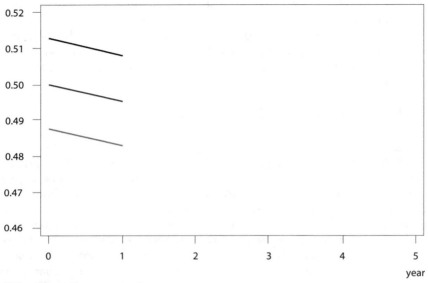

UIRP = uncovered interest rate parity

Source: Authors' illustration.

UIRP applies over time horizons of any length. Figure 3.2 displays the expected paths of the dollar-pound exchange rate when the five-year interest rate in the United States is 1 percentage point higher than in the United Kingdom. In each of these paths, the exchange rate is expected to decline 1 percentage point per year, and the cumulative decline in the exchange rate over the five-year period is 5 percent.[9]

Tying Things Down: Role of International Trade

By itself, financial market arbitrage determines only the expected future rate of change in exchange rates. What determines the current values of exchange rates? In other words, which among the paths shown in figure 3.2—or among many other paths with the same slope—is the right one? If financial markets care only that the dollar should be expected to depreciate 1 percent against the

---

9. More precisely, the cumulative decline is 4.9 percent because the 1 percent decline each year is applied to a value for the previous year that is gradually declining. In this example, the expected future interest rate differential is presumed to be constant over the next five years, but other patterns are possible. The average expected rate of depreciation over any horizon equals the difference between home and foreign interest rates with a term to maturity equal to that horizon.

Figure 3.2   Expected exchange rate paths with UIRP for five-year bonds

pounds per dollar

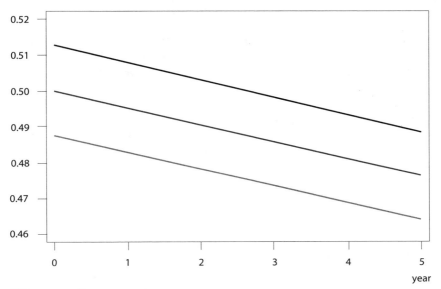

UIRP = uncovered interest rate parity

Source: Authors' illustration.

pound next year, who is to say whether the current exchange rate should be 0.5 pounds per dollar, or 5 pounds per dollar, or 0.05 pounds per dollar?

Answering this question involves the concept of arbitrage through international trade. It matters very much to consumers and producers whether the dollar-pound exchange rate is 0.05, 0.5, or 5. As any international tourist knows, the exchange rate is the conversion factor that allows us to compare prices abroad with those from home. A television, for example, that costs £500 will cost $1,000 when the dollar-pound exchange rate is 0.5, but only $100 if the dollar-pound exchange rate is 5.

A basic principle of international economics is that the prices of goods and services in different countries should be equal when converted into the same currency. This principle is known as the law of one price (LOP). Arbitrage through international trade tends to enforce the LOP, but, as described below, there are also contravening factors at work. In general, if a country's prices are lower than those of its trading partners, its exports will grow and its imports will shrink. There are two ways this can bring about a return to the LOP. First, the rising demand for exports in the country with cheaper goods may push up its prices, and the falling demand for exports in the more expensive country may push down its prices, until prices are equalized. Second, the trade surplus of the country with cheaper prices will cause it to accumulate net foreign assets. As discussed in more detail below, the growing net foreign assets of the cheaper country and the declining net foreign assets of the more expensive country may cause the currency of the more expensive country to fall relative to the currency of the cheaper country and thus equalize prices.

If the LOP holds for all goods and services in the long run, and if the baskets of goods and services consumed in different countries are similar, then average consumer prices are equal across countries in the long run when converted into the same currency using their respective exchange rates. This outcome is known as purchasing power parity (PPP).

The mathematical definition of PPP is shown in equation 3.5, where P_D is the average domestic price and P_F is the average foreign price (in foreign currency). The domestic price, P_D, should equal the foreign price, P_F, converted into domestic currency by the exchange rate, E. PPP is said to prevail when the ratio of the average domestic price to the average foreign price (adjusted by the exchange rate) equals 1.[10]

$$P_D = P_F / E \text{ or } E = P_F / P_D \tag{3.5}$$

The Real Exchange Rate

The real exchange rate (RER) is the ratio of domestic prices to foreign prices (adjusted by the exchange rate) for the economy on average (equation 3.6).

$$RER = E \times P_D / P_F \tag{3.6}$$

In principle, RER = 1 when prices are equalized on average and PPP prevails. However, the concept of an average price of consumer goods is not well defined; how does one express televisions, haircuts, and housing in terms of a common unit in order to calculate an average price? Instead, statistical agencies calculate consumer price indices (CPIs), which measure average changes in price over time from an arbitrary base year. The CPI is set to 100 in the base year; the change in the CPI each subsequent year equals the weighted average of the changes of the prices of every individual good included in the CPI, where the weights depend on how much people spend on each good. Because of the arbitrary choice of the CPI level in the base year, it is not clear whether the RER at any point in time is above or below PPP.[11] However, changes in the RER imply changes in average prices relative to PPP.

---

10. Appendix 3B reviews economic research on PPP.

11. The International Comparison of Prices Program at the University of Pennsylvania has developed measures of the average deviation of other countries' consumer prices relative to US consumer prices. However, these measures are based on heroic assumptions about the comparability of goods and services across countries. Also, as discussed in chapter 5, consumer prices generally include indirect taxes that are not relevant for arbitrage opportunities across countries.

If the forces of international trade and domestic competition in each country work gradually to restore the RER back toward PPP, then the exchange rate at some point in the future should be equal to the ratio of foreign to domestic prices. This means that the RER based on CPIs should return to the same value again and again over time. Over the long run, the average value of the RER should be the PPP value. We label this PPP value RER^{PPP}.

As discussed in appendix 3B, there is strong evidence of adjustment toward PPP over time. Studies indicate that half of any deviation from PPP tends to unwind within two to five years and that three-quarters of any deviation unwinds within four to ten years.[12] Thus, at any point in time, the best estimate of the RER 10 years into the future will be its PPP value, RER^{PPP}. Of course, random economic shocks may intervene to push RER away from RER^{PPP}, but these shocks are as likely to push RER up as to push it down. To a reasonable approximation, the expected value of RER 10 years from now, RER^{e10}, equals RER^{PPP}. If we assume $RER^{e10}=RER^{PPP}$ and we use the definition of RER contained in equation 3.6, we obtain equation 3.7 for the level of the nominal exchange rate expected in 10 years, E^{e10}.

$$E^{e10} = RER^{PPP} \times (P_F^{e10}/P_D^{e10}) \tag{3.7}$$

For interest rates on bonds that mature in 10 years, we can rewrite equation 3.4 as equation 3.8.[13]

$$E = E^{e10} \times (1 + I10_D)^{10} / (1 + I10_F)^{10} \tag{3.8}$$

Substituting the right-hand side of equation 3.7 for E^{e10} in equation 3.8 produces equation 3.9.

$$E = RER^{PPP} \times (P_F^{e10}/ P_D^{e10}) \times (1 + I10_D)^{10} / (1 + I10_F)^{10} \tag{3.9}$$

Equation 3.9 implies that today's exchange rate is linked not only to today's 10-year interest rates, but also to expected prices in both countries 10 years from today. Figure 3.3 shows how today's exchange rate is determined, based on equation 3.9. After 10 years, the exchange rate is expected to stabilize at $RER^{PPP} \times (P_F^{e10}/ P_D^{e10})$ (the dashed line in the figure), which depends on expected future prices; this stabilized rate is denoted by point B.[14] The slope of the path between today's exchange rate and point B is determined by the interest rates in both countries. In this example, the interest rate in the United States is assumed

---

12. As discussed in appendix 3B, this conclusion applies to economies at similar stages of development without major changes in relative net foreign asset positions.

13. For ease of notation, these are simple interest rates that compound once a year. The exponent, 10, reflects 10 years of compound interest.

14. The exchange rate will be constant in the long run only if inflation rates are equal in the two countries. The analysis is more complicated if the two countries have different long-run inflation rates, but the essential insight is the same.

Figure 3.3 Expected exchange rate paths and future prices with UIRP for 10-year bonds and 10-year PPP

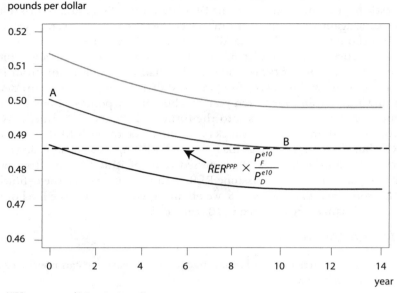

pounds per dollar

UIRP = uncovered interest rate parity
PPP = purchasing power parity

Source: Authors' illustration.

to be higher than in the United Kingdom. As shown in figures 3.1 and 3.2, when the US interest rate is higher than the UK interest rate, today's exchange rate is higher than the future exchange rate, but there are many exchange rate paths that slope downward over time. Three such paths are plotted in figure 3.3. Only one of these paths, however, crosses point B after 10 years. This path uniquely indicates the level of today's exchange rate, at point A.

In contrast to figure 3.2, in figure 3.3 the differential in expected future one-year interest rates is assumed to decline steadily and to be eliminated after 10 years; this is why the lines flatten out over time. One implication of a gradual return to PPP is that interest rate differentials can also be expected to gradually decline, at least for countries with similar inflation rates. In the long run, two countries with the same inflation rate must have the same interest rate, according to the UIRP model with long-run PPP.

What Moves Exchange Rates?

The combination of UIRP and long-run PPP embodied in equation 3.9 and figure 3.3 is the standard economic model of exchange rates. An important implication of this model is that movements in exchange rates are caused by movements in interest rates and changes in expected future prices. In particular, increases in domestic interest rates, decreases in expected future domestic prices, decreases in foreign interest rates, and increases in expected future foreign prices all cause the home currency to appreciate.[15] It is essential, however, to distinguish between movements in today's exchange rate and expected changes in the future.

Interest Rates

Equation 3.4 indicates that when domestic interest rates are higher than foreign interest rates, the future exchange rate will be lower than the current exchange rate. How then can a rise in the domestic interest rate cause the exchange rate to rise?

When the domestic interest rate is high, the exchange rate may be high, but it is expected to fall in the future back toward its long-run level. If the domestic interest rate rises further, the exchange rate will rise, but then it will be expected to fall even faster in the future. This property of the standard model—that a change in the interest rate differential causes the exchange rate to move in the opposite direction today from its expected change in the future—causes the most confusion.

The first panel of figure 3.4 redisplays the path of the exchange rate as plotted in figure 3.3, starting from the current exchange rate at point A. Now, however, the domestic interest rate increases after one year and the exchange rate jumps up to point C. The new path for the exchange rate returns to the PPP rate (point B) within 10 years, but it has a steeper slope because of the increased difference between the domestic and foreign interest rate.[16] The second panel shows that the reverse is also true. A decrease in the interest rate causes the exchange rate to fall (point C), but then the path of the exchange rate slopes downward less steeply or even begins to slope upward.

Expected Future Inflation

In the standard model, changes in relative expected future prices cause the exchange rate to move today but have no implications for the slope of the future path of the exchange rate as long as interest rates stayed fixed. The first panel of figure 3.5 shows what happens when there is a rise in expected future domestic prices 10 years in the future. Holding other variables constant, if P_D^{e10} rises, then $RER^{PPP} \times (P_F^{e10} / P_D^{e10})$ falls. In other words, if a country is expected to experience higher inflation in the future, then its currency is expected to depreciate over time to keep its prices equal to exchange-rate-adjusted foreign prices in the long run. Because neither domestic nor foreign interest rates have

---

15. There also may be feedback from exchange rates to interest rates, but under floating exchange rate systems this feedback is often relatively small, as explained in chapter 6.

16. For simplicity, convergence after a shock is always assumed to be complete after 10 years.

Figure 3.4   Effect of interest rate changes on the exchange rate

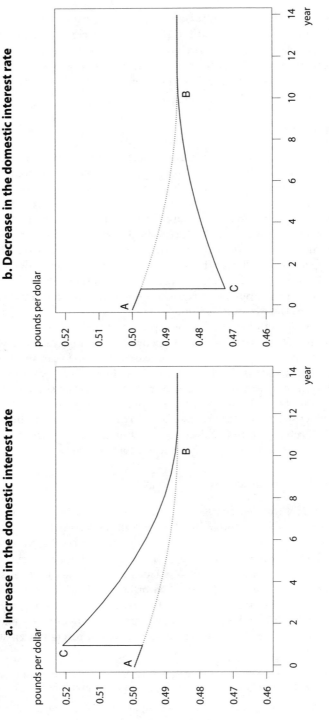

a. Increase in the domestic interest rate

b. Decrease in the domestic interest rate

Source: Authors' illustration.

Figure 3.5 Effect of domestic price changes on the exchange rate

a. Increase in expected future domestic prices

b. Decrease in expected future domestic prices

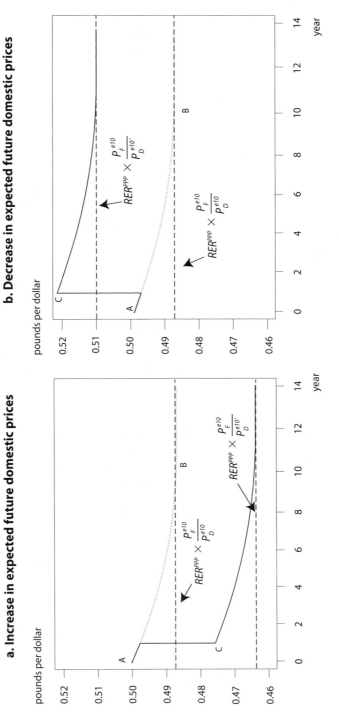

Source: Authors' illustration.

changed, the slope of the exchange rate path does not change, but the exchange rate jumps down to point C. Thus, the shift in today's exchange rate has no effect on the expected future rate of change of the exchange rate. The second panel shows the exchange rate path when expected future domestic prices fall.

Dominance of Financial Markets

As shown above, two key determinants of exchange rates are the goods markets (prices), which determine the long-run level of the exchange rate, and financial markets (interest rates), which determine the expected future rate of change of the exchange rate. The value of the exchange rate at any point in time depends on both. However, the volume of activity in the financial markets far outweighs the volume of transactions in the goods markets. It is because of the high volume of financial transactions, which are aimed at equalizing rates of return rather than the relative prices of goods, that deviations from PPP exchange rates are so large.

Financial transactions dominate the foreign exchange market not only for key international currencies, such as the dollar, euro, and yen, but also for currencies that play a less central role in global finance. For example, during the second quarter of 2010, total exports plus imports of goods and services per day in Australia and Sweden averaged $2.1 billion and $1.7 billion, respectively.[17] Yet, according to the Bank for International Settlements (BIS 2010), in April 2010, the average daily turnover of Australian dollars and Swedish kronor in the spot foreign exchange market was $111 billion and $19 billion, respectively. In other words, foreign exchange transactions were 10 to 50 times the volume of export and import transactions.[18]

If most foreign exchange transactions were associated with arbitrage in international trade, deviations from PPP would be much smaller.[19] Moreover, as described in the next section, there appears to be something else going on in financial markets besides the pure equalization of rates of return. This missing factor appears to be related to the riskiness of exchange rates.

How Adequate Is the Standard Model?

This section assesses how well the standard model of exchange rates explains actual exchange rate movements.

---

17. This calculation is based on an assumption of 20 trading days per month. Data are from the IMF's *International Financial Statistics* database.

18. Spot transactions in the US dollar were $1,188 billion per day and US exports plus imports of goods and services were $70 billion per day. The corresponding multiple is 17.

19. As discussed in chapter 6, not all trade flows are motivated by arbitrage, so that deviations from PPP may arise even in the absence of purely financial transactions.

First the Good News: Interest Rates and Price Levels Do Matter

Research shows that exchange rates do respond in the right direction to some changes in interest rates, as predicted by the standard model and shown in figure 3.4. In particular, when central banks unexpectedly raise policy interest rates, their currencies show a tendency to appreciate immediately. Also, longer-term interest rate increases linked to news that an economy is growing more strongly than expected, and thus may require higher future short-term policy interest rates, tend to cause a currency appreciation.

Exchange rates also have been shown to move in line with the ratios of foreign to domestic price levels over long periods of time. Some studies find that the RER returns to a constant value in the long run, consistent with our previous assumption of a fixed value of RER^{PPP}, especially for countries at similar stages of economic development. Other studies find evidence that RER^{PPP} may drift slowly over time. In particular, countries with fast-growing per capita income tend to have rising RERs.[20] As discussed later in this chapter, changes in countries' net foreign assets also may have long-lasting effects on their RERs. Overall, however, almost all studies agree that movements in long-run RER^{PPP} are gradual and that there is a strong tendency for surprise movements in the RER to unwind over time as exchange rates and relative prices move back into line. The tendency for exchange rates and relative prices to move together is most pronounced during episodes of high inflation or hyper-inflation, as discussed in box 3.1.

Now the Bad News: Interest Rates and Price Levels Do Not Explain Much

Studies show that the vast majority of monthly or annual changes in exchange rates cannot be explained by changes in relative interest rates, by changes in expected future exchange rates, or by expected future relative price levels. There are large, unexplained discrepancies between exchange rate behavior and the UIRP model. As mentioned, exchange rates tend to move in the correct direction in the relatively small number of instances when interest rate movements are related to news about the strength of economic activity or the stance of monetary policy. On average, however, changes in exchange rates are only weakly correlated with changes in interest rates on a monthly or yearly basis, and the correlation typically goes in the opposite direction from that implied by the standard model.

To understand these results, consider equation 3.10, which is the loga-

---

20. This effect occurs because productivity tends to rise faster for tradable goods than for nontradable goods. This drives up the price of nontradable goods relative to the price of tradable goods. If the RER for tradable goods returns to 1, then the overall RER cannot return to 1 because nontradables prices rise relatively more in the faster-growing country, hence its RER increases over time. Appendix 3B discusses research on this topic.

Box 3.1   Purchasing power parity (PPP) during hyperinflation

Hyperinflations are episodes when a country's price level soars by hundreds of percent per year or more. These create a natural test of the PPP hypothesis: If the exchange rate does not move as quickly as prices, the real exchange rate (RER) will deviate from PPP by a large and growing amount. The rapidity of price changes during periods of hyperinflation means that any other factors influencing the exchange rate will be dwarfed. Thus, the link between the price level and the exchange rate should be clearly visible.

Figures B3.1.1 and B3.1.2 display the two sides of equation 3.5 for two episodes of hyperinflation: Brazil in the late 1980s and early 1990s and Zimbabwe in the mid-2000s. In each case, the domestic price level (local consumer price index [CPI]) soared by many orders of magnitude. The forces of international arbitrage through trade caused a comparable depreciation of the domestic currency, as evidenced by the increase in the exchange-rate-adjusted foreign price level, proxied by the US CPI expressed in local currency. The parallelism of the adjustment in the case of Brazil is striking. For Zimbabwe, the exchange rate adjusted in steps, as the government repeatedly tried to fix the exchange rate only to abandon the peg months later when the forces of arbitrage proved too strong.

The ratio between the two lines in each figure is the RER (not shown). Although this ratio was not constant over these episodes, especially in Zimbabwe, its movements were transitory and tiny compared with the movements in prices.

Figure B3.1.1   Hyperinflation in Brazil

index, January 1987 = 1

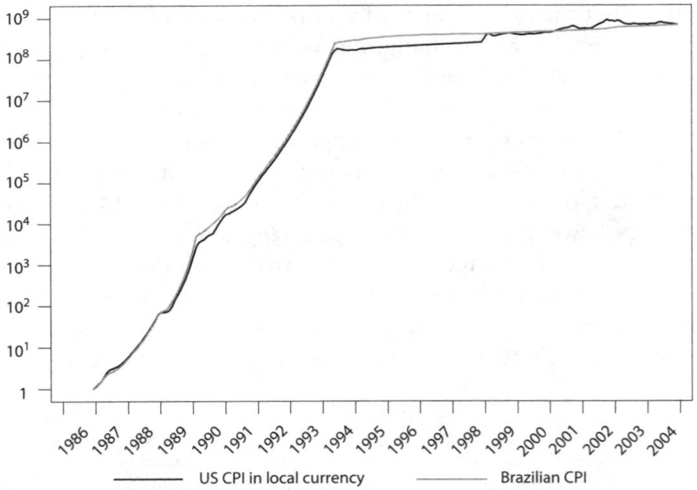

——— US CPI in local currency   ——— Brazilian CPI

CPI = consumer price index

Source: IMF *International Financial Statistics* database.

(box continues next page)

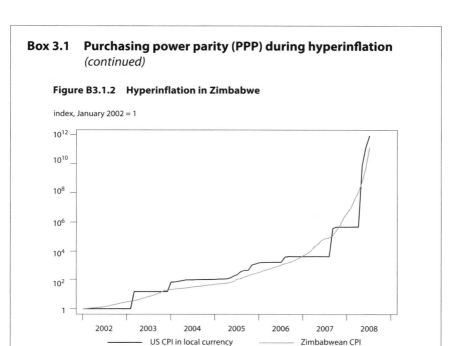

Box 3.1   Purchasing power parity (PPP) during hyperinflation
(continued)

Figure B3.1.2   Hyperinflation in Zimbabwe

index, January 2002 = 1

CPI = consumer price index

Source: IMF *International Financial Statistics* database.

rithm of the reciprocal of equation 3.4.[21] The solid line in figure 3.6 is the right-hand side of equation 3.10—that is, the difference between foreign (UK) and domestic (US) one-year interest rates.

$$\log(E^{e1}) - \log(E) = I1_F - I1_D \tag{3.10}$$

A key difficulty in testing the UIRP model is that we do not know the market's expectation of the one-year-ahead exchange rate, E^{e1}. One approach is to assume that any errors in the market's expectation are small and random. In that case, if we substitute the actual value of the next year's exchange rate for the expected value, any discrepancies should be small and temporary. The dashed line in figure 3.6 is the logarithmic difference between the next year's exchange rate and the current year's exchange rate. If the expected and actual values are close, then the dashed line is roughly equal to the left-hand side of equation 3.10 and the dashed line and the solid line should be close together. In figure 3.6, the two lines are very different and have essentially no correlation.

---

21. The interest rate differential $(I1_F - I1_D)$ is based on the fact that $\log(X/Y) = \log(X) - \log(Y)$ and on the approximation that $\log(1+Z) = Z$ for small values of Z, such as most interest rates in decimal form.

Figure 3.6 The UIRP model at one-year horizon (United States versus United Kingdom)

percentage points

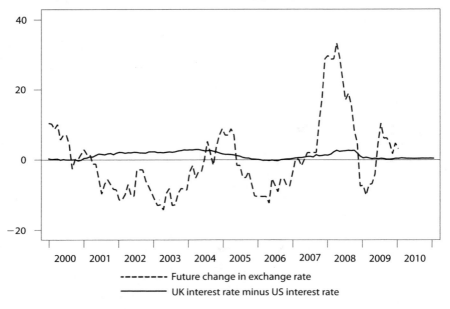

-------- Future change in exchange rate
———————— UK interest rate minus US interest rate

UIRP = uncovered interest rate parity

Notes: This figure uses one-year interest rates on government bonds and one-year-ahead changes in the dollar-pound exchange rate. The lines correspond to the two sides of equation 3.10.

Sources: Datastream, IMF *International Financial Statistics* database, authors' calculations.

The results of comparisons of virtually all floating exchanges rates (not shown) are similar. This implies either (1) that expectations of exchange rates one year ahead are very prone to error, or (2) that there is something important missing from equation 3.10.

Figure 3.7 displays both sides of equation 3.10 for a fixed exchange rate, between the Hong Kong dollar and the US dollar. Hong Kong has pegged its currency at HK$7.8 per US dollar since 1983. Financial market participants have long held a high degree of confidence in this peg, and so there is little room for any error in expectations of the future exchange rate. (Note that the vertical scale has been magnified by a factor of 10 compared with figure 3.6 in order to better distinguish the two lines.) The interest rate differentials fluctuate by roughly the same amount in figures 3.6 and 3.7, yet the exchange rate changes in figure 3.6 are more than 10 times larger and much more volatile than in figure 3.7. It is no surprise that exchange rates are less volatile when they are fixed by a central bank, but it may be a surprise that interest rate differentials are no less volatile under a fixed exchange rate regime. The gap between

Figure 3.7 The UIRP model at one-year horizon (United States versus Hong Kong)

percentage points

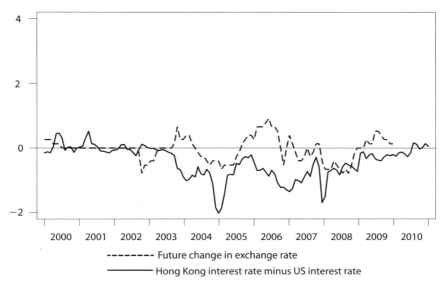

UIRP = uncovered interest rate parity

Notes: This figure uses one-year interest rates on government bonds and one-year-ahead changes in the US dollar–Hong Kong dollar exchange rate. The lines correspond to the two sides of equation 3.10.

Sources: Datastream, IMF *International Financial Statistics* database, authors' calculations.

the two lines is much smaller under a fixed exchange rate, but the correlation, although slightly positive at 0.18, is not significantly greater than zero. Even under this credibly fixed exchange rate, something is noticeably putting a wedge between the two sides of equation 3.10.

Are the gaps between the two lines in each figure driven mainly by errors in expectations about the future exchange rate? It is plausible that such errors could be important to the dollar-pound exchange rate because it is highly volatile, and so most of the movements in the dashed line may have been unexpected. However, it is much less plausible that there were large errors in expectations about the pegged rate between the US dollar and the Hong Kong dollar. Is it possible, however, that (relatively) small errors in expectations could have driven the (relatively) small gaps between the lines in figure 3.7?

Two alternative measures of the expected one-year-ahead US dollar–Hong Kong dollar exchange rate can be tested to see if they reduce the gap between the two lines in figure 3.7: (1) the (constant) 10-year average value of the exchange rate and (2) the current value of the exchange rate. Neither of these shrinks the gap between the dashed and the solid lines; moreover, they both reduce the correlation between the interest rate differential and the expected exchange rate change. Furthermore, the value of the expected year-ahead exchange rate that was needed at each point to eliminate the gap between the lines (not shown) was outside the official band set by the Hong Kong Monetary Authority for most of 2004 through 2008. In light of the fact that the actual exchange rate has never been outside the official band in the past 11 years, this measure does not provide a good estimate of the expected future exchange rate.[22] Therefore, it seems likely that errors in measuring the expected future exchange rate are not the only—or even the most important—reason for the breakdown of the UIRP model applied to the exchange rate between the US and Hong Kong dollars.

One way to get around the problem of measuring expectations of future exchange rates is to take advantage of long-run PPP. As discussed above and in appendix 3B, fluctuations in the long-run RER^{PPP} are very small for countries at a similar stage of development. This finding implies that the expected value of RER 10 years ahead (RER^{e10}) is nearly constant over time at the value RER^{PPP}. In equation 3.11, R10 refers to the 10-year real interest rate on indexed bonds.[23] RER^{PPP} should be nearly constant, and so log(RER) should be nearly parallel to the 10-year real interest rate differential times 10.

$$\log(RER) = \log(RER^{PPP}) + 10 \times (R10_D - R10_F) \qquad (3.11)$$

Figure 3.8 shows that the logarithm of the dollar-pound RER is more volatile than the 10-year real interest rate differential times 10, although the difference in volatility is not as striking as in figure 3.6. Nevertheless, the low correlation (0.12) between the two lines suggests that something important is missing from the standard UIRP model.

Further Exchange Rate Puzzles

There are other puzzling observations that call into question the standard UIRP model and suggest the presence of a missing factor. The high volatility of both nominal and real exchange rates under floating exchange rate systems was thoroughly documented first by Mussa (1986). He observes that, when nominal exchange rates are allowed to float, they are far more volatile than CPIs or other broad price indices. This holds true across many countries and time periods, including before World War II. Because the RER is the ratio

---

22. It may be that during 2004–08 market participants assigned a small probability to a change in the Hong Kong monetary regime, which might have pushed the expected future exchange rate outside the official band. If so, it demonstrates the serious difficulty in achieving complete credibility of even the hardest of fixed exchange rate regimes.

23. The real interest rate is the nominal interest rate minus the expected inflation rate. Inflation-indexed bonds pay a nominal interest rate equal to the rate of inflation plus a fixed real return. Appendix 3A shows that one can derive a version of equation 3.10 for RER in terms of the real yields on 10-year inflation-indexed bonds. This is the basis for equation 3.11.

Figure 3.8 The URIRP model at 10-year horizon (United States versus United Kingdom)

percentage points

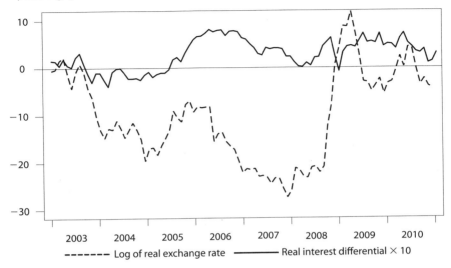

------- Log of real exchange rate   ——— Real interest differential × 10

URIRP = uncovered real interest rate parity

Notes: This figure uses 10-year indexed bond yields and the logarithm of the real dollar-pound exchange rate. The lines correspond to the two sides of equation 3.11 (minus the constant RER^{PPP}).

Sources: IMF *International Financial Statistics* database, Federal Reserve, Bank of England, authors' calculations.

of two CPIs times the nominal exchange rate, the RER is volatile when the nominal exchange rate is volatile and CPIs are stable. By clamping down on nominal exchange rate volatility, fixed exchange rate systems also clamp down on RER volatility.

Flood and Rose (1995) confirm that nominal exchange rates continued to be more volatile a decade later, and they look for an empirical explanation.[24] According to equation 3.9, more volatile exchange rates should be associated with more volatile relative interest rates or more volatile long-run expected relative prices. In addition to interest rates and price levels, Flood and Rose also look at the volatility of many other macroeconomic variables. They are unable to find any variables that consistently became either more or less volatile when countries moved from fixed to floating exchange rates. They conclude that some feature of the foreign exchange market must have changed. In other words, the standard model of exchange rates is missing something important.

Figure 3.9 shows that these findings remain valid. The 12-month changes of RERs between countries that have fixed exchange rates (first panel) are much

---

24. Mussa's results also are confirmed by Baxter and Stockman (1988).

Figure 3.9 Bilateral real exchange rates

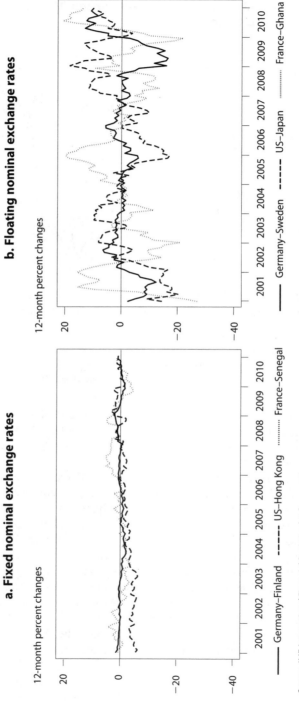

a. Fixed nominal exchange rates

12-month percent changes

——— Germany–Finland ------ US–Hong Kong .... France–Senegal

b. Floating nominal exchange rates

12-month percent changes

——— Germany–Sweden ------ US–Japan .... France–Ghana

Source: IMF *International Financial Statistics* database.

less volatile than the changes of RERs between countries that have floating exchange rates (second panel).

A common view during the 1980s and 1990s was that more stable inflation rates would promote stability among floating exchange rates. Former Chairman of the US Council of Economic Advisors Beryl Sprinkel (1991) stated it this way: "To the extent major countries continue moving toward more stable growth and greater price stability, exchange rates will become more stable." According to former Federal Reserve Chairman Paul Volcker (1995) "[t]he most important prerequisite for exchange rate stability—the rock upon which all else must rest—is a strong sense of commitment of the major powers to reasonable price stability." Describing the process of convergence in Europe prior to the launch of the euro, the president of the German Bundesbank, Ernst Welteke (2001) said "[e]xchange-rate stability presupposes domestic price stability. This perception was the first step towards concentration on monetary stability, and thus on a continuous convergence of inflation rates towards a lower level and more stable exchange rates."

Figures 3.10, 3.11, and 3.12 show how this common view is proven false by the experience of the past 20 years. Each panel displays data for one economy compared with the rest of the advanced economies.[25]

Figure 3.10 shows that relative CPIs have become less volatile in recent decades in all the advanced economies except the United States, where the relative CPI was less volatile to start. Figure 3.11 shows that long-term interest rate differentials also have become less volatile in recent decades in all the advanced economies. In contrast, figure 3.12 shows that exchange rates have not become less volatile in recent decades. The figure tracks effective exchange rates, which are a trade-weighted average of an economy's bilateral exchange rates (in this case against the other advanced economies) and provide a convenient summary measure of an economy's overall exchange rate with the rest of the world.

The standard model, as summarized by equation 3.9, implies that exchange rate volatility moves in line with the volatility of relative prices and interest rate differentials.[26] Decade-by-decade volatilities of each of these three variables are listed for each advanced economy in table 3.1. The downward trends in the volatility of relative prices and long-term interest rate differentials are striking: Their volatility reached a four-decade low in the 2000s in all of these economies.[27] Yet, there is no visible trend in the volatility of exchange rates. The

---

25. The focus is on volatility at the four-quarter (one-year) horizon rather than over shorter intervals because it is generally believed that longer-lasting swings in exchange rates have the greatest potential to cause harm. Looking at even longer intervals, say five years, does not change the basic results of these figures, although it would blur the boundaries between decades.

26. In principle, changes in the volatility of relative prices and interest rate differentials might not affect the volatility of exchange rates if the covariance of relative prices and interest rate differentials moves in an offsetting direction. This is not the case for any of these economies.

27. The only exception is for volatility of relative prices in the United States, which exceeded its previous low average by a mere 0.1 percentage point.

Figure 3.10 Relative consumer price indices, advanced economies (four-quarter changes)

percent

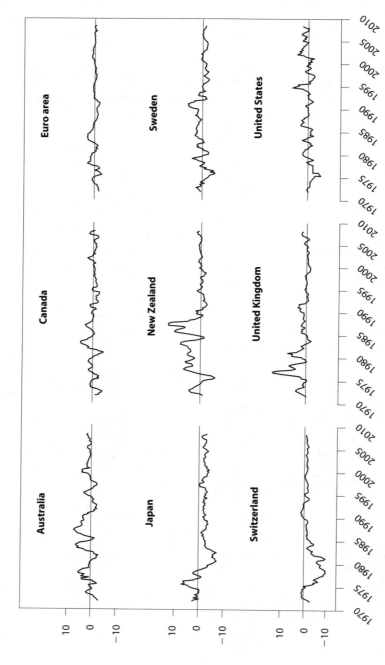

Source: Bank for International Settlements.

Figure 3.11 Long-term interest rate differentials, advanced economies (four-quarter changes)

percentage points

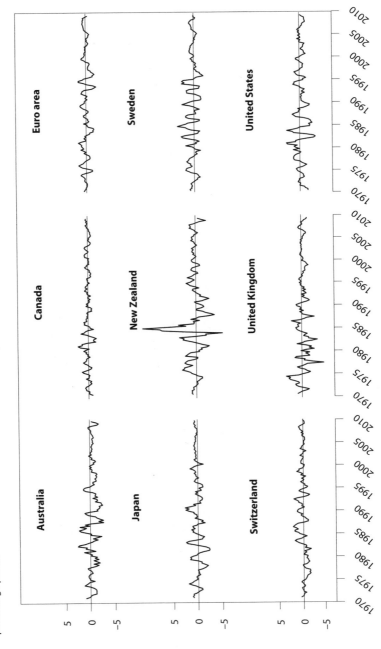

Source: IMF *International Financial Statistics* database.

Figure 3.12   Nominal effective exchange rates, advanced economies (four-quarter changes)

percent

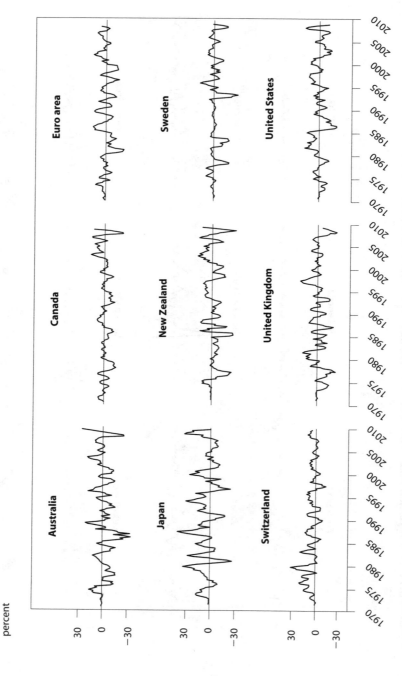

Source: Bank for International Settlements.

Table 3.1   **Volatility of relative CPIs, long-term interest rate differentials, and exchange rates in advanced economies, 1970–2009**
(standard deviations of four-quarter percent changes)

Country	1970s	1980s	1990s	2000s
Relative CPI				
Australia	2.2	3.0	1.6	1.0
Canada	1.7	2.1	1.0	1.0
Euro area	1.5	1.5	0.7	0.4
Japan	3.6	1.7	0.8	0.8
New Zealand	3.4	4.1	1.1	0.6
Sweden	2.2	1.0	2.5	0.8
Switzerland	3.5	2.2	1.0	0.3
United Kingdom	3.7	1.8	1.2	1.0
United States	2.3	1.4	2.0	1.5
Average	**2.7**	**2.1**	**1.3**	**0.8**
Long-term interest rate differential				
Australia	0.8	1.4	0.9	0.4
Canada	0.5	0.8	0.4	0.4
Euro area	0.6	0.8	0.9	0.4
Japan	1.0	1.2	0.9	0.3
New Zealand	1.1	3.2	1.0	0.7
Sweden	0.8	1.2	1.2	0.4
Switzerland	0.6	1.0	0.7	0.3
United Kingdom	1.5	1.2	0.6	0.4
United States	0.8	1.6	0.7	0.5
Average	**0.8**	**1.4**	**0.8**	**0.4**
Nominal effective exchange rate				
Australia	7.0	11.3	6.8	9.1
Canada	5.4	4.2	4.1	7.6
Euro area	3.4	8.0	6.7	6.1
Japan	9.8	11.0	11.1	9.4
New Zealand	7.0	8.7	6.7	9.5
Sweden	5.1	5.5	7.8	5.5
Switzerland	7.0	5.7	5.3	3.4
United Kingdom	7.1	7.8	7.6	6.4
United States	4.4	9.2	5.3	7.3
Average	**6.2**	**7.9**	**6.8**	**7.2**

CPI = consumer price index

Notes: Long-term interest rate is the yield on 10-year government bonds. Nominal effective exchange rate is the "narrow" measure from the Bank for International Settlements website, www.bis.org.

Sources: IMF *International Financial Statistics* database, Bank for International Settlements, and authors' calculations.

absence of any linkage between exchange rate volatility and the volatility of the other variables argues strongly for a missing factor in the standard model.

This unexplained exchange rate volatility has caused two developers of the theory of optimal currency areas to become outspoken critics of the modern floating exchange rate system. Nobel prize winner Robert Mundell (2011) favors a permanent peg of each country's currency at par (that is, each currency unit equals the other in value) to a global currency unit managed by the International Monetary Fund (IMF). Stanford University professor Ronald McKinnon (2010) favors regional fixed exchange rates (for example, within Asia, the Americas, and Europe), with substantial stabilization of exchange rates between the major regions. Both Mundell and McKinnon place a high value on the benefits of currency stability and a low value on the benefits of independent monetary policy. Other public figures including former Federal Reserve Chairman Paul Volcker (2000) and French President Nicolas Sarkozy[28] have stated publicly that exchange rates are too volatile and that the international monetary system should be reformed in order to damp, and possibly even to eliminate, this volatility.

The Missing Factor: Currency Risk Premiums

Financial economists call the missing factor in the UIRP model a risk premium because it is tied to the riskiness of the arbitrage that underpins UIRP. The fact that the expected future exchange rate, E^{e1}, in equation 3.4 is uncertain makes arbitrage between $I1_D$ and $I1_F$ risky—investors cannot be sure that the future exchange rate will be the value they expect. Note that the risk inherent in such arbitrage is two-sided: The future exchange rate may end up either higher or lower than expected, and thus the returns to holding domestic versus foreign bonds may end up being either higher or lower. We know that risk is the key to the missing factor in UIRP because a version of interest rate parity without this risk fits the data well, as discussed below. Also, as shown in figure 3.7, the magnitude of the missing factor is smaller when the risk of the future exchange rate is perceived to be smaller, as in a credibly fixed exchange rate.[29]

---

28. See Angela Doland, "Sarkozy Looks to Limit Exchange Rate Swings," Associated Press, August 25, 2010.

29. Appendix 3A also discusses the risk premium; no study has yet been able to link the risk premium systematically to any observable measure of risk. The appendix also discusses other strands of research on exchange rate behavior that do not appear to fit into the UIRP-plus-risk-premium framework. On deeper examination, however, most of this other research either provides potential explanations for the risk premium or describes the market mechanisms underlying arbitrage. A notable exception is chartist analysis, which seeks to identify patterns in the data that have predictive power but does not appeal to the arbitrage forces that underlie UIRP. Most economists doubt that chartism provides any durable insights into the behavior of exchange rates, but appendix 3A discusses economic research that considers the implications for risk premium behavior when a class of investors follows chartist or other analysis not grounded in the UIRP framework.

The Promise of Covered Interest Rate Parity

A domestic investor can eliminate the exchange rate risk when arbitraging between domestic and foreign bonds by hedging the proceeds of foreign bonds using the one-year-ahead forward exchange rate, F1.[30] Similarly, a foreign investor can hedge the proceeds of domestic bonds using the same forward exchange rate. This arbitrage relationship, known as covered interest rate parity (CIRP)—because the forward rate "covers" the risk—is shown in equation 3.12. As discussed in appendix 3A, studies show that CIRP does very well in explaining the behavior of advanced economy currencies and that today's exchange rate moves very closely with the forward exchange rate and relative interest rates.[31] The expected profits from such an arbitrage tend to be small because the risk is small—all the elements of the arbitrage (E, F1, $I1_D$, and $I1_F$) are known in advance and there is no need to predict the future.

$$E / F1 = (1 + I1_D) / (1 + I1_F) \tag{3.12}$$

The only difference between UIRP and CIRP is the substitution of the expected future exchange rate (E^{e1}) by the forward exchange rate (F1). Thus, a direct implication of the good fit of CIRP and the poor fit of UIRP is that forward rates are poor predictors of future exchange rates. Indeed, to a large extent, banks determine the forward rates they are willing to offer their clients based on the riskless arbitrage implied by equation 3.12 rather than any prediction of the future exchange rate.

Adding a Risk Premium to UIRP

Equation 3.13 adds a one-year risk premium, RP1, to UIRP, arising from the riskiness of arbitrage between domestic and foreign bonds when the future exchange rate is not known in advance.[32] The risk premium reflects investors' preferences and prejudices between investments in different currencies. These may be linked to concerns about political environments or policy frameworks, the nature of investors' portfolios, the expected correlations of asset returns with consumption patterns, or other factors.

$$E / E^{e1} = (1 + I1_D) / [(1 + I1_F) \times (1 + RP1)] \tag{3.13}$$

---

30. A forward exchange contract is a promise to buy or sell a given quantity of foreign currency at a specific future date for a price that is fixed in advance.

31. Discrepancies appeared during the financial crisis of 2008–09 that seem to be related to the perceived riskiness of the banks quoting the forward exchange rates. In other words, investors had some doubt that the banks would be able to honor their forward contracts. CIRP does not hold well for many developing-economy currencies because of restrictions on cross-border investing.

32. In general, the risk premium may differ with the horizon of the UIRP relationship.

When investors feel less comfortable about holding bonds denominated in domestic currency, they demand a higher expected return in order to hold domestic-currency bonds; this higher return is the risk premium. For example, in equation 3.13, when the risk premium is positive (RP1 > 0), the expected return to holding domestic bonds is greater than the expected return to holding foreign bonds. When the risk premium is negative (RP1 < 0), the expected return to holding foreign bonds is greater than the expected return to holding domestic bonds.

An increase in RP1 tends to push down the exchange rate today (so that it is expected to rise in the future), to raise the domestic interest rate, and/or to lower the foreign interest rate. Under floating exchange rates, it is generally believed that risk premiums mainly affect exchange rates, whereas with fixed exchange rates, risk premiums operate primarily through interest rates. However, as discussed in appendix 3A, there is some evidence that under floating exchange rates risk premiums can affect both exchange rates and interest rates simultaneously. These simultaneous effects can explain why statistical tests of UIRP often find that interest rates and exchange rates move in the "wrong" direction relative to each other.

Risk Premiums Are Large and Volatile

Risk premiums are not just fleeting phenomena; they have a long-run impact on exchange rates. The solid lines in figure 3.13 are the RERs based on CPIs between Australia and the United Kingdom (first panel) and between France and the United States (second panel). The dashed lines are a measure of the 10-year risk premiums between these assets as described in equation 3A.8 of appendix 3A.[33] Almost all the movement in the RER is accounted for by movement in the risk premium; very little of the movement in the RER remains to be explained by the standard model. This pattern is common across most floating RERs.

Risk Premiums and the Mussa-Flood-Rose Puzzle

The addition of a risk premium to the standard model of exchange rates goes a long way toward explaining the puzzles of exchange rate volatility, especially because the movements in risk premiums are very large, as shown in figure 3.13. The primary force behind exchange rate volatility is not volatility of interest rates or expected future price levels but volatility of risk premiums. It is not surprising, then, that the reduced volatility of interest rates and inflation rates over the past 20 years has had little effect on the volatility of exchange

---

33. The dashed line also includes any change in the expected RER 10 years ahead. As discussed in appendix 3B, economic studies show that such changes are small and gradual, at least between economies at similar stages of development. They certainly cannot explain the occurrences of double-digit-percentage jumps in the dashed lines within periods of less than a year.

Figure 3.13   Long-term risk premiums and real exchange rates (minus constant mean)

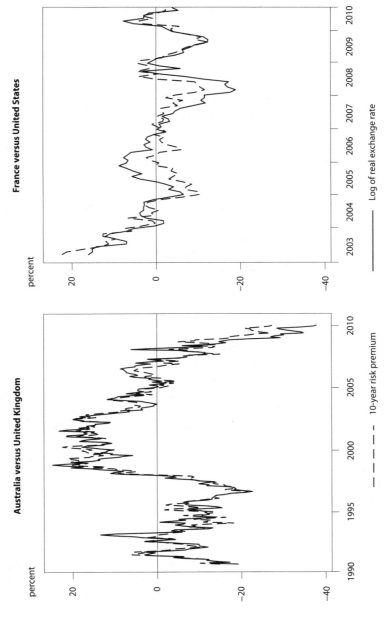

Australia versus United Kingdom

France versus United States

percent

percent

Notes: The 10-year risk premium is defined as 10 × RP10 in equation 3A.8.

Sources: IMF *International Financial Statistics* database, Federal Reserve, Bank of England, Agence France Trésor, Reserve Bank of Australia, authors' calculations.

- - - - - 10-year risk premium

——— Log of real exchange rate

rates. The combined effects of interest rates and expected inflation rates are limited to the small gap between the two lines in figure 3.13.

Risk Premiums Are More Volatile under Floating Exchange Rates

Risk premiums are present in both fixed and floating exchange rate systems. However, by greatly restricting exchange rate movements, fixed exchange rate systems reduce the perceived risk in financial arbitrage across currencies and thus reduce the level and volatility of risk premiums. Figure 3.14 displays 10-year risk premiums between France and three important trading partners: Germany, Italy, and the United Kingdom. The risk premium versus the United Kingdom is calculated using 10-year inflation-indexed bonds under the assumption that the French-UK RER always is expected to return to a constant value of RER^{PPP} after 10 years, as assumed in figure 3.13. The risk premiums against Germany and Italy are calculated using equation 3.13 at the 10-year horizon under the assumption that France, Germany, and Italy will remain in the euro area for at least the next 10 years, and thus $E = E^{e10}$. The risk premium is simply the difference between 10-year nominal bond yields in the home currency and in the foreign currency. Figure 3.14 shows that, although risk premiums are present in all three RERs, they are considerably larger and more variable when the exchange rate is floating than when it is fixed.

As Flood and Rose (1995) assert, floating exchange rate systems are inherently characterized by large and volatile risk premiums across currencies. These risk premiums are much smaller under fixed exchange rate systems. The higher volatility of risk premiums under floating exchange rate systems is a key piece of the Mussa puzzle of why RERs are much more volatile under floating rate systems than under fixed rate systems.

The puzzle remains, however, why the reduced volatility of inflation and interest rates has had so little effect on the volatility of the risk premium. This is true for other financial markets, too. For example, increases in economic stability have not damped the volatility of risk premiums in the equity or real estate markets. Indeed, some have argued that a stable economic environment can encourage an unsustainable decline in the risk premiums on financial and real assets such as equities and housing, creating bubbles in asset prices. The subsequent popping of such bubbles generally implies a sharp rebound in the risk premium on the underlying asset. If economic stability does not reduce the volatility of asset prices in general, then it should be no surprise that it does not reduce the volatility of exchange rates.

An intriguing feature of this analysis is the self-fulfilling nature of risk premium volatility under floating exchange rates. When exchange rates are free to float, they can be volatile. When they are volatile, the risk premium is large and may be volatile. When the risk premium is large and volatile, exchange rates are volatile, thereby justifying the large risk premiums. The volatility of exchange rate risk premiums also is spurred by the unusual two-way nature of exchange rate risk: The currency that is safe for some investors is risky for

Figure 3.14 Risk premiums under fixed and floating exchange rates

percent

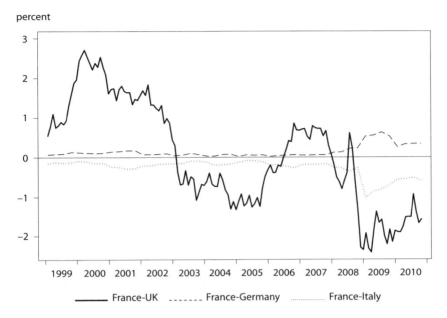

Sources: IMF *International Financial Statistics* database, Bank of England, Agence France Trésor, authors' calculations.

others, and vice versa.[34] Thus, it is not only the size but also the sign of the exchange rate risk premium that can change. Other risky assets, such as equities and real estate, always have positive risk premiums.

Portfolios and Risk Premiums

Economists have made little progress in explaining risk premiums, but it is widely believed that investor portfolios play some role. In the UIRP model, investors are assumed to be willing to hold unlimited amounts of bonds in whichever currency yields a higher expected return. A more plausible assumption is that, at least beyond some point, it takes a higher expected return to induce investors to hold more bonds in a given currency. In this view, the relative supplies of bonds in different currencies should have an important effect on risk premiums (Branson and Henderson 1985; Blanchard, Giavazzi, and Sa 2005). An increased supply of bonds in a given currency should raise the risk premium on that currency. Another plausible assumption is that investors

---

34. This two-sided nature of exchange rate risk may increase the volatility of the risk premium, but it should also reduce the magnitude of the risk premium because one investor's risky asset is another investor's safe asset.

prefer to hold bonds denominated in their home currencies. In this view, risk premiums should be lower on bonds denominated in the currencies of countries with more and wealthier investors.

Net Foreign Assets and Risk Premiums

Combining these two plausible assumptions implies that risk premiums should be higher on bonds denominated in the currencies of countries that have borrowed more from abroad than they have lent.[35] Such countries have negative net foreign assets (NFA). Note that what matters is the net position, not the gross position. Investors in all countries may desire to hold diversified portfolios of domestic and foreign assets, but an increase in the expected relative return on a country's assets induces investors to hold more of that country's assets *relative* to other countries' assets.[36]

Equation 3.14 adds this effect to the UIRP relationship while leaving a role for additional components of the risk premium that are exogenous to portfolio patterns. RPP refers to the component of the risk premium that is based on portfolio positions; it is a negative function of the NFA of the home country—that is, higher NFA reduces RPP. By definition, the NFA of the rest of the world are equal and opposite in sign to those of the home country, and so they do not need to be included in equation 3.14.[37] RPX refers to the component of the risk premium that is exogenous.

$$E / E^{e1} = (1 + I1_D) / [(1 + I1_F) \times (1 + RPP1 (NFA)) \times (1 + RPX1)] \qquad (3.14)$$

Several studies have found that NFA positions do help to explain the behavior of exchange rates in the long run, consistent with equation 3.14 (Faruqee 1995, Gagnon 1996, Lane and Milesi-Ferretti 2002).[38] However, portfolio positions contribute very little to the daily, monthly, and yearly fluctuations in exchange rates. Thus, the seemingly exogenous risk premium component (RPX) is the dominant factor behind most of the volatility of exchange rates.

---

35. This result assumes that countries tend to borrow in their own currency and lend in foreign currency. This assumption accurately describes all advanced economies and some developing countries. However, many developing countries both borrow and lend in foreign currencies, in which case the implications of net borrowing or lending for the exchange rate are less clear.

36. Note that there are two independent forces at work. Investors wish to hold a diversified portfolio in order to minimize total risk; this means that investors in each country will want to hold some assets of the other country. But the factors discussed above still affect the *relative* amounts of home and foreign assets.

37. For exchange rates between two countries in a world of multiple trading partners, RPP depends on NFAs in both the home and foreign country.

38. These studies focus on the behavior of private investors. A relatively recent phenomenon is the accumulation of large portfolios of foreign assets by central banks and governments, a topic discussed in chapter 8.

Appendix 3A
Evidence on Interest Rate Parity

Short-Term Interest Rate Parity
Studies Reject Uncovered Interest Rate Parity (UIRP)

Many researchers have tested the UIRP relationship, expressed in equation 3.4, using interest rates with relatively short maturities ranging from one day to one year. The key difficulty in testing this relationship is that we do not directly observe the expected future exchange rate. A common approach is to assume that expectations held by financial market participants are not systematically wrong. Define the random error in market forecasts of the future exchange rate, u_{t+1}, as in equation 3A.1. If the actual future exchange rate, E_{t+1}, is higher than expected, u_{t+1} is positive.

$$u_{t+1} = \log(E_{t+1}) - \log(E_t^{e1}) \tag{3A.1}$$

If the expectations error, u_{t+1}, is uncorrelated with the interest rate differential a statistical test of UIRP can be conducted using equation 3A.2, which is based on the logarithm of equation 3.4 with E^{e1} replaced using equation 3A.1 and using the approximation $\log(1+I1) = I1$.

$$\log(E_{t+1}) - \log(E_t) = (I1_{Ft} - I1_{Dt}) + u_{t+1} \tag{3A.2}$$

According to research surveys by Engel (1996) and Chinn (2006), studies overwhelmingly reject a coefficient of 1 on the interest rate differential in equation 3A.2. Indeed, studies often find a negative coefficient, which suggests a tendency for the residual term to be negatively correlated with the interest rate differential. Studies also find very low R^2s for equation 3A.2, implying that interest rate differences do not explain much of the exchange rate movements. Chaboud and Wright (2005) find support for UIRP at horizons that just barely cover the accrual of daily interest on bank deposits, but this result vanishes when the horizon is lengthened for even a few hours.

Engel, Mark, and West (2008) note that the large residuals in equation 3A.2 and the near random-walk behavior of exchange rates should not be surprising in light of the fact that interest rate differentials are also highly persistent. The exchange rate can be modeled as an infinite discounted sum of future fundamental factors that drive both interest rates and exchange rates.

When the fundamentals are close to a random walk, the exchange rate will be close to a random walk and the forecast error in exchange rates will be large. Their results suggest that it may be useful to look at the fit of UIRP over a long time horizon, a topic we will return to below.

Studies Support Covered Interest Rate Parity (CIRP)

An alternate measure of the expected future exchange rate is the forward rate (or futures rate) in financial markets.[39] Engel (1996) and Chinn (2006) both report that CIRP (equation 3.12) holds very well for advanced-economy currencies.[40] This result almost certainly reflects the lack of risk in arbitraging interest rates across countries when the future conversion rate is locked in advanced. Indeed, banks typically price forward rates for their customers based on the interest rate differential between the two currencies. Significant deviations from CIRP generally occur only when capital controls prevent investors from obtaining bonds or bank deposits in either of the two currencies involved.[41] In light of the close connection between interest rate differentials and forward exchange rates, it is not surprising that forward rates are typically found to be no better at predicting future exchange rates than interest rate differentials.

Mixed Results Using Survey Data on Future Exchange Rates

Studies of short-term UIRP that use surveys of expected future exchange rates have mixed results (Froot and Frankel 1989, Chinn and Frankel 1994, Gourinchas and Tornell 2002, Chinn 2006). Although these studies do not clearly support UIRP, they do not reject it as strongly as studies that use actual future exchange rates. One interpretation is that exchange rate forecast errors are importantly correlated with interest rates. Under this interpretation, standard tests using actual future exchange rates are biased, but it is not clear why forecast errors should be systematically related to interest rates. Another, perhaps more plausible, interpretation is that survey participants' responses about expected future exchange rates are influenced by published forward rates, which would explain why these statistical results lie between those based on actual future exchange rates (which reject UIRP) and those based on forward rates (which accept CIRP).

Explaining the Negative Coefficient in UIRP

Chinn and Meredith (2004) and Engel and West (2006) suggest that the negative coefficient in short-term UIRP regressions may reflect monetary policy reactions to movements in currency risk premiums. These studies take the exis-

---

39. Forward rates are based on individual contracts with banks. Futures rates are traded on centralized exchanges and have a limited range of maturity dates.

40. Indeed, in Engel's survey, the left- and right-hand sides of equation 3.12 (in logarithms) were treated as equivalent substitutes to be placed on the right-hand side of equation 3A.2 for testing UIRP.

41. Notable deviations in CIRP also arose between the dollar and the euro (and sterling) during the financial crisis of 2008–09. These probably reflect perceived liquidity and/or credit risks at a number of large banks.

tence of time-varying risk premiums as given. Their goal is to explain why these risk premiums induce the typical inverse correlation between changes in relative interest rates and changes in the exchange rate. According to these studies, an increase in the risk premium that depreciates the currency also causes the central bank to raise the short-term interest rate. Because the currency tends to appreciate gradually toward PPP after the initial shock, a negative correlation is induced between the future exchange rate change and the foreign minus domestic interest rate. This effect may be present even if the central bank does not respond directly to the exchange rate, as long as the exchange rate affects other variables, such as inflation and output, to which the central bank does respond. Both studies are able to explain some of the negative correlation in short-term data.[42]

Mark (2009) identifies structural changes in both US and German monetary policy behavior in the past few decades. He shows that modeling the learning process about these policy changes improves the ability of the Engel and West model to explain the negative coefficient in UIRP tests.

Do Exchange Rates Respond at All to Interest Rates?

An alternative test of UIRP starts with long-run UIRP, as in equation 3.9, using 10-year bond yields. Taking the first difference of the logarithm of equation 3.9 yields equation 3A.3, where we have assumed that $\Delta RER^{PPP} = 0$ and used the approximation that $\log(1+I10)=I10$.

$$\Delta\log(E_t) = \Delta\log(P^{e10}_{Ft}/P^{e10}_{Dt}) + 10 \times \Delta(I10_{Dt} - I10_{Ft}) \tag{3A.3}$$

Changes in expected price levels far in the future are not directly observable, making it hard to test equation 3A.3.[43] Nevertheless, if unobserved price expectations are not correlated with changes in bond yields, then changes in exchange rates should be positively related to changes in relative bond yields. However, regressions of the change in the exchange rate on the changes in home and foreign bond yields have very low R^2s, and often the coefficients have the wrong sign.[44] These results may arise either because changes in bond yields are correlated with changes in long-run expected price levels or because the residual of equation 3A.3 (that is, the risk premium) is correlated with changes in bond yields.

Recently, some studies have attempted to estimate equation 3A.3 using only

---

42. Bansal and Dahlquist (2000) reject UIRP for most developing economies, but they do not obtain negative coefficients, which may reflect less aggressive central bank stabilization of inflation in developing economies.

43. As is shown below, for economies and time periods in which long-term inflation-indexed bonds exist, it is possible to construct estimates of expected future price levels.

44. Often, the regression is specified in terms of the change in relative bond yield, which forces the coefficients on the domestic and foreign bond yields to be equal and opposite in sign.

periods in which the changes in bond yields are not likely to be associated with changes in expected future price levels or the risk premium. Fair (2003), Faust et al. (2007), and Andersen et al. (2007) show that changes in bond yields in the minutes immediately following news releases about the state of the economy or monetary policy are correlated with exchange rates in the direction implied by equation 3A.3. Focusing on very short windows (as short as five minutes) around the news releases ensures that the movements are caused by the news events and not by other factors. This connection is strongest for news about real economic activity and monetary policy. Interestingly, for news about inflation, the correlation is very low, consistent with the hypothesis that news about inflation affects both domestic bond yields and long-run expected domestic price levels in the same direction.[45] Equation 3A.3 implies that an increase in the domestic bond yield that occurs simultaneously with an unobserved increase in long-run expected domestic prices should have a smaller (or even negative) effect on the exchange rate. Overall, these studies show that exchange rates do respond to interest rates, as predicted by the standard UIRP model.

Long-Term Interest Rate Parity

Uncovered Nominal Interest Rate Parity

Most studies of UIRP have examined the links between short-term interest rates and short-term expected changes in exchange rates. This focus likely reflects the greater availability of data on short-term interest rates and the fact that it takes a very long sample in order to calculate a sufficiently large number of long-term changes in the exchange rate. For example, with 20 years of data, one can calculate only 10 years of 10-year changes in the exchange rate. Moreover, these 10-year changes in exchange rates have a high degree of overlap, inducing autocorrelated errors in the regression. However, as data samples have lengthened and data on long-term interest rates have become more widely available, researchers have explored UIRP over longer horizons.

Chinn (2006) reviews previous studies and conducts new tests which show that UIRP holds better for five-year and ten-year horizons than for the standard one-month to one-year horizons.[46] The coefficients on the interest rate differentials at the longer horizons, at around 0.7, are much closer to their theoretical

---

45. Clarida and Waldman (2008) find that positive inflation surprises tend to cause currencies to appreciate, especially for countries whose central banks have a strict inflation target, presumably because markets expect higher inflation to cause central banks to raise interest rates aggressively.

46. Bekaert, Wei, and Xing (2007) subsequently challenged the view that UIRP holds better at long horizons. They test UIRP in a monthly vector auto-regression (VAR) framework, using the VAR coefficients to calculate expected future exchange rates. They find somewhat less strong rejections of UIRP than in standard regression tests at short horizons, but their tests find little difference in the performance of UIRP at different horizons. A key difference between their approach and that of other studies of UIRP at long horizons is that Bekaert, Wei, and Xing (2007) use VAR predictions of 60-month-ahead exchange rates, whereas other studies used the actual 60-month changes. There may be a systematic inefficiency of VARs, which generally have short lags, in predicting so far ahead.

value of 1. However, the R^2s remain low in all cases, consistent with substantial remaining risk premiums. If economies tend to return to steady-state paths in the long run, it may be that long-term expectations of exchange rates are more accurate than short-term expectations. A related explanation, suggested by Chinn, is that long-horizon data may smooth out transient noise and thus reduce the errors-in-variables problem. Finally, the monetary policy interaction proposed by Chinn and Meredith (2004) and Engel and West (2006) may be more important at short horizons. For longer horizons, the impact of monetary policy is less apparent and thus the negative bias is smaller. Nevertheless, the low R^2s in Chinn's tests still imply that unexplained risk premium shocks are an important driving factor in exchange rates even at long horizons.

Uncovered Real Interest Rate Parity (URIRP)

Edison and Pauls (1993) implement an approach based on the assumption that real exchange rates (RERs) return toward purchasing power parity (PPP) over time. (Appendix 3B discusses the evidence in support of long-run PPP.) This assumption allows for construction of a test of long-term UIRP that does not require the calculation of long-term changes in exchange rates or the assumption that forecast errors are uncorrelated with interest rates. However, it does require an estimate of the expected long-run inflation rate in order to calculate a long-run real interest rate. In their study, Edison and Pauls (1993) find little support for long-run URIRP, but this negative result may reflect a short sample and/or a poor estimate of long-run inflation expectations.

The emergence of long-term bonds with returns indexed to inflation allows a new implementation of long-run URIRP. Note that the expected price level 10 years ahead can be expressed in terms of today's price level and the expected inflation rate over the next 10 years (equation 3A.4), where INF^e is expected inflation. Substitute the right-hand sides of equation 3A.4 and its analog for the foreign country for P^e_{Dt+10} and P^e_{Ft+10} in equation 3.9 and add a risk premium as in equation 3.13. Then define the gross real interest rate as the gross nominal interest rate divided by the gross average expected inflation rate over the next 10 years (equation 3A.5). Recall that the RER is the exchange rate times the ratio of domestic to foreign prices (equation 3A.6). Collecting terms yields the long-term URIRP equation allowing for a risk premium (equation 3A.7). Equation 3A.8 is the logarithm of equation 3A.7.

$$P^e_{Dt+10} = P_{Dt} \times (1 + INF^e_{Dt+1}) \times (1 + INF^e_{Dt+2}) \times ... \times (1 + INF^e_{Dt+10}) \qquad (3A.4)$$

$$(1 + R10_{Dt})^{10} = (1 + I10_{Dt})^{10} / [(1 + INF^e_{Dt+1}) \times (1 + INF^e_{Dt+2}) \times ... \times (1 + INF^e_{Dt+10})] \qquad (3A.5)$$

$$RER_t = E_t \times P_{Dt}/P_{Ft} \qquad (3A.6)$$

$$RER_t = RER^{PPP} \times (1 + R10_{Dt})^{10} / [(1 + R10_{Ft}) \times (1 + RP10_t)]^{10} \qquad (3A.7)$$

$$\log(RER_t) = \log(RER^{PPP}) + 10 \times [R10_{Dt} - R10_{Ft}] - 10 \times RP10_t \qquad (3A.8)$$

Using 10-year indexed bonds allows us to test this URIRP relationship without any need to measure expected future variables, as long as 10 years is long enough for the RER to return to PPP. Regressions of equation 3A.8 treating the risk premium as an unobserved residual reveal that the risk premium is very large and has an autoregressive root near 1 for all country pairs. Thus, the risk premium is nonstationary. To obtain a stationary regression, we take the first difference of equation 3A.8, shown as equation 3A.9. According to equation 3A.9, the change in RER should equal 10 times the change in $R10_D - R10_F$. The intercept should be zero.[47]

$$\Delta \log(RER_t) = 10 \times \Delta [R10_{Dt} - R10_{Ft}] - 10 \times \Delta RP10_t \qquad (3A.9)$$

Table 3A.1 presents estimates of this relationship using real yields on 10-year indexed bonds. The coefficients on $R10_D - R10_F$ are usually significantly positive and never significantly negative. But the p-values for the test of URIRP show that they are significantly less than the theoretical value of 10 in every case but the US-Australian RER. Thus, it appears that even at the 10-year horizon, the risk premium often is correlated with the real interest rate differential.

The constant terms are not statistically significant. The largest estimated constant, −0.5 for the US-Australian RER, implies an average rate of depreciation of the US dollar relative to the Australian dollar of ½ percent per month in real terms. The coefficients on the real interest differential are not noticeably changed by dropping the constant terms.

The residuals of some of these regressions are positively autocorrelated. A first-order moving-average (MA(1)) error coefficient of around 0.25 is induced whenever a continuous-time random walk variable is averaged over discrete time intervals (Working 1960). The RERs are based on monthly averages of consumer prices and exchange rates and so are subject to this MA(1) error. After allowing for an MA(1) error, there is no remaining autocorrelation in the residuals, except marginally for the Australian-UK RER. Thus, the results suggest that the unobserved long-term risk premiums are close to driftless random walks.

The regression R^2s are low, and the root mean squared errors (MSEs) of the regressions are almost as large as the monthly standard deviations of the real exchange rates themselves, implying that movements in $R10_D - R10_F$ are only a small factor behind movements in real exchange rates. These regression root MSEs of 2 to 3 percent per month are larger than any plausible error that might arise from expectations of incomplete return to PPP within ten years.[48] These results suggest strongly that the risk premium is by far the most important driver of exchange rate behavior.

---

47. A nonzero intercept indicates a trend or stochastic drift in either RER^{PPP} or the risk premium.

48. See appendix 3B for further discussion.

Table 3A.1   Long-term uncovered real interest rate parity (URIRP)
(monthly changes, August 1986–November 2010)

	US-UK	US-CA	US-AL	US-FR	CA-UK	AL-UK	FR-UK
$\Delta(R10_D{-}R10_F)$	1.87	3.71**	9.55***	6.09***	3.75**	2.76*	−1.08
	(2.73)	(1.80)	(2.71)	(1.79)	(1.80)	(1.42)	(1.48)
CONSTANT	−0.04	−0.41	−0.50	−0.21	0.21	0.12	0.07
	(.34)	(.28)	(.38)	(.30)	(.22)	(.20)	(.18)
Test of URIRP (*p*-value)	.003	.001	.868	.029	.001	.000	.000
MA(1)	0.24***	0.29***	0.41***	0.14	−0.02	0.15*	−0.02
	(.08)	(.08)	(.15)	(.15)	(.09)	(.09)	(.09)
R^2 (OLS)	.01	.08	.35	.14	.06	.04	.01
Number of observations	94	93	94	94	117	292	146
Portmanteau tests for autocorrelation of residual (*p*-values)							
1 month	.80	.86	.88	.93	.98	.76	.99
3 month	.75	.85	.45	.92	.66	.17	.48
12 month	.65	.72	.74	.92	.52	.05	.31
Root MSE	2.64	2.12	2.60	2.55	2.44	2.94	2.23
Std. dev. ΔRER	2.75	2.32	3.45	2.78	2.53	3.03	2.24
10 × Std. dev. $\Delta(R10_D{-}R10_F)$	1.36	1.81	1.77	1.57	1.61	1.88	1.53

AL = Australia; CA = Canada; FR = France; UK = United Kingdom; US = United States; $R10_D{-}R10_F$ = real interest rate differential; MA(1) = first-order moving average error; OLS = ordinary least squares; MSE = mean squared errors; Std.dev. = standard deviation; RER = real exchange rate

Notes: This table presents results of Box-Jenkins regressions of equation 3A.9 with first-order moving-average error using 10-year constant maturity real yields on indexed bonds. The Canadian real yield is from benchmark bonds with 20–30 years to maturity. French bond data start in October 1998, Canadian bond data start in March 2001, and US bond data start in January 2003. The R^2 statistics are from OLS regressions of equation 3A.9, which yielded very similar coefficients. Huber-White standard errors are in parentheses. ***, **, and * denote statistical significance at the 1, 5, and 10 percent levels, respectively.

Sources: Authors' calculations based on data from Bank of Canada, Bank of England, Federal Reserve Board, Agence France Trésor, Reserve Bank of Australia, and IMF *International Financial Statistics* database.

Models of Risk Premiums

Engel's (1996) survey covers papers that augment UIRP with models of the risk premium. These models typically are based on risk aversion in consumption and generally are estimated using short-term interest rates. Engel concludes that both the magnitude of exchange rate volatility and the negative correlation typically estimated between future exchange rate changes and interest rate differentials are not consistent with proposed models of risk premiums.

Lustig and Verdelhan (2007) revisit consumption-based risk aversion and the exchange rate risk premium. They show that returns on high-yielding currencies tend to be positively correlated with US consumption growth and are thus risky, whereas returns on low-yielding currencies tend to be negatively correlated with US consumption growth and are thus a natural hedge for US investors. The amount of risk aversion required to explain observed risk premiums is extremely high but is comparable to that required to explain the risk premium in equity markets. Lustig and Verdelhan (2007) do not explain the source of these correlations nor do they examine risk from the point of view of foreign investors.

Alvarez, Atkeson, and Kehoe (2007) and Gust and Lopez-Salido (2009) propose theoretical models in which risk premiums are driven by monetary policy changes to expected inflation in the presence of frictions in asset allocation. Neither study tests its model against the data. (Gust and Lopez-Salido focus on the equity premium.) These models may not be very relevant in the modern world in which inflation has been—and is expected to remain—remarkably stable.

Backus et al. (2010) show that some versions of monetary policy interest rate rules can generate risk premiums consistent with the failure of short-run UIRP in a formal asset pricing model under relatively strict assumptions (e.g., PPP holds continuously). They do not present evidence to show that monetary policy rules in practice are responsible for the behavior of exchange rate risk premiums.

Plantin and Shin (2006) develop a theoretical model of trading frictions that slow down the initial reaction of the exchange rate to a change in the fundamentals (interest rates and inflation expectations). This creates an extended period in which the exchange rate earns excess returns (risk premium) followed by a random and sudden reversal. Farhi et al. (2009) argue that the risk of sudden reversals ("rare disasters") explains about 25 percent of exchange rate risk premiums in advanced economies. Burnside et al. (2008) suggest that sudden reversals ("peso events") may explain most of the risk premium in exchange rates, but they argue that the driving factor is not a large loss during the reversal but an increase in the stochastic discount factor (rate of time preference in consumption). They do not explain why the discount factor moves so suddenly.

Jorda and Taylor (2009) propose that the deviation of the RER from a predicted value based on UIRP and long-run PPP provides a good measure of the size and direction of a potential future sudden exchange rate movement of the kind studied by Farhi et al. (2009). They use this measure to design a trading strategy that is relatively safe yet still earns excess returns, suggesting that currency risk premiums remain a puzzle.

Ito and Chinn (2007) relate the magnitude of risk premiums to various country characteristics. They find that inflation variability and per capita income are associated with larger risk premiums but that capital account openness and financial development are associated with smaller risk premiums, at least in developing economies.

Engel (2010) argues that there are two contradictory components of risk premiums in exchange rates. The first component, which has been the subject of most attempts to explain risk premiums, is the tendency for currencies with high interest rates to appreciate further in the short run. The second component, which receives much less attention, is the tendency for currencies with high interest rates to depreciate over the long run by even more than predicted by UIRP. Engel (2010) suggests that the behavior of monetary policy may play a role in creating these apparently contradictory tendencies, but he does not model the connection, stating that it "is not straightforward."

Other Approaches to Exchange Rates

Theoretical Models

An important group of studies has relaxed the assumption that most or all economic agents are rational. Some of these studies include models with "noise traders," who may be following chartist strategies or may be influenced by rumors and herd behavior (Jeanne and Rose 2002, De Grauwe and Grimaldi 2006, Burnside et al. 2011). These studies also include a group of rational traders, who try to arbitrage away excess profits. If the rational traders are risk averse or lack sufficient access to capital, the market equilibrium is importantly influenced by the noise traders and strict UIRP will not hold. Note, however, that from the point of view of the rational traders, it can be said that UIRP with a risk premium does hold. The rational traders earn the risk premium as compensation for the risk they bear in trying to stabilize against the noise traders. These models generally do not lead to interesting insights concerning the behavior of the risk premium over time, but that is not their objective. De Grauwe and Grimaldi (2006), however, do stress the tendency for noise traders to extrapolate trends, which may contribute to the negative coefficient in short-term UIRP tests because an increase in the interest rate causes a currency to continue to appreciate for some time after the interest rate stops rising.

Rather than introduce pure noise traders, Bacchetta and van Wincoop (2007) invoke modest limitations on rationality for all traders. They argue that a combination of random-walk expectations of future exchange rates (which typically cannot be rejected statistically) and infrequent portfolio adjustment can explain the failure of UIRP. With random-walk exchange rate expectations, currencies with higher interest rates are more attractive. With staggered and infrequent portfolio adjustment, the upward pressure on a currency from a rise in the domestic interest rate is stretched out over several months or quarters, which explains the tendency for high-interest-rate currencies to appreciate rather than depreciate, as the UIRP model predicts.[49]

---

49. In this respect, their model is similar to that of Plantin and Shin (2006) and has an implication similar to that of De Grauwe and Grimaldi (2006).

Empirical Models

A number of studies focus on the dynamics of exchange rate adjustment using high-frequency (minute-by-minute and even second-by-second) data on order flows to foreign exchange dealers.[50] This literature has little to say on the UIRP-PPP standard model, as interest earnings typically accrue only at the daily frequency. Rather, it illuminates the underlying micro structure of the foreign exchange market and how exchange rates adjust in the very short run.

Meese and Rogoff (1983) and Cheung, Chinn, and Pascual (2005) test a variety of empirical models of exchange rates, many based loosely on the standard model with ad hoc terms to capture elements of the risk premium or of long-run drifts in PPP, and others based on fundamental drivers of interest rates and inflation rates. Meese and Rogoff (1983) famously find that none of the empirical models of the 1970s are able to predict exchange rates significantly better than simply assuming a random walk (that is, that the future exchange rate equals today's exchange rate plus a white noise random error). Cheung, Chinn, and Pascual (2005) find weak evidence that some models outperformed a random walk for some exchange rates or some forecast horizons but that no model consistently forecasts well across all exchange rates and horizons.

Engel, Mark, and West (2008) conduct joint tests of UIRP and various fundamental models of interest rate differentials. They show that their models are usually able to predict future exchange rates better than a random walk at the 16-quarter horizon but only occasionally do their models improve on a random walk forecast at the one-quarter horizon.

---

50. See, for example, Killeen, Lyons, and Moore (2006) and the papers cited therein.

Appendix 3B
Evidence on Long-Run Purchasing Power Parity

The Rogoff Survey Article

Rogoff (1996) shows that deviations from the law of one price (LOP) are large for some goods, such as Big Mac hamburgers, and small for others, such as gold. Deviations from the LOP are highly correlated with exchange rates, both for aggregate price levels and for price indices at a high level of disaggregation. Engel and Rogers (1996) present evidence that LOP deviations between pairs of cities are much more volatile when the cities have different currencies than when they share the same currency.

Despite the overwhelming evidence against the LOP and PPP in the short run, Rogoff (1996, 647) asserts that most economists "instinctively believe in some variant of purchasing power parity (PPP) as an anchor for long-run real exchange rates (RERs)." This instinct finds strong support in episodes in which one of the countries under study has high inflation, as shown in box 3.1. However, many early studies of long-run PPP between countries with relatively low inflation typically are not able to reject the counterhypothesis that RERs follow a random walk, i.e., that relative prices do not return to PPP. These studies focus on the 20 years or so after the breakdown of the Bretton Woods fixed exchange rate system in 1973. If reversion to PPP happens slowly over many years, it may be hard to detect it convincingly in samples of only 20 or 30 years.

In order to increase the power of tests against a null hypothesis of a random walk, Frankel (1986) and Edison (1987) greatly lengthen the sample period (to about 100 years) and are able to reject the hypothesis that RERs follow a random walk. Further studies confirm their findings. Typically, these studies find that the RER returns toward a stable long-run value at the rate of 10 to 30 percent per year. This convergence to PPP often is reported in terms of the "half-life" of PPP deviations—in other words, the length of time it takes for the RER to cover half the distance to PPP. According to Rogoff (1996), estimated half-lives are remarkably concentrated around three to five years. The slow convergence of PPP deviations helps to explain why a long sample is needed to have a high degree of confidence that PPP really holds in the long run.

An alternative approach that gained popularity in the 1990s was to test for long-run PPP in panel data sets (time series for several countries) under the assumption that long-run PPP or the lack thereof is common to all countries. Using post-1973 data, studies typically find that long-run PPP holds, with roughly the same three- to five-year half-life that is estimated in the 100-year samples for individual countries.[51]

A caveat noted by Rogoff (1996) is that evidence on long-run PPP is

---

51. Early panel studies are criticized by O'Connell (1998), who shows that the presence of cross-country correlation biases the test statistic for stationarity. Subsequent studies, discussed below, find evidence of long-run PPP even after taking this bias into consideration.

stronger for countries at similar stages of development. According to a model first advanced by Harrod (1933) and later developed by Balassa (1964) and Samuelson (1964), rapidly developing economies tend to have faster productivity growth in traded goods. This productivity growth depresses traded goods prices relative to prices of nontraded goods. If PPP holds over traded goods, then nontraded goods prices tend to rise in faster-growing countries relative to slower-growing countries. A RER that includes nontraded goods prices tends to rise permanently for fast-growing countries.

A final point raised by Rogoff (1996) is that cumulative current account surpluses may tend to raise a country's RER in the long run. In studies not covered by Rogoff's survey, Faruqee (1995), Gagnon (1996), and Lane and Milesi-Ferretti (2002) find evidence of long-run PPP augmented by a significant effect of net foreign assets.

Studies Since 1996

Edison, Gagnon, and Melick (1997) show that a more powerful statistical test proposed by Horvath and Watson (1995) is able to reject the hypothesis of no long-run PPP in post-1973 data for 10 of 26 bilateral exchange rates. This is rather strong evidence in favor of long-run PPP given the shortness of the sample. The evidence for PPP is much stronger for RERs with Germany than with the United States, perhaps reflecting Germany's greater exposure to trade and the proximity of Germany to many of the countries in the sample.

Papell and Prodan (2003) find significant evidence for long-run PPP in the RERs of 8 of 16 countries over roughly 100-year samples (bilateral exchange rates against the United States). In countries where the hypothesis of no long-run PPP cannot be rejected, there is some evidence for structural breaks or trends, perhaps owing to Harrod-Balassa-Samuelson (HBS) effects.

Cheung, Lai, and Bergman (2004) replicate the Rogoff findings of half-lives of three to five years using standard linear methods for bilateral RERs of France, Germany, Italy, Japan, and the United Kingdom against the United States from 1973 through 1998. They reject a unit root in all cases except Japan. They also show that most of the adjustment to long-run PPP occurs via the nominal exchange rate rather than via price levels.

Taylor (2002) examines more than a century of RER data on 20 mainly industrial countries. He finds evidence of mean reversion in all countries. For 17 of the 20 countries he rejects a unit root in trade-weighted RERs at the 10 percent significance level or better. He finds some evidence of a time trend or drift in the PPP exchange rate (RER^{PPP} in the terminology of this chapter), but the rate of change of RER^{PPP} is usually quite small. The median rate of change of RER^{PPP} (in absolute value) is 0.3 percent per year. Only in the case of Japan does the trend rate exceed 1 percent per year. These drifts are relatively steady over time, so that the innovation, or surprise, component in any year has a standard deviation well below 0.3 percent. This finding suggests that changes in expectations about RER^{PPP} 10 years ahead should be very small, as assumed implicitly in figures 3.8 and 3.13 and the regressions of table 3A.1. Taylor (2002) also finds that the volatility of RERs is noticeably larger under floating exchange rates than under fixed exchange rates, but the rate of reversion to PPP is not strongly affected by the exchange rate regime. He finds half-lives concentrated in the range of two to five years.

In their review article, Taylor and Taylor (2004) find support for both HBS and portfolio effects on the long-run real exchange rate. They argue that estimates of mean reversion to PPP are likely to be biased downward if such effects are not controlled for. They also argue that trade barriers and transportation costs are likely to create a nonlinearity in reversion to PPP. When deviations from PPP are small, the profits from arbitrage may not be sufficient to cover these costs. For moderately large deviations of 5 to 10 percent, Taylor, Peel, and Sarno (2001) find half-lives of just over two years, and they find even shorter half-lives for very large deviations of 20 percent or more. The evidence in Taylor and Taylor (2004) shows that mean reversion is especially pronounced during periods of high inflation, perhaps because temporary deviations are larger during such periods.

Lothian and Taylor (2008) examine 180 years of French, UK, and US data for evidence of the HBS effect in RERs. They posit that the HBS effect is correlated with relative real GDP per capita. In a specification with nonlinear mean reversion, they find significant evidence of such an effect in the UK-US RER but not in the UK-French RER. For the UK-US RER, the HBS effect is relatively flat from 1821 until 1895, and then it predicts a gradual depreciation of the UK RER of about 0.2 percent per year until 1975, after which it flattens out again. Lothian and Taylor (2008) find that the HBS effect explains very little of short-run fluctuations in the RER but that it can account for as much as 9 percent of variations over a seven-year horizon.[52]

Chong, Jorda, and Taylor (2010) estimate the HBS effect in a panel of 21 OECD countries from 1973 through 2008. As in Lothian and Taylor (2008), the HBS effect is modeled as proportional to the ratio of real GDP per capita between the countries whose RER is being examined. When the effect is constrained to be equal in each country, it is estimated that the RER appreciates by 0.57 to 0.78 percent of any increase in the ratio of real GDP per capita, depending on whether the RER is measured relative to the United States or to the whole world. However, estimates differ considerably across countries when they are not constrained to be equal, and some have the wrong sign. For comparison, the analogous coefficient in Lothian and Taylor (2008) for the UK-US RER from 1821–2001 is 0.24. For the OECD countries, the ratio of real GDP per capita moves slowly over time and rarely exceeds a rate of 1 percent, and so the constrained HBS effects estimated by Chong, Jorda, and Taylor (2010) imply only a slow drift over time in RER^{PPP}.

---

52. In principle, the explanatory power of the HBS effect should continue to grow over longer horizons, but the sample is not long enough to permit accurate measurement of the HBS effect at horizons much longer than seven years.

Cheung, Chinn, and Fujii (2008) study the HBS effect in a sample dominated by developing countries over the post–World War II period. They find a statistically significant effect, but the magnitude of this effect is highly sensitive to sample selection and modeling assumptions. Johnson et al. (2009) discuss some of the problems with the Penn World Table data used by Cheung, Chinn, and Fujii (2008). They show that the HBS effect is highly significant in a cross-section of developing countries; there is a strong tendency for absolute price levels to be higher in countries with a higher real per capita GDP (using PPP-adjusted GDP).

Lee and Tang (2007) use OECD sectoral data to test for PPP with an HBS effect. They find strong evidence for PPP with a long-run positive effect of labor productivity on the RER but no consistent effect of total factor productivity on the RER. Moreover, they show that the labor productivity effect on the RER operates through the RER for tradable goods, not through the RER for nontradable goods, which is at odds with the theory behind the HBS effect. One potential explanation is that fast-growing economies improve the quality of the tradable goods they produce and that this quality improvement is incorrectly measured as a price increase.

Imbs, Mumtaz, and Rey (2003) demonstrate theoretically that estimates of the half-life of deviations in the RER based on an aggregate price index in general will be higher than the weighted average of the half-lives of the individual relative prices. Using EU consumer price data for specific goods in different countries, they show that the average half-life of reversion to the LOP is 14 months, whereas the estimated half-life using an aggregate of the same data is 27 months.[53] However, their results imply that there are significant categories of goods with half-lives much greater than the 27 months estimated in the aggregate. Because goods with longer half-lives tend to have larger deviations from the LOP, they have larger effects on PPP deviations in aggregate price indices than their spending share would imply. Although Imbs, Mumtaz, and Rey (2003) make an interesting point concerning differences in half-lives across individual goods, their average estimates are not relevant for the overall behavior of consumer prices, which are dominated by those goods with long half-lives of return to the LOP.

Bergin, Glick, and Wu (2009) show that relatively rapid reversion to the LOP for prices of specific goods (as in Imbs, Mumtaz, and Rey 2003) reflects the effects of idiosyncratic shocks that average out in aggregate indices. After removing these idiosyncratic effects, they find that the half-lives of reversion to the LOP for specific goods are similar to the half-lives of RER reversion to PPP for aggregate price indices. They also confirm the result of Cheung, Lai, and Bergman (2004) that most of the reversion to PPP occurs through the exchange rate rather than through price levels. Parsley and Popper (2010) also

---

53. The aggregate half-life among EU countries is smaller than the average among OECD countries more broadly, probably reflecting greater proximity and lower trade costs.

find that deviations from the LOP for specific goods have a strong common element with deviations from PPP for broad price indices.

Conclusions

On balance, the broad consensus from numerous studies of long-run PPP is that RERs do tend to revert to equilibrium slowly over time and that almost all of this reversion occurs within 10 years of any shock. However, in some cases, equilibrium RERs seem to drift gradually over time, possibly reflecting the effects of differential rates of development (HBS) or portfolio effects through net foreign asset accumulation.

4

Do Volatile Exchange Rates Reduce Economic Output?

> Chasuble: *I suppose you know all about relations between Capital and Labour?*
> Cecily: *I am afraid I am not learned at all. All I know is about the relations between Capital and Idleness—and that is merely from observation.*
> —Oscar Wilde, *The Importance of Being Earnest*

In principle, volatile exchange rates may reduce long-run economic output through wasted expenditures on foreign exchange transactions, costly adjustments in the structure of the economy, and the damping effects on international trade and business investment of exchange rate uncertainty. On the other hand, giving up monetary policy independence to peg the exchange rate may reduce long-run economic output through costly swings in overall economic activity and in inflation and through the damping effects on business investment of uncertainty about future activity and inflation.

This chapter shows that volatile exchange rates do increase spending on financial transactions by a small amount. The only way to substantially reduce such expenditures is to adopt a common global currency, which is not a viable option for the foreseeable future. The chapter also shows that volatile exchange rates do discourage international trade to a modest extent, although other factors appear to be much more important in explaining differences in trade across countries.

Most important, there is no apparent effect from volatile exchange rates— one way or the other—on the level of economic output or the long-run growth rate of an economy. Many other factors appear to be far more important than the exchange rate regime in explaining the large differences across economies in levels of output per capita or long-run rates of economic growth.

Volatile Exchange Rates and Financial Transactions

As discussed in chapter 3, the level of trading activity in global foreign exchange markets far exceeds the requirements of international trade. It also far exceeds the reported gross flows of cross-border investment. Much of this trading activity is the result of financial market participants taking short-term positions in response to uncertainty and volatility in exchange rates. But much of it also may result from short-term cross-border positions in underlying financial instruments, such as bonds and equities, which are unrelated to exchange rate volatility.

Foreign Exchange Market Turnover

Table 4.1 provides an overview of some foreign exchange transactions in currencies with pegged exchange rates and in currencies with floating exchange rates. The Bank for International Settlements (BIS 2010) reports transaction data for only three pegged currencies: the Danish krone, which is pegged to the euro, and the Chinese renminbi and Hong Kong dollar, which are pegged to the US dollar. For comparison with the Danish krone, the table includes transactions in the Norwegian krone, which floats freely. For comparison with the Hong Kong dollar, the table includes the Singapore dollar, which has a managed float.[1] For comparison with the Chinese renminbi, the table includes transactions in the Indian rupee, which has a managed float. Because Hong Kong is an entrepôt for Chinese trade, the table also includes combined entries for the renminbi and Hong Kong dollar. Finally, the table includes trading in all currencies (corrected for double counting) as well as trading in world equity markets.[2]

The first column of table 4.1 lists annualized turnover in the foreign exchange market for each currency. The second column lists the average growth rate of turnover in the previous nine years. Annual turnover grew rapidly for all currencies except the Danish krone. Turnover in foreign exchange markets grew roughly twice as fast as turnover in equity markets.

It is common to measure the turnover of financial transactions relative to the market value of the underlying assets. For example, the memorandum line of the table shows that global trading in equity markets in 2009 was roughly two times global equity market capitalization. Transactions in the foreign exchange market involve claims on bank deposits. Thus, two measures of the value of the assets underlying foreign exchange transactions are total bank deposits and external bank liabilities, and columns 3 and 4 show the ratios of foreign exchange turnover to these measures.[3] Foreign exchange transactions also are required to

---

1. As shown in table 2.1, the IMF classifies Singapore as a soft peg (other managed arrangement) but it is more appropriately characterized as a managed float because the central bank regularly updates its basket target in light of domestic economic conditions.

2. Each currency transaction is recorded twice, reflecting that two currencies are involved. This is appropriate for analysis of total transactions in the currency of a given country, but at the global level it overstates the number of transactions by a factor of two.

3. The BIS defines external bank liabilities to include claims by foreigners on a country's banks (mainly deposits) plus any liabilities of the banks to domestic residents that are denominated in foreign currency.

Table 4.1   Spot foreign exchange turnover in selected currencies, 2010

Currency	Annual spot foreign exchange turnover (trillions of dollars) (1)	Turnover growth, 2001–10 (percent annual rate) (2)	Ratio of turnover to 2010 total bank deposits (3)	2010 external bank liabilities (4)	2009 gross balance of payments transactions (5)	2009 GDP (6)
Pegged exchange rate						
Danish krone	1	5	7[a]	4	3	4
Hong Kong dollar	5	14	7[b]	9	4	22
Chinese renminbi	2	81	0.2	n.a.	0.7	0.4
Hong Kong + China	7	18	0.6	n.a.	2	1.3
Floating exchange rate						
Norwegian krone	3	19	12[a]	16	6	8
Singapore dollar	4	21	14	5	5	21
Indian rupee	3	31	4[b]	36	4	3
All currencies (no double counting)	373	16	6[c]	14	7	6

	Stocks traded in 2009 (trillions of dollars)	Trading growth, 2001–09 (percent annual rate)	Ratio of trading to market value	Ratio of trading to GDP
Memorandum: World equity	81	9	2	1.4

n.a. = not available

a. For Denmark and Norway, ratios are based on M2.
b. For Hong Kong and India, ratios are based on 2009 deposits.
c. These deposits are global "money + quasi money" for 2008 from World Bank, *World Development Indicators*.

Notes: The Bank for International Settlements (BIS) surveys refer to average daily foreign exchange trading in the month of April. These data are annualized under the assumption of 250 trading days per year. Double counting arises because each transaction is recorded under two currencies; this has a major effect on the dollar and the euro, which are the main vehicle currencies. Global totals are divided by two to correct for double counting, but the individual country data are not adjusted. The external bank liabilities data refer to June 2010.

Sources: BIS (2010), BIS Locational Banking Statistics database, IMF *International Financial Statistics* database, World Bank *World Development Indicators* database (equity data), and authors' calculations.

support international trade and cross-border investment, and column 5 displays the ratio of foreign exchange turnover to gross balance of payments transactions.[4] The table also shows turnover relative to GDP (column 6).

---

4. Gross balance of payments transactions are the sum of the absolute values of all categories of current account and financial account flows reported by the IMF. The financial account flows

All the turnover ratios are higher for the floating Norwegian krone than for the fixed Danish krone. Similarly, all the turnover ratios are higher for the floating Indian rupee than for the fixed Chinese renminbi. The comparison of turnover ratios between the floating Singapore dollar and the fixed Hong Kong dollar is less clear-cut: Some are higher, some are lower, and some are similar. Hong Kong's role as an entrepôt for Chinese trade may distort the Hong Kong turnover data. This is supported by the fact that when the Chinese and Hong Kong data are added together, the resulting turnover ratios are all lower than the corresponding ratios for both Singapore and India.[5]

Overall, these results support the view that floating exchange rates increase the volume of transactions in the foreign exchange market. However, even in countries with a fixed exchange rate, foreign exchange transactions exceed the needs of international trade and cross-border investment by a considerable margin, as shown in column 5. This excess trading activity likely reflects short-term cross-border positioning in underlying financial instruments, such as bonds and equities, for reasons unrelated to speculation or hedging of volatile exchange rates. Trading in equity markets is growing rapidly, and although it is not growing as rapidly as trading in foreign exchange markets, it is growing faster than both equity market capitalization and world GDP. One source of this growth is the rise in gross cross-border asset holdings, which have grown much faster than GDP in countries that report such data. This trend toward portfolio diversification across borders likely will support continued growth in foreign exchange transactions regardless of exchange rate regime.

Derivatives Markets

Derivatives contracts are another important source of foreign exchange trans-action costs.[6] Financial derivatives have grown tremendously in all financial markets in recent years. According to BIS (2010), combined global turnover in foreign exchange forward, swap, and options contracts exceeds turnover in spot transactions by nearly 70 percent. Table 4.2 outlines the size of global derivatives markets in terms of the notional value of the contracts. In other words, an option to buy $1 million of foreign currency is valued as a $1 million derivative. If the underlying market for foreign exchange derivatives is taken to be global bank deposits, then the foreign exchange derivatives market is roughly equal in size to the underlying market. In comparison, the notional value of interest rate derivatives is nearly six times the size of the global bond

---

reflect net transactions within each category over the course of 2009, for example foreign purchases and sales of a class of domestic assets are netted out, but foreign purchases of domestic assets are not netted against domestic purchases of foreign assets.

5. These comparisons also are distorted by international capital controls in China and India. China's controls are widely viewed to be stricter than India's, and they probably contribute to reduced turnover in the renminbi.

6. Financial derivatives are contracts whose value depends on the price of an underlying asset.

Table 4.2   Global financial derivatives, 2010 (trillions of US dollars)

	Derivative type			
	Foreign exchange	**Interest rate**	**Credit**	**Equity**
Notional value of contracts	63	549	31	13
Underlying market	58	94	94	49

Notes: Interest rate derivatives refer to those in a single currency. Notional amounts are the sum of over-the-counter data (June) and organized exchanges data (September). Underlying market data are for "money + quasi money" in 2008 (foreign exchange), domestic plus international debt securities in September 2010 (interest rate and credit), and 2009 market capitalization of listed companies (equity).

Sources: BIS (2010), BIS securities database, and World Bank *World Development Indicators* 2010 database.

market. The notional value of credit and equity derivatives, though large, is notably smaller than the underlying markets. Clearly, foreign exchange derivatives are important, but their volume is not obviously out of line with derivative activity in other financial markets.

Foreign Exchange Transaction Costs

A widely cited study by Emerson, Gros, and Italianer (1990) argues that EU citizens would save 0.3 to 0.4 percent of GDP per year in foreign exchange transaction costs after the launch of the euro.[7] The study examines four types of transaction costs: (1) direct business expenses on foreign exchange transactions, (2) direct consumer expenses on foreign exchange transactions, (3) in-house business costs for managing exchange rate variability, and (4) improvements in cross-border payments technology that would be mandated by European law. The first three of these components are used here to estimate the worldwide cost of all foreign exchange transactions as of 2010. (The fourth component is omitted because laws on cross-border payments technology can be adopted with or without currency reform.)

Direct Business Expenses on Foreign Exchange Transactions

Direct business costs of foreign exchange transactions, including those of financial businesses, can be estimated using total reported transactions (both interbank and bank-customer and including all foreign exchange derivative transactions) and multiplying by half of the bid-ask spread in the wholesale

---

7. This estimate is based only on the costs of internal EU transactions, given that countries outside the European Union would continue to have separate currencies. The study also assumed that the euro would be adopted by all 15 existing EU members. It did not consider that some EU countries would stay out of the euro area, that new countries would join, or that trade and cross-border investment would grow relative to GDP.

market.[8] (Businesses whose transactions are smaller than those of the whole-sale market are included in the estimate of direct consumer costs.) For whole-sale trades between the three major currencies (dollar, euro, and yen), the typical bid-ask spread is 1 basis point; this category represents 45 percent of all transactions. For trades between these currencies and those of the other large advanced economies, typical bid-ask spreads are 2 to 4 basis points; this category represents 32 percent of all transactions. For trades between the major currencies and smaller advanced economies or larger emerging market economies, typical bid-ask spreads are 5 to 10 basis points. Finally, for all other trades, bid-ask spreads are more than 10 basis points, in some cases much more. The last two categories represent 23 percent of all transactions.

Almost all (98 percent) of reported currency transactions involve at least one of the three major currencies. Ultimate transactions between non-major currencies generally are transacted in two steps involving first the purchase and then the sale of a major currency. Some derivatives transactions have higher spreads than these, especially for contracts with maturities of 30 days or more, but the overwhelming majority have maturities of 7 days or less (BIS 2010), and thus do not have significantly higher spreads than those on spot transactions.

Based on these spreads and volumes, total wholesale foreign exchange transaction costs in 2010 were about $185 billion, or 0.3 percent of estimated 2010 world GDP.[9] Banks may charge higher spreads than these to their business customers, but the overwhelming share of these transactions (87 percent) occur between banks. Indeed, some of the transactions undoubtedly occur between different branches or subsidiaries of the same bank, in which case the assumed bid-ask spreads surely exaggerate the cost. Moreover, as discussed in Emerson, Gros, and Italianer (1990), each customer transaction may be supported by one or more interbank transactions, and so attributing a higher cost to the customer transactions at the same time that we add in the cost of interbank transactions would lead to double counting. Also, the true cost to society is based on the resources devoted to foreign exchange transactions and not on the pricing strategies of banks. By convention, foreign exchange transactions are a profit center for banks, which use these fees to cross-subsidize other transactions that are provided for free. Therefore, this methodology likely overstates the true resource cost to society of these transactions. On balance, however, $185 billion is a plausible upper bound of the direct costs of large-scale foreign exchange transactions.

---

8. Transaction volume data are from BIS (2010). Bid-ask spreads are based on personal contacts with traders at hedge funds and large commercial banks. The cost of an individual transaction is half of the bid-ask spread because a purchase at the ask rate and a sale at the bid rate constitutes two transactions with a total cost equal to the bid-ask spread.

9. This reflects an assumed average bid-ask spread of 10 basis points for the third and fourth categories, which is probably too high because transactions are concentrated in the currencies of the relatively larger and more advanced economies, which have lower bid-ask spreads. Estimated 2010 GDP is from IMF (2011b).

Direct Consumer Expenses on Foreign Exchange Transactions

Smaller-scale retail transactions clearly are more expensive, but they are also tiny compared to the size of the wholesale foreign exchange markets. These transactions include the exchange of banknotes and traveler's checks, small-scale bank transfers, and credit card transactions by consumers and small businesses. Emerson, Gros, and Italianer (1990) estimate these costs to aggregate to about one-quarter of the total cost of large-scale transactions. Based on the estimate above of global wholesale foreign exchange transactions costs for 2010, these would be no more than $45 billion. Tourism and small business cross-border activities likely were relatively more important within Europe in 1990 than they are for the world as a whole in 2010, reflecting the high degree of economic integration in the European Union. Thus, this estimate of global retail transaction costs may be too high.

The plausibility of this estimate can be assessed using the accounts of two of the world's largest corporations engaged in retail foreign exchange transactions: Travelex and Western Union. For 2009, Travelex reports total revenues of $1 billion.[10] About half of these revenues derive from consumer foreign exchange transactions and half from processing international business payments and "outsourcing." The latter activities likely involve, but are not limited to, foreign exchange conversion; and so Travelex's total foreign exchange revenues were between $500 million and $1 billion in 2009. For 2010, Western Union reports total revenues of $5.2 billion, of which $1 billion are identified as "foreign exchange revenues."[11] On a worldwide basis, the retail foreign exchange industry is highly fragmented, with banks in all countries engaged in this business to some extent. Nevertheless, the fact that two of the largest firms in the industry have foreign-exchange-related revenues of no more than $1 billion each suggests that the global costs of retail foreign exchange transactions are most likely less than $45 billion.

In-House Business Costs for Managing Exchange Rate Variability

The in-house costs of managing a nonfinancial business in a world of volatile exchange rates range from keeping track of accounts in different currencies to designing strategies to hedge against exchange rate volatility, both operationally and financially. These costs do not include the direct costs of financial transactions and hedging, which are captured in the other components. Emerson, Gros, and Italianer (1990) estimate these in-house costs aggregate

---

10. Travelex claims to be "the world's largest retail foreign exchange specialist" as well as "the world's largest global non-bank wholesale foreign exchange supplier" and "the world's largest non-bank provider of commercial cross-border payments services." Travelex's annual reports are available at www.travelex.com.

11. According to its website (www.westernunion.com), Western Union operates in 200 countries and territories with 445,000 agents.

to about half of the direct cost of wholesale transactions, but this estimate is acknowledged to be the least precise of the three components. Their estimate is based loosely on responses to a questionnaire sent to six nonfinancial companies in Europe as well as a study of small and medium enterprises in Belgium. Applying this ratio globally in 2010 implies an upper bound on in-house business costs of $90 billion.

The Scope for Reducing Foreign Exchange Transaction Costs

Altogether, the three components sum to an upper bound on foreign exchange transaction costs of $325 billion in 2010, or 0.5 percent of world GDP. Eliminating these costs would require that the entire world adopt a common currency. The savings to any one country from joining a regional currency union are much lower; they are roughly proportional to the fraction of the country's total international trade and cross-border investment conducted within the region. On average, if a country conducts half of its trade and investment with other members of a currency union, it could expect to save half its estimated transaction costs, or no more than 0.25 percent of GDP.

Note that only a fraction of these savings can be achieved by pegging exchange rates. If a hard peg is highly credible, it can reduce costs of managing exchange rate volatility. But pegged exchange rates still require extra transactions and bookkeeping relative to a common currency. For example, Denmark—with its highly credible and long-lived peg to the euro—has spot foreign exchange transactions equal to three times its gross international trade and cross-border investment and an even higher volume of transactions in foreign exchange derivatives. In a world in which the major currencies float against each other, a country saves relatively little in transactions cost by pegging its currency to those of its immediate neighbors.

Moreover, it is not obvious that foreign exchange transaction costs represent a pure waste of resources. The growth of financial activity relative to overall economic activity is widespread across the advanced economies and in many developing economies, too. In each of the Group of 7 (G-7) highly industrialized economies, the share of GDP originating in the finance industry has increased by 10 to 15 percentage points in a steady trend since 1970. This increase almost surely reflects technological and financial innovations and is spread across a wide range of markets, including equities, real estate, bonds, and foreign exchange.

Volatile Exchange Rates and International Trade

Rose (2000) reports a stunning empirical regularity: Countries in a currency union conduct 200 to 400 percent more trade with each other than normally expected based on their sizes, locations, and other factors. Subsequent research by Rose and others scaled back these implausibly large estimates by taking more careful account of other factors that affect trade, but they still find large estimated increases in trade, on the order of 50 percent (Rose and van Wincoop 2001, Rose 2008). Similarly, countries that peg their currency to that of another country tend to have higher trade with the target country, although the effect is much smaller than for a currency union (Klein and Shambaugh 2010, Qureshi and Tsangarides 2010).

All these estimates still may be too large to be true. In particular, it is very difficult to disentangle the causality. Does a currency union (or a pegged exchange rate) promote more trade between member countries? Or are countries that trade a lot with each other (or want to trade a lot with each other) more likely to form a currency union (or peg their exchange rates)? An interesting statistical finding that points to causality running from trade to a pegged exchange rate is that two countries that peg to the same anchor country actually trade slightly less with each other, even though they each trade more with the anchor country. This suggests that peripheral countries choose to peg to countries with which they already trade a lot and that this choice has little effect on their trading patterns. If causality ran instead from exchange rate stability to trade, one would expect trade between peripheral countries pegged to the same currency to be high.

Even if reducing exchange rate variability against a given country is presumed to increase trade with that country, and even if the reduction in exchange rate variability is presumed to come without any cost in higher variability of output and inflation, there is another issue to consider. If the increase in trade within a currency union (or between countries with a pegged exchange rate) comes at the expense of less trade with countries outside the union, the economic benefits are correspondingly reduced. For this reason, it is important to look at the effects of the exchange rate regime on total trade, not just on trade with specific countries.[12]

The formation of the euro area provides a natural test of the effects of exchange rate stability on trade. Baldwin (2006) and Lane (2006) find that trade among members of the euro area increased between 5 and 15 percent more than would otherwise have occurred. They also find little evidence of any reduction in trade with countries outside the euro area. These findings raise the possibility that creation of the euro area may have slightly boosted output among member countries.[13] Of course, greater trade links are no proof of a positive output effect. As discussed in chapter 7, the lack of an independent monetary policy exacerbated the fiscal problems of several peripheral members of the euro area in 2010 and 2011, which in turn has hampered economic growth. The long-run effects of this lack of policy independence have yet to be determined.

---

12. Rose and van Wincoop (2001) factor this into their conclusions.

13. Higher trade raises output only to the extent that it increases specialization and efficiency in production and variety in consumption. The efficiency and variety effects on output are only a small fraction of the increase in trade volumes.

Table 4.3 outlines the effects on trade of the creation of the euro area for selected European countries. The table focuses on total trade, rather than internal trade, because it is a better indicator of the potential for increased output. The first column displays trade as a share of GDP in the five years from 1989 through 1993. The second column displays the trade share in the most recent five years for which data are available, 2005–09. The third column displays the net increase in trade between 1989–93 and 2005–09. To better isolate the maximum effects caused by the euro, the years immediately before and after its adoption in 1999 are excluded.[14] However, the results are not noticeably different when the 10-year period 1989–98 is compared with the 10-year period 2000–09.

The upper part of the table displays trade shares for the 12 countries that were members of the euro area as of 2001. The lower part of the table displays trade shares for six countries that were members of the European Free Trade Area (EFTA) but not the euro area in 2001.[15]

The average increase in trade as a share of GDP for euro-area countries is 32 percentage points, which is 11 percentage points higher than the average increase for the other EFTA countries. The GDP-weighted increase for euro-area countries is 25 percentage points, which is also 11 percentage points higher than the GDP-weighted increase for the other EFTA countries. These numbers are at the high end of the estimates cited above that the common currency increased trade by around 5 to 15 percent, or by somewhat less as a share of GDP. However, the difference in trade growth between euro-area countries and the other EFTA countries is not even close to being statistically significant. Many of the other EFTA countries experienced higher increases in trade than those experienced by many euro-area countries. In fact, excluding the two outliers, Luxembourg and Norway, the average trade increases are equal across the two groups.[16] Moreover, during 2005–09 all of the other EFTA countries had higher trade shares than several of the most important euro-area countries. This suggests that there may be less scope for trade increases in economies that already trade a lot.

The countries listed in table 4.3 that have close trade links to Central and Eastern European countries experienced more rapid trade growth than other European countries. These include Austria, Finland, Germany, and Sweden. On the other hand, France, Portugal, and the United Kingdom have weaker trade links with Eastern Europe, and they have more slowly growing trade shares. These differences appear to be driven by the interaction of rapid

---

14. Some researchers argue that the effect of the common currency on trade started a few years before its 1999 launch. It probably also continued for several years afterward.

15. All members of the euro area are members of EFTA. The new euro area and EFTA members from Central and Eastern Europe are not included because changes in their economies were dominated by the transition from socialist to market economies.

16. Excluding these outliers has little effect on the GDP-weighted increases.

Table 4.3 Exports and imports as share of GDP in selected European countries (percent)

Country	1989–93	2005–09	Net increase
Euro area members as of 2001			
Austria	71	107	36
Belgium	129	159	30
Finland	50	83	33
France	43	53	10
Germany	49	83	34
Greece	46	55	9
Ireland	113	155	42
Italy	38	55	17
Luxembourg	188	308	120
Netherlands	108	137	29
Portugal	61	69	8
Spain	36	57	21
Euro area average	78	110	32
GDP-weighted average	52	77	25
Selected European Free Trade Association (EFTA) members			
Denmark	70	99	29
Iceland	63	85	22
Norway	71	74	3
Sweden	59	94	35
Switzerland	70	97	27
United Kingdom	49	58	9
EFTA average	64	85	21
GDP-weighted average	57	71	14

Source: Organization for Economic Cooperation and Development (OECD) National Accounts database.

development in Eastern Europe with geographic proximity, not with currency union.[17]

Excluding merchandise trade with Central and Eastern Europe would reduce the GDP-weighted net increase of euro-area trade from 25 to 19 percent of GDP, whereas it would reduce the GDP-weighted net increase of other EFTA trade from 14 to 12 percent of GDP.[18] The excess trade growth of the euro area

---

17. Trade is not likely to have been affected much by the fact that a few of the eastern countries are planning to join the euro area soon (or recently joined). Most are not planning to join in the foreseeable future. The gravity model used by most researchers on this topic does take geographic distance into consideration.

18. This calculation is based on merchandise exports and imports to developing Europe, Czech

over the non-euro EFTA countries thus would be reduced from 11 percentage points to 7 percentage points. Moreover, this adjustment covers only goods trade and not services trade, and so it may underestimate the effect of trade between Western and Eastern Europe. Overall, the evidence indicates that the common currency has had a moderate positive effect on trade, but this cannot be asserted with a high degree of confidence.

Taking a more global perspective, it is worth noting that despite high exchange rate volatility across the major regions, trade and cross-border investment have continued to grow relative to world GDP. According to the International Monetary Fund (IMF 2011b), world GDP in US dollars grew at an average annual rate of 5.3 percent from 1990 to 2010. During the same period, world exports grew at an average annual rate of 7.7 percent. Over the past 10 years, both GDP and exports have grown even faster, averaging 6.8 percent and 8.8 percent, respectively. Data on cross-border investment is less comprehensively available, but for countries that report to the IMF's Coordinated Portfolio Investment Survey, total cross-border portfolio asset holdings increased at a very rapid 14.3 percent per year from 2001 through 2009. Altogether, there seems to be little evidence that currency volatility is a significant drag on growth of trade and cross-border investment.

Direct Evidence on Output and Growth

Even if volatile exchange rates were found to increase transaction costs and reduce international trade, the bottom line for the overall effect on economic well-being is the effect on economic output. In principle, higher transaction costs, lower trade, and wasteful resource shifts across economic sectors may reduce an economy's long-run output or GDP.[19] But these effects may be more than offset by the beneficial effects of more stable inflation and output, which a central bank can pursue through the use of monetary policy when the exchange rate is free to float. In the end, the question is an empirical one. This section examines the effects of exchange rate volatility on long-run economic growth and the level of output. (Chapters 5 and 6 explore the relationship between volatility of exchange rates and the *volatility* of output and inflation.)

Republic, Slovak Republic, and Slovenia from the IMF's *Direction of Trade Statistics* database. For Belgium and Luxembourg, these data are available only on a combined basis, and so there is no unweighted average calculated for the euro area as in table 4.3.

19. There is a measurement problem because consumer spending on foreign exchange transactions is included in GDP even though it provides no real benefit to consumers. However, this is by far the smallest component of foreign exchange transaction costs, well under 0.1 percent of GDP, and the other components are not included in GDP. Indeed, to the extent that businesses produce less final output because of the resources they devote to foreign exchange transactions, these costs should lower measured GDP.

Exchange Rate Volatility and Economic Output

A casual observation reveals no clear connection between output and exchange rate volatility or the exchange rate regime. It is possible for economies of all sizes and income levels to operate with either a fixed or a floating exchange rate. There are large advanced economies and small advanced economies at both ends of the spectrum of exchange rate regimes (see table 2.1). Even the otherwise rather similar Nordic economies of Finland and Sweden are at opposite ends of the spectrum. Among developing economies, there is a tendency for smaller economies to be on the fixed end of the spectrum, but there are exceptions such as Albania, Armenia, Mauritius, and even tiny Seychelles (population 87,000). Giant China, on the other hand, has a relatively fixed exchange rate.

Therefore, to gauge the effects on output of exchange rate stability, it is helpful to rank countries according to the variability of their exchange rates. Note that it is impossible for any one country to stabilize its exchange rate against all other countries unless all countries have a fixed exchange rate. Therefore, a country that desires to peg its exchange rate can choose only one anchor currency against which to stabilize.[20] The anchor generally can be assumed to be the currency of the country's most important trading or investing partner, which maximizes any benefits on trade or cross-border investment.

According to the IMF (2010), the overwhelming majority of countries with an exchange rate anchor use either the US dollar or the euro as their reference currency. A small number of countries use a basket of currencies, and even fewer use an individual currency other than the dollar or euro. For the former countries, the (unspecified) basket can be reasonably approximated by the IMF's special drawing right (SDR), which is a basket of the dollar, euro, yen, and UK pound; the latter countries are not included in this analysis.[21] Table 4.4 lists the standard deviation of the exchange rate for each country, calculated on a monthly basis against the dollar, the euro, or the SDR from 2000 through 2009 (the reference currency is that which yields the lowest standard deviation).[22] The table also displays population and per capita GDP (output) in dollars adjusted by purchasing power parity (PPP).[23]

---

20. It is possible to stabilize against a weighted average of more than one currency, sometimes referred to as a currency basket, but in that case the stabilization against any individual currency is incomplete.

21. The dropped countries are Bhutan, Brunei Darussalam, Kiribati, Lesotho, Namibia, Nepal, and Swaziland.

22. For Japan, the United Kingdom, and the United States, the SDR is excluded because it is defined in terms of these currencies and the euro. Members of the euro area are assigned a volatility of 0 because their currencies are fixed to each other. The ranking essentially would be unaffected in terms of the monthly changes in the exchange rate, as the correlation between the standard deviations in levels and in changes is 0.98.

23. In order to compare real output across countries, it is common to adjust for differences in price levels. The World Bank's PPP-adjusted GDP data express each country's GDP in terms of US

Table 4.4   Exchange rate volatility, income, and population, selected countries, 2000–2009

	Country	Standard deviation of exchange rate	Reference currency	2009 GDP per capita (PPP) (thousands of dollars)	2009 population (millions)
1	Belgium	0.0	EUR	36	11
2	Austria	0.0	EUR	38	8
3	United Arab Emirates	0.0	USD	58	5
4	Spain	0.0	EUR	33	46
5	Antigua and Barbuda	0.0	USD	19	<1
6	Panama	0.0	USD	13	3
7	Grenada	0.0	USD	8	<1
8	Portugal	0.0	EUR	25	11
9	Dominica	0.0	USD	9	<1
10	Finland	0.0	EUR	35	5
11	Montenegro	0.0	EUR	13	1
12	Germany	0.0	EUR	36	82
13	Luxembourg	0.0	EUR	84	<1
14	Djibouti	0.0	USD	2	1
15	Turkmenistan	0.0	USD	7	5
16	St. Lucia	0.0	USD	10	<1
17	Lebanon	0.0	USD	13	4
18	Saudi Arabia	0.0	USD	23	25
19	Italy	0.0	EUR	32	60
20	St. Kitts and Nevis	0.0	USD	15	<1
21	Qatar	0.0	USD	91	1
22	Belize	0.0	USD	7	<1
23	France	0.0	EUR	34	63
24	Netherlands	0.0	EUR	41	17
25	Ireland	0.0	EUR	41	4
26	Jordan	0.0	USD	6	6
27	Syria	0.0	USD	5	21
28	El Salvador	0.0	USD	7	6
29	Greece	0.3	EUR	30	11
30	Cape Verde	0.4	EUR	4	1
31	Gabon	0.4	EUR	14	1
32	Mali	0.4	EUR	1	13
33	Chad	0.4	EUR	1	11
34	Burkina Faso	0.4	EUR	1	16
35	Niger	0.4	EUR	1	15
36	Senegal	0.4	EUR	2	13
37	Cameroon	0.4	EUR	2	20
38	Benin	0.4	EUR	2	9

(table continues next page)

Table 4.4 Exchange rate volatility, income, and population, selected countries, 2000–2009 *(continued)*

	Country	Standard deviation of exchange rate	Reference currency	2009 GDP per capita (PPP) (thousands of dollars)	2009 population (millions)
39	Republic of Congo	0.4	EUR	4	4
40	Guinea-Bissau	0.4	EUR	1	2
41	Togo	0.4	EUR	1	7
42	Equatorial Guinea	0.4	EUR	32	1
43	Comoros	0.4	EUR	1	1
44	Bosnia and Herzegovina	0.4	EUR	8	4
45	Estonia	0.5	EUR	19	1
46	Denmark	0.5	EUR	37	6
47	Bulgaria	0.5	EUR	13	8
48	Trinidad and Tobago	0.7	USD	26	1
49	Nicaragua	0.9	SDR	3	6
50	Former Yugoslav Republic of Macedonia	0.9	EUR	11	2
51	Croatia	1.9	EUR	20	4
52	Cambodia	2.5	USD	2	15
53	Guatemala	2.6	USD	5	14
54	Lithuania	2.9	EUR	17	3
55	Maldives	3.0	USD	5	<1
56	Latvia	3.1	SDR	15	2
57	Switzerland	3.3	EUR	45	8
58	Singapore	4.0	SDR	51	5
59	Peru	4.2	SDR	9	29
60	Samoa	4.3	SDR	4	<1
61	Albania	4.4	EUR	8	3
62	Slovenia	4.6	SDR	27	2
63	Norway	4.6	EUR	56	5
64	Algeria	4.7	SDR	8	35
65	Tunisia	4.7	SDR	8	10
66	Hungary	4.7	EUR	20	10
67	Kyrgyzstan	4.9	SDR	2	5
68	Morocco	4.9	EUR	4	32
69	Malaysia	5.1	USD	14	27
70	Thailand	5.1	SDR	8	68
71	Vietnam	5.1	USD	3	87
72	Mauritania	5.1	USD	2	3
73	Australia	5.3	EUR	39	22
74	Vanuatu	5.5	EUR	4	<1
75	India	5.8	USD	3	1155
76	Sweden	5.9	EUR	38	9

(table continues next page)

Table 4.4 Exchange rate volatility, income, and population, selected countries, 2000–2009 *(continued)*

	Country	Standard deviation of exchange rate	Reference currency	2009 GDP per capita (PPP) (thousands of dollars)	2009 population (millions)
77	China	5.9	SDR	7	1331
78	Kenya	6.3	USD	2	40
79	Canada	6.7	EUR	38	34
80	Kazakhstan	6.8	SDR	12	16
81	Sudan	6.9	SDR	2	42
82	Azerbaijan	7.1	USD	10	9
83	Georgia	7.2	SDR	5	4
84	Tonga	7.2	USD	4	<1
85	Uganda	7.3	USD	1	33
86	Mauritius	7.3	USD	13	1
87	Fiji	7.3	SDR	5	1
88	Moldova	7.4	SDR	3	4
89	Yemen	7.4	USD	2	24
90	New Zealand	7.7	EUR	29	4
91	Mongolia	7.8	USD	4	3
92	Russia	8.1	SDR	19	142
93	Israel	8.1	SDR	28	7
94	Bolivia	8.7	USD	4	10
95	Poland	8.7	EUR	19	38
96	Indonesia	8.8	USD	4	230
97	Japan	8.8	USD	32	128
98	Honduras	8.9	USD	4	7
99	Philippines	9.2	USD	4	92
100	Serbia	9.3	USD	12	7
101	Chile	9.9	SDR	14	17
102	Bangladesh	10.0	USD	1	162
103	Papua New Guinea	10.1	SDR	2	7
104	Ethiopia	10.1	USD	1	83
105	Nigeria	10.2	USD	2	155
106	South Korea	10.5	SDR	27	49
107	Lao People's Democratic Republic	10.6	USD	2	6
108	Czech Republic	10.8	EUR	25	10
109	Slovak Republic	10.8	EUR	22	5
110	Mexico	11.0	USD	14	107
111	Sri Lanka	11.3	USD	5	20
112	United Kingdom	11.4	EUR	36	62
113	Pakistan	11.9	USD	3	170

(table continues next page)

Table 4.4 Exchange rate volatility, income, and population, selected countries, 2000–2009 *(continued)*

	Country	Standard deviation of exchange rate	Reference currency	2009 GDP per capita (PPP) (thousands of dollars)	2009 population (millions)
114	Colombia	12.5	SDR	9	46
115	Rwanda	12.7	USD	1	10
116	Ukraine	12.8	USD	6	46
117	Armenia	13.8	EUR	5	3
118	Romania	14.9	USD	14	21
119	Botswana	15.0	USD	13	2
120	Liberia	15.6	USD	<1	4
121	South Africa	15.6	SDR	10	49
122	Tanzania	15.8	USD	1	44
123	Solomon Islands	15.9	USD	3	1
124	Burundi	16.8	USD	<1	8
125	Mozambique	16.9	USD	1	23
126	Zambia	17.1	USD	1	13
127	United States	17.9	EUR	46	307
128	Sierra Leone	18.5	USD	1	6
129	Egypt	18.6	USD	6	83
130	Paraguay	20.0	USD	5	6
131	Brazil	20.0	SDR	10	194
132	Madagascar	20.4	USD	1	20
133	Costa Rica	20.7	USD	11	5
134	Jamaica	21.3	USD	8	3
135	Iceland	21.5	SDR	38	<1
136	Tajikistan	22.1	USD	2	7
137	Haiti	24.2	USD	1	10
138	Ghana	25.3	USD	2	24
139	Turkey	27.4	USD	14	75
140	The Gambia	28.0	USD	1	2
141	Uruguay	29.2	USD	13	3
142	Uzbekistan	30.6	EUR	3	28
143	Seychelles	30.7	USD	20	<1
144	Malawi	31.8	USD	1	15
145	Belarus	32.0	USD	13	10
146	Dominican Republic	33.6	USD	8	10
147	Libya	34.0	USD	17	6
148	Guinea	39.2	USD	1	10
149	Venezuela	44.6	USD	12	28
150	Argentina	46.6	USD	15	40
151	Iran	67.5	USD	12	73
152	Angola	72.4	USD	6	18

(table continues next page)

Table 4.4 Exchange rate volatility, income, and population, selected countries, 2000–2009 (continued)

	Correlations across all countries	
	Standard deviation of exchange rate	GDP per capita
GDP per capita (p-value)	−0.1520 (0.0615)	
Population (p-value)	0.2049 (0.0113)	−0.0767 (0.3478)
	Correlations excluding euro area and Gulf Cooperation Council	
	Standard deviation of exchange rate	GDP per capita
GDP per capita (p-value)	−0.0416 (0.6289)	
Population (p-value)	0.2328 (0.0062)	−0.0971 (0.2591)

PPP = purchasing power parity; USD = US dollar; EUR = euro; SDR = special drawing rights

Notes: Countries in currency unions are listed first, and then countries are listed according to exchange rate volatility (standard deviation of exchange rate).

Sources: IMF International Financial Statistics database, World Bank World Development Indicators 2010 database, and authors' calculations.

Countries in currency unions and with pegged exchange rates are listed first. In comparing between tables 2.1 and 4.4, note that table 2.1 is based on a country's exchange regime in 2010 only, whereas table 4.4 is based on exchange rate behavior during the 10 years from 2000 through 2009. Note that members of the two African currency unions are listed as having a small amount of exchange rate variability, reflecting their joint movements against the euro, even though members' currencies remained fixed against each other (the difference in their ranking would be minimal if they were listed as having zero volatility against each other).

As table 4.4 reveals, there is little correlation between per capita GDP or population size and exchange rate variability. There is a clustering of countries with especially high per capita GDP near the top of the table, but this reflects the fact that a number of rich countries in Europe belong to the euro area and that some rich countries in the Gulf Cooperation Council (GCC) peg their currencies to the US dollar.[24]

---

dollars at US prices. Because prices for many services are lower in developing economies than in the United States, their GDP levels are higher in PPP terms than in terms of market prices.

24. The GCC countries included in table 4.4 are Qatar, Saudi Arabia, and United Arab Emirates.

The bottom section of table 4.4 displays the correlations across each column in the table. The first set of correlations includes all countries in the table. These correlations are all small, but the negative correlation between exchange rate variability and per capita GDP is almost statistically significant and the positive correlation between exchange rate variability and population is strongly significant.[25] In short, smaller countries are more likely to peg their exchange rates, larger countries are more likely to float, and richer countries may be more likely to peg. The second set of correlations excludes the countries in the euro area and the GCC. If we are interested in whether exchange rate variability reduces per capita GDP, excluding these countries is appropriate because (1) the European common currency was created long after its member countries had become rich and thus cannot be viewed as the cause of their high per capita GDP and (2) the choice of exchange rate regime clearly had no effect on the oil deposits in the Persian Gulf. In both of these groups, causality, if any, runs from high output to a fixed exchange rate. For this set, the correlation between exchange rate variability and population remains strong, but the correlation between exchange rate variability and per capita GDP essentially drops to zero and is far from being statistically significant.

These results are corroborated by Rose (2010), who shows both graphically and statistically that there are no significant differences in the patterns of per capita GDP across categories of exchange rate regimes using any of the four classification schemes described in box 2.1 (Levy-Yeyati and Sturzenegger 2003, Reinhart and Rogoff 2004, Shambaugh 2004, IMF 2010).

It is important to recognize that correlations are no proof of causation nor is a lack of correlation proof of a lack of causation. If rich countries generally are those with better economic governance and more stable economic policies, it should be no surprise to find that they have greater stability in a wide range of economic variables, including exchange rates. This would indicate a negative correlation between exchange rate variability and per capita GDP, which is evident to a modest extent in table 4.4, but it does not indicate that exchange rate variability reduces output. The following subsection looks at attempts to identify causal effects on economic output from exchange rate regimes (and hence volatility).

Exchange Rate Volatility and Economic Growth

Because differences in per capita GDP across countries arise from many factors, such as natural resources, geography, history, and political and economic institutions, and because many countries have changed exchange rate regimes over time, most researchers focus on the effect of exchange rate

---

Data on per capita GDP are not available for other GCC countries, and therefore they are not included.

25. Statistical significance is denoted by the p-values in parentheses. A lower p-value denotes greater significance. A standard benchmark for significance is a p-value less than 0.05.

regimes on the growth rate of output rather than on the level of output. The idea is that, if a fixed exchange rate raises output in the long run and if countries sometimes change between fixed rates and floating rates, then countries with fixed rates should grow faster on average than countries with floating rates.[26] In their recent survey of research on exchange rate regimes, Klein and Shambaugh (2010) report that many studies find a statistically significant negative effect of a fixed exchange rate regime on growth compared with a floating exchange rate regime. However, this result disappears when some other explanatory factors for economic growth are included, such as initial GDP per capita, initial investment rate, population growth, and geographic effects. In a similar analysis with a different set of explanatory factors, Ghosh, Ostry, and Tsangarides (2010) also find no consistent effect of exchange rate regime on economic growth.[27]

Rose (2010) examines the effect of exchange rate regime on growth using a complete set of controls for countries and years instead of additional variables. Rose's results are summarized in table 4.5, each row of which reports the estimated effect of the given regime on economic growth (in annual percentage points) relative to growth under a pegged exchange rate.[28] For example, the entry of 0.8 in the narrow crawl column for the IMF (2010) de facto classification implies that countries with a crawling exchange rate peg grow 0.8 percentage points per year faster than countries with a fixed peg or currency union. The largest and most significant effect is −4.3 percentage points under a free fall in the Reinhart and Rogoff (2004) classification, but this result almost surely reflects reverse causation from a weak economy to a depreciating exchange rate. Moreover, it is not clear to what extent a free fall really is an exchange rate regime as opposed to a temporary response to an economic crisis. None of the classification schemes produces statistically significant evidence of a difference in growth between a pegged and a freely floating regime, or nonpegged regime under the Shambaugh (2004) classification.

Overall, exchange rate volatility does not appear to be an important factor affecting economic growth or output over the long run. There is little difference in average growth rates under pegged exchange rates or floating exchange

---

26. If exchange rate variability affects the long-run level of GDP per capita, the effect on the growth rate should die out over time whenever a country remains in the same exchange rate regime for a long period of time.

27. Their study finds that developing economies with intermediate exchange rate regimes tend to grow faster than economies with fixed or freely floating exchange rates. However, their definition of intermediate includes managed floats in which monetary policy targets inflation and output while foreign exchange intervention is used to damp exchange rate fluctuations. As discussed in chapter 8, such a regime is feasible when capital is not highly mobile. A key factor behind the good outcomes for many economies with a managed float is that monetary policy is free to pursue domestic stabilization.

28. Rose uses a different aggregation of the IMF categories than is shown in table 2.1. The narrow crawl category is a subset of table 2.1's soft peg category with the remainder of the soft peg category included in Rose's managed float category.

Table 4.5   Comparative effects of floating and fixed exchange rate regimes on economic growth (annual percentage points)

Exchange rate classification system	Exchange rate regime			
	Narrow crawl	Managed float	Free float	Free fall
Reinhart and Rogoff	−0.3	−1.0*	0.5	−4.3**
	(0.4)	(0.5)	(1.2)	(0.6)
IMF (de facto)	0.8*	0.5	0.2	
	(0.3)	(0.4)	(0.5)	
	Intermediate	Float		
Levy-Yeyati and Sturzenegger	−1.5**	−0.5		
	(0.4)	(0.4)		
	Nonpegged			
Shambaugh	0.3			
	(0.3)			

Notes: Each row reports the estimated effect of the given regime on economic growth in annual percentage points relative to growth under a pegged exchange rate. Robust standard errors in parentheses. * and ** denote significance at 5 and 1 percent levels, respectively.

Sources: Rose (2010, table 2), drawing on Reinhart and Rogoff (2004), IMF (2010), Levy-Yeyati and Sturzenegger (2003), and Shambaugh (2004).

rates. Other factors appear to be far more important than exchange rate regimes in explaining growth differences across economies.

Level of the Exchange Rate and Economic Growth

In popular discourse, the level of the exchange rate often is viewed as more important than the volatility of the exchange rate or the exchange rate regime. As discussed in chapter 6, although a deliberate depreciation of the exchange rate can temporarily boost an economy's growth rate, this effect is fleeting, and it causes inflation to rise. High inflation, in turn, reduces economic growth in the long run.[29]

Countries that restrict international capital mobility may find it possible to grow rapidly for a prolonged period by keeping the currency undervalued while keeping monetary policy tight to prevent inflation. Ghosh, Ostry, and Tsangarides (2010) present evidence that some developing economies with managed floating exchange rates have faster growth than their peers that have pegged exchange rates or free floats and that this growth is not associated with

---

29. Khan and Senhadji (2001) show that inflation rates above roughly 10 percent in developing economies and 3 percent in advanced economies have a negative effect on growth. This result is not sensitive to the specification of the test or outliers in the data.

high inflation. But this evidence is sensitive to the way regimes are classified. Chapter 8 revisits this topic, in the context of the implications of incomplete capital mobility in developing economies.

Conclusions

The world could eliminate foreign exchange transaction costs by adopting a common global currency. Short of this unlikely event, regional common currencies provide only modest reductions in transaction costs, and few savings are to be had by maintaining separate but firmly fixed exchange rates. Currency unions—and, to a lesser extent, pegged exchange rates—may increase trade between the member countries to a moderate degree, but other factors appear to be more important in explaining differences in the level of trade across countries.

The ultimate harm from higher foreign exchange transaction costs and lower trade is a possible reduction in the level of economic output or the long-run economic growth rate. Volatile exchange rates also might reduce economic output through wasteful shifts in investment across sectors of the economy. On the other hand, a fixed exchange rate may reduce economic output in the long run by preventing monetary policy from stabilizing inflation and domestic economic activity. Direct tests of the effect of the exchange rate regime on economic output or long-run economic growth find no measurable effect one way or the other.

Do Volatile Exchange Rates Destabilize Inflation and Output?

Moderation is a fatal thing, Lady Hunstanton. Nothing succeeds like excess.
—Lord Illingworth in Oscar Wilde's *A Woman of No Importance*

Chapter 3 made the case that floating exchange rates are excessively volatile. Chapter 4 showed that this volatility has no measurable effect on the long-run level of economic output. This chapter explores whether volatile exchange rates cause inflation and output to be volatile. We focus especially on volatility over horizons of a year or more, as daily—and even monthly—fluctuations in exchange rates are not likely to have a large effect on inflation and output.

Floating exchange rates are associated with higher and more volatile inflation in many developing economies. However, in these cases, it is unstable monetary policy that causes the volatility in both inflation and the exchange rate. For most advanced economies in recent decades (and increasingly in some developing economies), monetary policy has succeeded in stabilizing inflation rates despite highly volatile exchange rates.

There is little overall correlation between exchange rate volatility and swings in output. For advanced economies in recent decades, even very large movements in exchange rates generally have not destabilized output. Indeed, movements in exchange rates often help stabilize output.

The key to achieving stable inflation and output under floating exchange rates is to have a central bank that actively pursues these goals. As outlined in chapter 2, low inflation and stable employment (or output) are the official objectives of many central banks. But the question still remains why large swings in nominal exchange rates cause such large swings in real exchange rates (RERs). Why don't exports and imports move by whatever it takes to arbitrage prices across countries? And why don't large movements in exports and imports destabilize inflation and output? There are four reasons, the first two of which are most important.

- Product differentiation plays the most important role. Consumers tend to prefer goods and services produced in their home countries and therefore do not consider goods produced in other countries to be close substitutes.

- Trade barriers also play a significant role. Many consumer services, in particular, are intrinsically difficult to trade, including, for example, health care, restaurant meals, and retailing. Trade in some goods also entails high costs, either because they are expensive to transport or because they face high tariffs or other trade barriers in importing countries.

- Price discrimination across markets by producers of branded products plays a minor role.

- Lags in the adjustment of trade volumes and prices are unimportant.

Plan of This Chapter

In this chapter, we explore whether exchange rate volatility induces volatility in inflation and output or employment. Economists generally view the effect of the exchange rate on output to be very similar to its effect on employment. Therefore, this analysis focuses either on output or on employment, depending on the circumstances, but not on both. The analysis also focuses on time horizons of a year or more, which reflects the fact that levels of inflation, output, and employment move slowly from month to month. This also corresponds well to the analysis of business cycles, which are swings in economic activity with a mean duration of roughly four years (although individual cycles may vary in length from one year to more than 10 years). Daily or even monthly exchange rate volatility has little effect on overall economic activity; rather, it is the swings in exchange rates lasting more than a few months that have the potential to destabilize inflation, output, and employment.

The next section describes the research on the effects of exchange rates on volatility in inflation and output. The following section examines five cases in which very large exchange rate movements were not associated with any noticeable destabilization of inflation and employment. The remaining sections explore the features of the economy that allow inflation and output to be stable despite instability in exchange rates.

Lessons from Economic Research

As described in chapter 3, exchange rates continue to be volatile even though inflation has become much more stable. Likewise, output volatility also has declined over the past 25 years in the advanced economies.[1] In a widely read and

---

1. The decline in the volatility of inflation and output has been called "the Great Moderation" (Blanchard, Dell'Ariccia, and Mauro 2010). It is not yet clear whether the Great Recession of 2008–09 marks the return of more volatile output, but inflation, at least, has remained remarkably stable.

well-regarded paper, Obstfeld and Rogoff (2000) refer to the puzzlingly weak links between exchange rates and the rest of the economy as the "exchange rate disconnect." This section examines the evidence for an exchange rate disconnect that insulates inflation and output from the volatility of exchange rates.

Volatility in Inflation

Many studies show that for developing economies, inflation tends to be lower when the exchange rate is firmly fixed (Ghosh, Gulde, and Wolf 2002; Rogoff et al. 2003; Ghosh, Ostry, and Tsangarides 2010; Klein and Shambaugh 2010). However, the same studies find no evidence that fixed exchange rates deliver lower inflation in advanced economies. These results are not sensitive to the system used to classify exchange rate regimes, but they do not examine the effect of the exchange rate regime on the volatility of inflation. Because higher inflation is more volatile than low inflation, any effect exerted by the exchange rate regime on the level of inflation surely affects the volatility of inflation as well.[2] As discussed below, the difference in results for developing and advanced economies appears to result from a difference in the behavior of monetary policy.

Another approach to the question of whether volatile exchange rates cause volatility in inflation is to assess whether specific large movements in the exchange rate cause correspondingly large movements in inflation. In the popular press, currency depreciation is strongly linked with inflation. For example, the opinion pages of the *Wall Street Journal* routinely castigate the Federal Reserve every time the dollar falls substantially, warning that high inflation is just around the corner.[3] Over the past 25 years, these warnings have always been proven wrong, yet the concern is not entirely without merit. Gagnon (2009b, 2010) examines episodes of large and persistent depreciations in advanced economies. He shows that, in the 1970s and early 1980s, some episodes of currency depreciation led to rising inflation,[4] but that since 1985, large currency depreciations have not led to rising inflation in the advanced economies.

Figure 5.1 displays information on seven large depreciations identified by Gagnon (2010) between 1985 and 1993.[5] The vertical axis shows the change in

---

2. For the countries shown in table 4.4, the correlation between the average level of inflation and the standard deviation (volatility) of annual inflation is 0.93 from 1999 through 2009.

3. See for example, David Ranson and Marc Miles, "What If It's Trade that Drives Currencies?" *Wall Street Journal,* July 1, 1987; Laura Cohn, "Dollar Weakness Is Seen Threatening Soft Landing if Inflation Is Rekindled," *Wall Street Journal,* April 17, 1995, C4; and E. S. Browning, "Weak Dollar Worries Investors—Sharp Drop in the Currency May Boost US Inflation, Weigh Down Confidence," *Asian Wall Street Journal,* December 22, 2003, M1.

4. The US dollar depreciation of 1978 was not large enough to be included in Gagnon's sample, but it was followed by rising inflation.

5. The episodes are Australia and Greece in 1985, the United States in 1986, Finland in 1992, and Italy, Spain, and Sweden in 1993.

Figure 5.1   Change in inflation rate after large currency depreciation

change in inflation (percentage points)

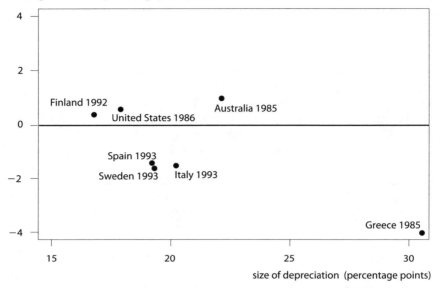

Note: The change in inflation is the average GDP inflation rate in the 8 quarters after the start of the depreciation minus the average inflation rate in the 8 quarters before the depreciation. The depreciation is measured as the percent change in the nominal effective exchange rate over the 4 quarters after the start of the depreciation.

Source: Gagnon (2010).

the rate of inflation in the two years after the depreciation relative to the two years before the depreciation. The horizontal axis shows the size of the depreciation, measured as the four-quarter change in the nominal effective exchange rate. In these episodes, highly volatile exchange rates did not cause volatility in overall inflation. As Gagnon (2009a) discusses, the noticeable decline in inflation in Greece after 1985—which occurred despite the large currency depreciation—reflects tightened monetary and fiscal policy used to fight the high inflation that preceded the depreciation.

Why is exchange rate volatility sometimes associated with inflation volatility and sometimes not? The answer is monetary policy. Several recent papers (listed in appendix 5C) show that the effect of the exchange rate on inflation is smaller when inflation is low and stable. One of these papers (Gagnon and Ihrig 2004) links this development both theoretically and empirically to changes in monetary policy that occurred in almost all advanced economies, mainly during the 1980s. In particular, central banks in many countries began to target a low rate of inflation, either explicitly or implicitly. For some countries, this policy change required a switch from a fixed to a floating exchange rate, but for others (mainly in Europe) it was achieved by fixing more firmly to the currency of a country with stable inflation (primarily Germany). These policy developments are responsible for the secular decline in inflation rates and inflation volatility in advanced economies that is described in chapter 3.

Historically, many developing economies with floating exchange rates have had inflationary monetary and fiscal policies. It is this record of undisciplined policy that gives rise to the association between floating exchange rates and higher inflation in developing economies. However, in recent years, some developing economies have adopted monetary policies aimed at low and stable inflation, often in the context of increased exchange rate flexibility. In a study that includes developing economies, Kuttner and Posen (2001) show that central bank autonomy and an inflation targeting framework lead to lower and more stable inflation rates. Appendix 5C reviews evidence that developing economies with lower and more stable rates of inflation experience smaller inflation-related effects from exchange rate volatility.

Volatility in Output/Employment

The exchange rate affects output through its influence on exports and imports; this is the arbitrage through international trade described in chapter 3. Cross-country studies generally find that output is more volatile under a pegged exchange rate than under a floating rate, but the difference across regimes is small and is sensitive to the sample and to the system of regime classification (Ghosh, Gulde, and Wolf 2002; Rogoff et al. 2003; Ghosh, Ostry, and Tsangarides 2010). As with inflation volatility, the behavior of monetary policy is critical in determining how exchange rate volatility affects the volatility of output. Gagnon (2010) shows that sudden large depreciations in advanced economies are not associated with recession unless they were caused by inflationary monetary and fiscal policies that were subsequently reversed. Large currency depreciations have been followed by accelerations in output growth when they were caused by monetary policy actions aimed at stimulating the economy. Figure 5.2 displays output growth during the two years after the same large depreciations shown in figure 5.1. With the exception of Greece in 1985, growth rates were moderate or even slightly above average. As noted above, the Greek government tightened monetary and fiscal policy aggressively after the depreciation of 1985 in order to fight inflation, and this deliberate policy tightening caused a recession.

The experiences of developing economies are more varied, reflecting in part the wide divergence in monetary and fiscal policy behavior among these economies. An additional factor is the existence of a substantial amount of debt, either public or private, that is denominated in foreign currency. Studies show that foreign-currency debt can offset or even reverse the standard result that currency depreciation stimulates output growth through net exports (Allen et al. 2002, Arteta 2005, Towbin and Weber 2011). Moreover, foreign-currency debt reduces the ability of monetary policy to stabilize output under a floating exchange rate (Bergin, Shin, and Tchakarov 2006). Chapter

Figure 5.2 GDP growth rate after large currency depreciation

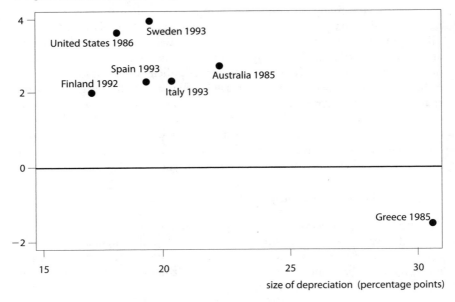

GDP growth rate (percentage points)

Note: The GDP growth rate is the average growth rate of real GDP in the 8 quarters after the start of the depreciation. The depreciation is measured as the percent change in the nominal effective exchange rate over the 4 quarters after the start of the depreciation.

Source: Gagnon (2010).

7 explores this issue in more detail, but for the most part this chapter focuses on economies without significant amounts of foreign-currency debt, which includes all the advanced economies and an increasing number of developing economies.

The Global Financial Crisis of 2008

The main causes and consequences of the global financial crisis of 2008 and the subsequent Great Recession are not related to exchange rate regimes (Blanchard, Dell'Ariccia, and Mauro 2010). The main causes are related to lax financial regulation and supervision in the United States and Europe. A number of auxiliary factors are also cited, ranging from overly loose monetary policy in advanced economies to excess reserve accumulation in developing economies (Palais-Royal Initiative 2011). But exchange rate regimes are absent from most of these lists. The hardest hit economies include those with both floating and fixed exchange rates, as do the least affected economies.

Figure 5.3   United States in the 1980s

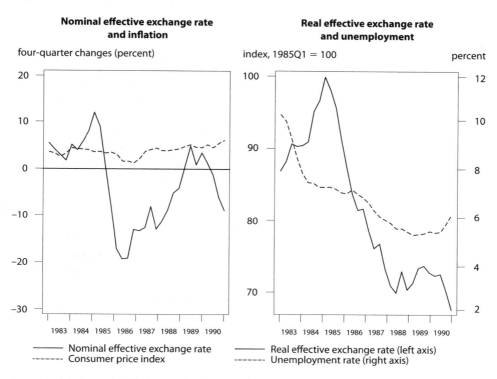

Nominal effective exchange rate
and inflation

four-quarter changes (percent)

Real effective exchange rate
and unemployment

index, 1985Q1 = 100

percent

——— Nominal effective exchange rate
------- Consumer price index

——— Real effective exchange rate (left axis)
------- Unemployment rate (right axis)

Sources: Bank for International Settlements, IMF *International Financial Statistics* database.

Five Historical Examples

This section presents five case studies of exchange rate volatility that was not
associated with volatility in inflation and employment: four instances of large
and sudden currency depreciations that were not caused by inflationary monetary policy and one sudden large currency appreciation (which occurs more
rarely).

United States in the 1980s

The left panel of figure 5.3 displays the changes in the 1980s in the US nominal
effective (or trade-weighted) exchange rate (NEER) and US inflation, shown by
the consumer price index (CPI).[6] The figure begins in 1983 and thus excludes

---

6. The effective exchange rates used in figures 5.3 through 5.7 are the "narrow" measures from the
Bank for International Settlements website, except for Brazil, for which only the "broad" measures
are available. The narrow measures exclude developing countries that have high inflation. The
inflation rates and unemployment rates are from the IMF *International Financial Statistics* database.

the disinflation that occurred during 1980–82 and was the explicit goal of US monetary policy. The dollar appreciated from 1980 through early 1985, partly as a result of loose fiscal policy and tight monetary policy, which kept US interest rates high relative to foreign interest rates, but also because of a sustained decline in the risk premium on US assets relative to foreign assets.[7] Beginning in the second quarter of 1985 and through 1988, the dollar depreciated sharply and fell a cumulative 35 percent. This remarkable reversal was not associated with any dramatic change in the interest rate differential between bonds denominated in dollars and those denominated in other currencies or by any change in expectations of long-run relative inflation rates; it mainly reflected a reversal of the previously falling risk premium on dollar assets. In other words, the dollar bubble popped. Despite this enormous depreciation, however, US inflation was remarkably steady. The only noticeable development in inflation was the temporary reduction in 1986 associated with the decline in global oil prices.

The right panel of figure 5.3 displays the US real effective exchange rate (REER) and the US unemployment rate. From 1983 through early 1985, the dollar appreciation did not cause any increase in the unemployment rate, although it may have slowed the rate of decline. From mid-1985 through early 1988, the depreciation may have contributed to a moderate further decline in unemployment. This example is not to deny that RERs can have important economic effects, but rather to point out that large swings in RERs are not incompatible with stable and sustainable economic growth.

Sweden in the Early 1990s

The left panel of figure 5.4 shows the rates of change in the Swedish NEER and CPI during the 1990s. The NEER was relatively stable from 1990 through mid-1992, and inflation was moderately high but declining.[8] In late 1992 and 1993, the NEER dropped sharply after Sweden abandoned its exchange rate peg in November 1992. In 1994 and 1995 it declined slightly further, and it rose moderately in 1996. On balance, between mid-1992 and early 1997, the Swedish currency depreciated 20 percent. Despite many fears at the time, Swedish inflation (net of the temporary effect of a tax hike in 1993) was not noticeably affected by the sharp depreciation.[9] Indeed, the substantial decline

---

7. A declining risk premium on dollar assets is implied by the fact that the dollar continued to appreciate even as the interest rate differential on US versus foreign bonds began to decline and there was little movement in expectations of long-run inflation in the United States relative to the rest of the world.

8. According to IMF (1993), increases in value-added tax rates contributed significantly to measured inflation in 1990, 1991, and 1993.

9. Sveriges Riksbank (1993) shows that there was a modest increase in expected inflation immediately after the depreciation, but this increase was largely reversed by late 1993 as it became clear that underlying inflation was not rising.

Figure 5.4 Sweden in the early 1990s

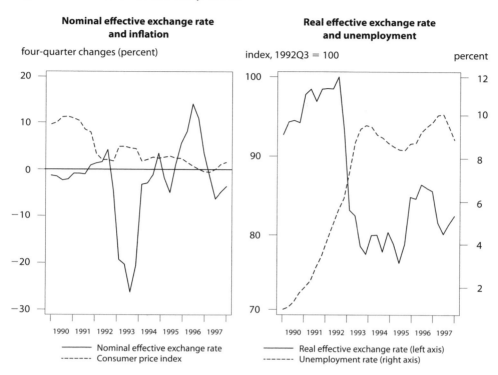

Nominal effective exchange rate and inflation

Real effective exchange rate and unemployment

four-quarter changes (percent)

index, 1992Q3 = 100   percent

——— Nominal effective exchange rate
------- Consumer price index

——— Real effective exchange rate (left axis)
------- Unemployment rate (right axis)

Sources: Bank for International Settlements, IMF *International Financial Statistics* database.

of inflation during 1991–92 not only was maintained, but inflation declined even a bit further by late 1996.

The right panel of figure 5.4 shows that the Swedish depreciation in late 1992 and 1993 was preceded and accompanied by rising unemployment. Unemployment stabilized soon after the depreciation and even fell modestly thereafter. The mild appreciation of late 1995 may have contributed to a modest rise in unemployment in 1996. Overall, there is no evidence that the sharp decline in the REER in 1993 destabilized the Swedish economy. Indeed, the opposite conclusion seems to be more plausible, namely that depreciation stabilized the unemployment rate without elevating the inflation rate.

New Zealand in the Late 1990s

The left panel of figure 5.5 displays the rates of change of New Zealand's NEER and CPI around the time of the Asian financial crisis of 1997–98. The currency appreciated steadily in the run-up to the crisis and then depreciated sharply in two stages during and after the crisis, falling a total of 25 percent between

Figure 5.5 New Zealand in the late 1990s

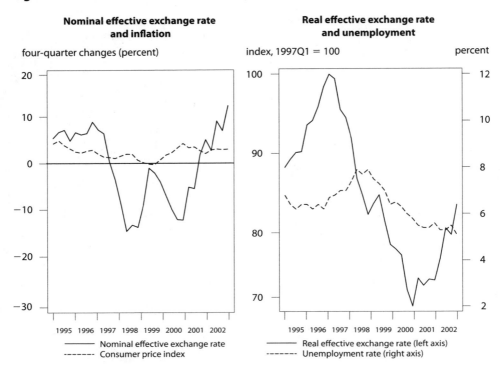

Nominal effective exchange rate and inflation

four-quarter changes (percent)

Real effective exchange rate and unemployment

index, 1997Q1 = 100   percent

Nominal effective exchange rate
Consumer price index

Real effective exchange rate (left axis)
Unemployment rate (right axis)

Sources: Bank for International Settlements, IMF *International Financial Statistics* database.

early 1997 and mid-2001. The depreciation may have been caused in part by expectations that the Reserve Bank of New Zealand would have to ease policy in response to the collapse of demand for New Zealand exports to economies affected by the financial crisis. Consistent with such expectations, the long-term interest rate in New Zealand declined. But the depreciation was considerably larger than can be attributed to relative bond yields, and movements in expected long-run inflation were very small, suggesting that the risk premium on New Zealand assets increased. Inflation fell a bit after the first stage of depreciation and then rose slightly with the second stage, but these movements were small and the CPI rose only 1.8 percent during 2001.

The right panel of figure 5.5 shows that the unemployment rate in New Zealand began to rise shortly before the REER began to decline, as the Asian financial crisis damped demand for New Zealand exports. The Reserve Bank of New Zealand initially reacted to the depreciation by tightening monetary policy, which contributed to the increase in the unemployment rate. However, the central bank reversed course after a few quarters. With a moderate lag, the depreciation and the policy U-turn appear to have stabilized the unemployment rate and set it on a downward path. New Zealand is the quintessential

Figure 5.6   Brazil at the millennium

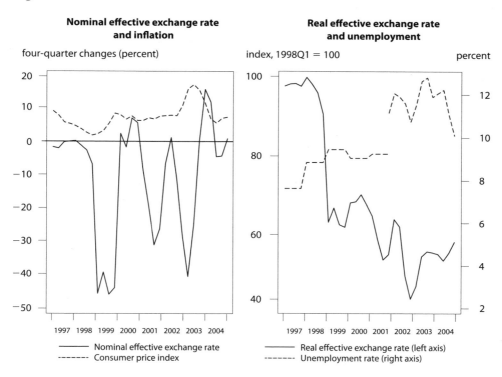

Nominal effective exchange rate and inflation

four-quarter changes (percent)

— Nominal effective exchange rate
------ Consumer price index

Real effective exchange rate and unemployment

index, 1998Q1 = 100   percent

— Real effective exchange rate (left axis)
------ Unemployment rate (right axis)

Note: Definition of unemployment was revised starting in 2001.

Sources: Bank for International Settlements, IMF *International Financial Statistics* database, back issues of the *International Financial Statistics Yearbook.*

small open economy, with just over 4 million people and total trade (exports plus imports) equal to 55 percent of GDP. These figures show that even small open economies can have reasonably stable inflation and output despite very large exchange rate swings.

Brazil at the Millennium

The left panel of figure 5.6 displays the rates of change of Brazil's NEER and CPI around the time of Brazil's financial crisis of 1999, the Argentine crisis of 2001, and the Brazilian election of 2002. Prior to 1999, the Brazilian real was on a crawling peg to the US dollar. The Brazilian government decided to let the real float in January 1999, as intense speculative pressure threatened to deplete Brazil's foreign exchange reserves and high interest rates strangled the economy. Brazil quickly moved to a regime of inflation targeting. Between early 1998 and early 2003, the currency depreciated an enormous 63 percent in three discrete steps. This depreciation reflected a combination of lower expected interest rates and higher expected inflation in Brazil as well as an increase in the risk premium on Brazilian assets. The first and third stages of the depreciation had small but noticeable effects on inflation. But inflation quickly came down after market participants realized that the newly elected president, Luiz Inácio Lula da Silva, was not going to embark on radical and inflationary policies. Moreover, in the context of Brazilian history, these effects on inflation were remarkably small.

The right panel of figure 5.6 shows that unemployment in Brazil had been rising before the first stage of depreciation. Rising unemployment probably contributed to the decline of inflation through 1998. After the first stage of depreciation, unemployment stabilized. Beginning in late 2001, the Brazilian government revised its procedures for measuring the unemployment rate, which led to a somewhat higher and more variable reported rate of unemployment. After adjusting for the gap between the old and new unemployment series in 2001Q3, there is little evidence that the large cumulative depreciation had much overall effect on the unemployment rate.

United Kingdom in the Late 1990s

The left panel of figure 5.7 displays the sharp appreciation of the UK pound that began at the end of 1996 and continued through early 1998. Contrary to expectations, there was no noticeable decline in inflation. The right panel shows that the cumulative real appreciation was about 20 to 25 percent. Again, there was no perceptible effect on the unemployment rate, which continued to drift downward steadily.

How Is the Economy Insulated from Exchange Rate Volatility?

Although exchange rate volatility is sometimes associated with volatility in inflation and output, these case studies show that it is also possible to have volatile exchange rates with stable inflation and output. Monetary policy is the critical factor that determines whether inflation and output are stable. But what features of the economy enable monetary policy to deliver inflation and output stability in the presence of such wide and persistent swings in RERs? And what prevents international trade imbalances from growing without bound when the RER deviates significantly from purchasing power parity (PPP)?

The rest of this chapter examines factors that weaken and prolong the trade and price responses to exchange rate shocks. It shows that the relatively slow and weak response of trade to the exchange rate is the reason RERs are able to have such large swings without destabilizing inflation and economic activity.

Trade Barriers, Trade Costs, and Taxes

As discussed in chapter 3, international trade connects the markets for goods and services in different countries. Goods tend to be exported from countries where they are cheaper and imported to countries where they are more expen-

Figure 5.7   United Kingdom in the late 1990s

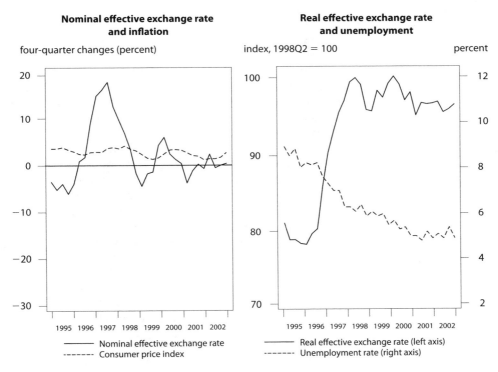

Sources: Bank for International Settlements, IMF *International Financial Statistics* database.

sive. This arbitrage tends to push prices back into equality, moving the RER toward PPP over time. However, there are a number of barriers and impediments to arbitrage by trade, which are explored in turn. As we will see, trade barriers and costs are not the only—and perhaps not even the most important—reason for the disconnect between exchange rates and inflation and output. But they are the most obvious explanation, so we start with them.

Insurmountable Barriers for Some Goods and Services

There are legal barriers to trade in some goods and services that prevent people from buying them from sources where they are cheaper. For example, there are official limits (quotas) on the quantity of sugar that can be imported into the United States.[10] When the dollar appreciates, foreign sugar producers who

10. These quotas are now specified as "tariff rate quotas." A fixed volume of sugar imports at a low tariff is allocated to exporting countries. Above this volume, sugar imports face a prohibitively high tariff, which stood at $0.40 per kilogram, more than 50 percent of the international price of sugar, as of January 2011.

would like to sell more sugar to US consumers are prevented from doing so by the import quota. As a result, the price of sugar in the United States rises above the world price (converted into dollars) when the dollar appreciates.[11] For services such as law, medicine, and accounting, professional licensing requirements and differences in national standards can prevent individuals in one country from accessing services from another country (including online or by telephone or mail). As a result, the prices of legal, medical, and other professional services in the United States rise above the prices of such services in other countries when the dollar appreciates, and they fall below foreign prices when the dollar depreciates.

In the Uruguay Round of trade negotiations, completed in 1994, countries agreed to abolish quotas and other nontariff restrictions for nonagricultural goods. The most significant set of quotas was contained in the Multi-Fiber Arrangement that restricted imports of textiles and clothing into many advanced countries. All remaining quota restrictions on textiles and clothing were eliminated as of 2005.[12] Reductions in quotas and other barriers for agricultural goods and services are being negotiated in the Doha Round.

Some services simply cannot be delivered between countries even in the absence of import quotas or other legal barriers—haircuts and housecleaning are classic examples of services that are physically impossible to deliver internationally, with minor exceptions such as in border cities.[13] Another important class of service that cannot be traded, strange as it may sound, is retail trade in the form of traditional in-person shopping.[14] Many, perhaps most, of the goods sold at such stores as Wal-Mart and Target are imported, but their retail store operations are nontraded services in each country in which they operate. The prices of goods sold at such stores therefore include a markup over the prices paid to the foreign producers in order to pay the salaries and other local service input costs that cannot be imported because they must be located near the consumers, including utilities, advertising, rent, and profit for the physical stores. Retail markups cannot be arbitraged directly across countries and so the prices of identical goods sold in different countries may differ for this reason. Studies show that these nontraded retail markups constitute between 30 and 70 percent of the price paid by consumers for imported goods (Berger et al. 2009).

---

11. Note that this barrier is one-sided. If the dollar were to depreciate enough, the world price in dollars might rise above the previous domestic price of sugar; this would cause the domestic price to rise because US sugar producers are free to export.

12. However, clothing and textiles continue to be an area of heightened trade friction, marked by a proliferation of anti-dumping and countervailing duty actions, as competitors in importing countries seek to limit imports.

13. Rationing of work visas is another barrier to the provision of services across countries. When a person moves to another country to work, he or she becomes both a producer and a consumer in the new country. However, the issue of migration is a complicated one that goes beyond the scope of this book.

14. Mail-order retailing can be traded across borders, as is discussed below.

Jensen and Kletzer (2005) estimate that 40 percent of the US labor force works in sectors that produce tradable goods and services and 60 percent works in sectors that produce nontradable goods and services. They stress that, despite the widespread view that services are not tradable, more US workers work in tradable service industries than in tradable manufacturing industries.

Costs of Trade

Even for goods and services that can be traded across borders, there are a wide range of trade costs that range from trivial to substantial. These include tariffs, which arise from official policy, and transport costs, which vary according to the mode and distance of transport and the perishability and weight of the product. High-value durable goods such as jewelry and electronics can be transported easily for only a small fraction of their value. Heavy goods, such as cement and mineral ores, are more expensive to transport. More perishable goods, such as fresh produce and cut flowers, may not survive a lengthy ocean voyage and require expensive air and truck transport, which greatly restricts their international trade.

Tariffs and transport costs can introduce ranges of relative price differences within which it is not possible to arbitrage from cheaper to more expensive countries. If a television set costs $100 in country A and $105 in country B and the cost of shipping it between the two countries is $10, it is not possible to earn a profit by arbitraging between the two markets, and international trade cannot reduce the price differential any lower than $10. There would be a similar damping effect if each country imposed a $10 (or 10 percent, in this example) tariff on TV imports, even if shipping were free. Although tariffs and transport costs do not completely prevent price arbitrage, they do place limits on how well arbitrage works. Large price differences are generally arbitraged away, but small differences may remain.

Hummels (2007) provides an excellent overview of transportation costs in trade. For the United States, transportation costs equal about 4 percent of the total value of imports. For New Zealand, which is much farther away from most of its trading partners, transportation costs equal about 8 to 10 percent of the total value of imports. Ocean transportation costs have fallen over time, but fluctuations in the price of oil make it difficult to estimate a clear trend. The rise of containerized shipping seems to have improved speed and tracking ability more than it has reduced cost. Hummels (2007) shows that exporters of manufactures are willing to pay on average almost 1 percent of the value of the good to reduce travel time by just one day. This preference for speed, combined with a tenfold decline in air transportation costs since the 1950s, has elevated the role of air shipping from insignificance to account for about one-third of US imports and half of US exports by value (excluding shipments to and from Canada and Mexico).

Table 5.1 lists average tariffs for selected product categories in the six

Table 5.1   Average tariffs for selected products, 2009 (percent)

Product group	Developing economies			Advanced economies		
	Brazil	China	India	European Union	Japan	United States
Animal products	8.9	14.8	33.1	23.2	12.3	2.5
Dairy products	15.1	12.0	33.7	49.4	147.5	16.2
Cereals	11.8	24.2	32.2	17.5	60.8	4.0
Sugar and confectionery	16.5	27.4	34.4	27.5	23.5	9.1
Beverages and tobacco	17.2	22.9	70.8	19.0	14.2	13.5
Minerals and metals	10.1	7.4	7.5	2.0	1.0	1.8
Petroleum	0.2	4.4	3.8	3.1	0.6	1.5
Chemicals	8.3	6.6	7.9	4.6	2.2	2.8
Textiles	22.5	9.6	13.6	6.6	5.5	8.0
Clothing	35.0	16.0	16.1	11.5	9.2	12.1
Leather and footwear	15.7	13.4	10.2	4.2	9.7	4.0
Nonelectrical machinery	12.7	7.8	7.3	1.9	0.0	1.2
Electrical equipment	14.2	8.0	7.2	2.8	0.2	1.7
Transport equipment	18.1	11.5	20.7	4.3	0.0	3.0
Miscellaneous manufactures	15.3	11.9	8.9	2.7	1.2	2.6

Source: World Trade Organization, *World Tariff Profiles 2010.*

largest trading economies. Agricultural products generally have the highest tariffs, especially in the advanced economies.[15] Dairy products stand out, with an average tariff of 147 percent in Japan. Minerals, petroleum, and chemicals have relatively low tariffs in all the major economies. Various categories of machinery and equipment have moderate tariffs in Brazil, China, and India but very low tariffs in the European Union, Japan, and the United States.

In addition to tariffs, government policies can raise other costs to trade. Examples include health and safety, hygiene, and labeling standards that differ from those of the exporting country. World Trade Organization (WTO) members have agreed on rules that prevent the imposition of such costs in an arbitrary and discriminatory way. Nevertheless, they do raise trade costs.

Another cost of trade that is difficult to measure is the cost of establishing brand recognition and distribution networks in a new market, sometimes referred to as sunk costs. Sunk costs are not unique to trade, but they are an important factor in the decision to enter or exit a given foreign market.

---

15. Note that these average tariffs are calculated as total collected duties divided by total imports in each category. Thus, they understate the effects of prohibitive tariffs in some goods. For example, the US average tariff of 9 percent on sugar and sweets mainly reflects the low tariff rate paid on imports up to the quota volume and not the very high tariff that would apply to any imports above that quota.

Taxes

Indirect taxes such as sales taxes, value-added taxes, and excise taxes can create price differentials if they are levied at different rates across countries. Unlike tariffs, however, such taxes are not barriers to trade because they are imposed equally on imports and domestically produced goods. For example, a consumer in France must pay the same value-added tax on a wine imported from the United States or a wine made in France. Because of the tax, the price of wine may be higher in France than in the United States, but the tax is not a barrier to trade because it does not introduce a wedge between the price of imported and locally produced goods. In the presence of such taxes, arbitrage should return the RER to PPP on a before-tax basis. In other words, the producer's revenues should be the same in both countries, even if consumers pay more in one country.

If the tax rate is the same across countries, then the measured RER is the same on both a before-tax and an after-tax basis. However, if the tax rate is higher at home, then the RER will be higher on an after-tax basis than on a before-tax basis. As long as tax rates remain constant, the ratio of the after-tax RER to the before-tax RER will be constant. But, when the tax rate changes in one country, the after-tax RER will change relative to the before-tax RER. Because CPIs measure prices including indirect taxes, the CPI-based RER is an after-tax RER, and because long-run PPP stabilizes the before-tax RER, changes in indirect taxes will introduce permanent shifts in CPI-based RERs. Overall, the changes induced in the long-run RER from these tax considerations are small, although the effects on exchange-rate-adjusted relative prices for specific products can be noticeable.

How Important Are Trade Barriers, Trade Costs, and Taxes?

Trade barriers, trade costs, and taxes obviously play some role in preventing the equalization of consumer prices across countries. Indeed, in their influential paper, Obstfeld and Rogoff (2000) suggest that trade costs are the main reason underlying the exchange rate disconnect.

Figure 5.8 shows the importance of these factors in the case of gasoline. Gasoline is cheap to transport and faces low trade barriers, and so it can be readily arbitraged at the wholesale level across countries. As shown, the exchange-rate-adjusted relative price of gasoline imports between Germany and the United States is close to 1 and remarkably stable, despite large exchange rate movements. At the retail level, however, the price of gasoline includes a significant nontradable component related to distribution and retail costs as well as indirect tax rates that change with the price of gasoline.[16]

---

16. Unlike value-added taxes that are a constant fraction of the retail price, gasoline taxes include a significant component of volume-related tax (for example, cents per gallon) that cause the overall tax rate to vary inversely with the price.

Figure 5.8   Relative price of gasoline in Germany and the United States (exchange rate adjusted)

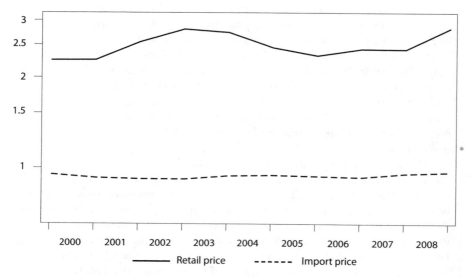

relative price

Retail price   ------ Import price

Sources: IMF *International Financial Statistics* database, US Energy Information Administration, Statistisches Bundesamt Deutschland, authors' calculations.

The retail markup and indirect taxes are much higher in Germany than in the United States, and as expected, the exchange-rate-adjusted price of gasoline at the retail level is higher in Germany than in the United States. The retail price is also much less stable and more greatly affected by the euro-dollar exchange rate than the import price.

For some goods and services, the effect of trade barriers is mitigated by possibilities for indirect arbitrage, as discussed in box 5.1. Indirect arbitrage operates when a close substitute for a nontradable good or service can be traded. For example, corn syrup is a substitute for sugar and is not subject to a US import quota.

At a broader level, although trade barriers, trade costs, and taxes are important, they are not the only reason for imperfect arbitrage between national markets through international trade. Indeed, studies show that RERs based on indices of tradable goods prices on a before-tax basis are highly correlated with RERs based on (after-tax) CPIs that include a wide range of nontradable goods and services (Engel 1999, Taylor and Taylor 2004). Figure 5.9 shows that, between the United States and Japan, movements in the RER based on manufactured goods at the producer level are essentially identical to movements in the CPI-based RER. Manufactured goods can be transported relatively cheaply between the United States and Japan, and they face low tariffs and few legal

Box 5.1 Indirect arbitrage

Despite the limitations on direct arbitrage imposed by trade barriers, indirect arbitrage may still occur through substitute goods and services that are tradable. For example, the United States has a strict quota on sugar imports but not on imports of corn syrup or the corn from which it is made.[1] The left panel of figure B5.1.1 shows the disconnect between sugar prices in the United States and in Brazil, a leading sugar producer. Not only are US prices always higher than Brazilian prices, but they are more insulated from global shifts in supply and demand. The right panel of figure B5.1.1 shows that US and Brazilian corn prices are closely connected, reflecting developments in the global market for corn, particularly after 2000, when the Brazilian government allowed the minimum price for corn to fall below the world price.[2]

The ability of food processors to substitute between sugar and corn syrup limits the effects of the sugar barriers on US prices for processed foods. A dollar appreciation that would lower the price of imported sugar in the absence of the sugar quota instead lowers the price of corn syrup and thus lowers US prices of foods that would otherwise be sweetened by using sugar. Because sugar and corn syrup are not perfect substitutes, however, this indirect arbitrage cannot fully undo the effects of the sugar quota on price differences between the United States and the rest of the world.

Another example of such substitution is mail-order catalogs. Ordering goods by mail order is not a perfect substitute for shopping at a local store because one cannot touch and test the goods in person and because there is a lag in delivery. Nevertheless, especially with the advent of the internet, mail ordering has become a substantial source of competition for brick-and-mortar retail outlets. Amazon.com reports that 48 percent of its sales in 2009 came from outside the United States. The L. L. Bean website reports that the company distributes catalogs in 160 countries.

Indirect arbitrage also can operate to the extent that changes in exchange rates affect the costs of producing goods and services, including those that are protected by high trade barriers or high trade costs. For example, a currency appreciation may decrease the cost of imported inputs to the production of a nontradable good, thereby putting downward pressure on its price even in the absence of direct competition from imports.

---

1. In fact, the United States exports corn, but the important point is that US producers can choose to sell their corn either at home or abroad. Their ability to arbitrage between the home and foreign markets keeps US corn prices equal to foreign corn prices in dollar terms.
2. According to Dutoit, Hernandez-Villafuerte, and Urrutia (2009), Brazil has a government-controlled minimum price regime for corn. Brazil was a net importer of corn until 2000 but subsequently became a net exporter, implying that the minimum price ceased to be binding after 2000.

(box continues next page)

Figure B5.1.1   US and Brazilian sugar and corn prices

Sources: IMF *International Financial Statistics* database, United Nations Commodity Trade Statistics database.

barriers to trade.[17] Producer prices for manufactures do not include indirect taxes that are included in CPIs; they also exclude the contribution to consumer prices that arises from nontradable local distribution and retailing costs. If the main sources of volatility and persistence in the CPI-based RER were trade barriers, trade costs, and taxes, then the RER in terms of producer prices for manufactured goods would be much more stable, with less persistent swings.[18] Figure 5.9 shows that between Japan and the United States, essentially all of the movement in the CPI-based RER is mirrored by the RER for manufactured goods based on producer prices. Clearly, other factors are at least as important—perhaps even more important—than trade barriers, trade costs, and taxes in explaining large and persistent swings in RERs.

---

17. Trade in manufactures between Japan and the United States is almost entirely composed of product categories with average tariffs of 3 percent or less, as shown in table 5.1. Assuming an average transportation cost of 4 percent (Hummels 2007), total trade and tariff costs should be about 5 to 7 percent. With trade costs of this magnitude, arbitrage should restrict the RER based on manufactured goods to a band from about 6 percent below PPP to about 6 percent above PPP. The RER for manufactured goods in figure 5.9 moves over a much wider range, suggesting that trade costs are not the only factor behind the exchange rate disconnect.

18. One difference between producer prices and consumer prices that works in the other direction is that producer prices cover only goods produced within a country, whereas consumer prices include prices of imported goods.

Figure 5.9   US-Japanese real exchange rates (RERs)

index, January 2000 = 100

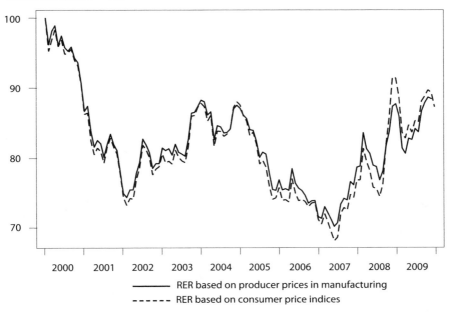

———— RER based on producer prices in manufacturing

– – – – – RER based on consumer price indices

Sources: IMF *International Financial Statistics* database, Bank of Japan, Bureau of Labor Statistics.

Product Differentiation and Brand Control

When two goods are identical, consumers will buy the one with the lower price. For such goods, a currency depreciation that raises the price of imports equally raises the price of domestic products. Such strong competition is reasonably descriptive of primary commodities and simple manufactured products. Figure 5.8 showed that the exchange-rate-adjusted relative price of gasoline at the import level is close to 1 and is highly stable. Figure 5.10 shows that exchange-rate-adjusted relative producer prices for primary commodities such as wheat, soybeans, petroleum, and tin also are close to 1 with relatively short-lived deviations. The CPI-based RERs for the same country-pairs are far more volatile than the exchange-rate-adjusted relative commodity prices.

Product Differentiation and Home Bias

Many traded goods are branded products that differ in important ways across producers. With such differentiated products, there generally does not exist a unique ratio of prices that is consistent with market equilibrium. For example, a depreciation of the dollar may raise the price for US consumers of a Volkswagen automobile relative to that of a Chevrolet. Some consumers will

Figure 5.10 Relative commodity prices (exchange rate adjusted) and real exchange rates (RERs)

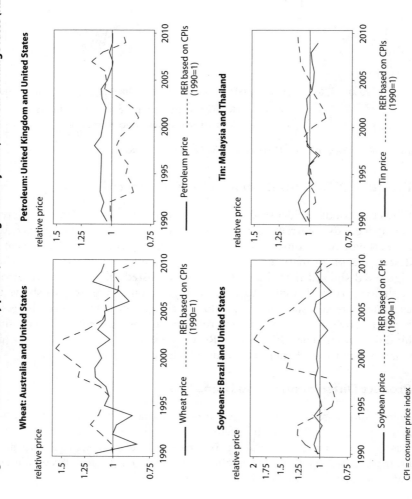

CPI = consumer price index

Sources: IMF *International Financial Statistics* database, authors' calculations.

switch from Volkswagens to Chevrolets, but many others will continue to buy Volkswagens. The market may remain indefinitely at a new equilibrium with higher Chevrolet sales and lower Volkswagen sales.[19]

Changes in the equilibrium relative prices of differentiated products do not cause changes in the RER, however, unless the shares of each brand differ across markets. The most common reason for different brand shares across markets is home bias: the tendency for consumers in each market to prefer locally produced goods. Consider a world in which automobiles are the only consumer good, and there are only two brands: Volkswagen (produced abroad in Germany) and Chevrolet (produced at home in the United States). If there is no home bias and half of consumers in each country buy each brand, then the change in the CPI in each country is simply the average of the changes in Volkswagen and Chevrolet prices. A 9 percent dollar depreciation raises the domestic US price of a Volkswagen by 10 percent.[20] Half of all prices rise by 10 percent and half remain unchanged, and so the US CPI rises by 5 percent (see figure 5.11).[21] For German consumers, the price in euros of a Chevrolet falls by 9 percent, and because Chevrolets comprise half of all unit sales, the German CPI decreases by 4.5 percent. Because of the depreciation of the dollar by 9 percent, the German CPI (measured in US currency) rises by 5 percent, which equals the rise in the US CPI, and thus the RER does not change.

The fall in the price of a Chevrolet relative to a Volkswagen is likely to increase Chevrolet's market share over time both at home and abroad. However, future changes in market share do not change the CPI as long as the prices of Chevrolets and Volkswagens remain constant in the future.[22] The assumption of no home bias does not require that brands have equal market shares; all that is required is that the market shares are the same in both countries. If Chevrolets initially had a larger market share both at home and abroad, the domestic (US) CPI would rise less and the foreign (German) CPI would fall more (as measured in foreign currency), but the RER would remain unchanged.

The stability of the RER after an exchange rate depreciation depends critically on the assumption of no home bias. If consumers in each country prefer

---

19. In the long run, Volkswagen may decide to build a factory in the United States in order to obtain the same low production costs as Chevrolet, but this process occurs over decades, not years.

20. The price of a Volkswagen rises by the same percentage the foreign currency appreciates. Surprising as it may seem, a 9 percent depreciation of the home currency in terms of the foreign currency implies a 10 percent appreciation of the foreign currency in terms of the home currency.

21. For simplicity, this example assumes that all of Volkswagen's costs are fixed in foreign currency and all of Chevrolet's costs are fixed in domestic currency. To the extent that imported parts are a significant component of either company's costs, this assumption may not hold. Studies generally find that foreign-currency-based costs are a small fraction of total costs for most producers in advanced economies.

22. The change in the price index is a weighted average of the changes of individual prices. Changes in market share change the weights used to calculate the price index, but they cannot affect the price index if the individual prices are not moving.

Figure 5.11 Effect of a nominal exchange rate depreciation on prices and real exchange rate with no home bias

index, year 0 = 100

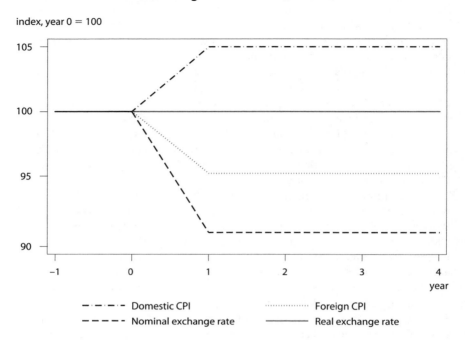

CPI = consumer price index

Source: Authors' illustration.

their home brand, a change in the exchange rate will change the RER. Returning to the above example, suppose that the home brand represents 90 percent of unit sales in each country (Chevrolet in the United States and Volkswagen in Germany). Now, if the dollar depreciates by 9 percent, the domestic US CPI increases by only 1 percent: The price of a Volkswagen rises by 10 percent, but Volkswagen has only a 10 percent weight in the CPI. The German CPI falls by 0.9 percent. In terms of US currency, the German CPI rises (roughly) by 9 percent, and the RER depreciates (roughly) by 8 percent, as shown in figure 5.12.

Home bias appears to be widespread. Verboven (1996) shows that domestic producers control a majority of sales in each of the four largest European automobile markets: Germany, France, Italy, and the United Kingdom. Home bias is reinforced by the presence of many producers who sell only in their home markets. For example, only 15 percent of US goods producers export to any other market (Bernard et al. 2007). Even in a relatively small economy such as Colombia, only about one-third of goods producers export their products (Das, Roberts, and Tybout 2007). Another recent study finds that in a sample of 32 developing economies, only one-third of firms surveyed had any exports

Figure 5.12 Effect of a nominal exchange rate depreciation on prices and real exchange rate with home bias

index, year 0 = 100

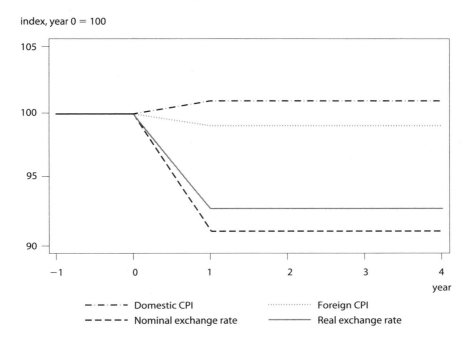

CPI = consumer price index
Source: Authors' illustration.

at all (Ricci and Trionfetti 2011).[23] The effect of home bias shown in figure 5.12 does not require domestic producers to have an absolute majority market share; all that is needed is that domestic producers have a larger market share in their home market than anywhere else.

Price Discrimination and Brand Control

The examples above assume that Chevrolet and Volkswagen charge the same prices at home and abroad. However, in the face of a dollar depreciation, Volkswagen may decide not to raise its price in the United States by the full amount of the dollar depreciation. In that case, the price charged in the US market, even at the wholesale level, will differ from that charged in Germany. (See box 5.2 on automobile prices across countries.) Through its control of the Volkswagen trademark and by restricting its warranty coverage to automo-

---

23. Moreover, the survey appears to have been tilted toward large firms, which are more likely to export.

Box 5.2 The international automobile market

The retail prices of four models of automobiles have been remarkably stable within the German, UK, and US markets over the past ten years, but movements in exchange rates have induced large swings when the prices of these same autos are converted into a common currency. These swings are comparable to those of the RERs between these countries. These results imply a very high degree of price discrimination, also known as pricing to market or incomplete pass-through.

Figure B5.2.1 displays the dollar-euro and pound-euro exchange rates during this period. The US dollar depreciated markedly and persistently against the euro in 2003 and 2004 and modestly and less persistently in 2007 and 2008. The UK pound depreciated moderately in 2003 and sharply in 2008 and 2009.

Figure B5.2.2 displays the price of BMW 7-series autos in each market.[1] The US price is for a slightly more powerful model than the German and UK price, and therefore the US price should be slightly higher, but this difference should be the same every year, with the exception of 2009 and 2010, when the German and UK comparison model changed and the US model did not. In fact, we do see a slight decline in the German and UK prices in 2009, consistent with the switch to a model with a less powerful engine. Nevertheless, the panels indicate that the price in each market was remarkably stable. The main deviation was a puzzling but temporary price surge in the United Kingdom in 2002. The lower right panel converts the UK and US prices into euros and redisplays the German prices. The dollar depreciation of 2003–04 is readily apparent in the declining US price in terms of euros (the dotted line) in those years. The pound depreciations of 2003 and 2009 are readily apparent in the declining UK price in terms of euros (the dashed line) during those years.

Figure B5.2.3 shows prices of the Volkswagen Passat in the same three markets. In Germany, the price is for the Passat 102. In the United Kingdom, the model number differs slightly by year, from 102 to 130 to 115 to 122. Volkswagen uses a different model labeling scheme in the United States. We examined the closest comparable model, the 1.8 from 2001 through 2005 and the 2.0 from 2006 through 2010. In each market, the local price of the Passat is fairly stable over time, although there is a noticeable uptick in the UK price in 2010. The lower right panel shows that, converted into euros, the US price dropped sharply along with the dollar in 2003–04. The UK price dropped noticeably with the pound in 2003 and again in 2009, before recovering about half of the 2009 decline in 2010.

Figure B5.2.4 shows prices of the Honda Civic in each of these markets.[2] German and UK prices are for Civic LS 1.4 from 2001 through 2005 and for Civic

(box continues next page)

Box 5.2   The international automobile market *(continued)*

Sport 1.8 from 2006 through 2010. US prices are for Civic DX from 2001 through 2005 and Civic EX from 2006 through 2010. The lines are broken between 2005 and 2006 to reflect this model shift—note the different axis scales for the two models. The prices are remarkably stable in each market, except for the United Kingdom in 2010. Once again, the pound depreciations of 2003 and 2009 and the dollar depreciation of 2003–04 show up in a marked divergence of prices after conversion into a common currency, as shown in the lower right panel. However, a bit more than half of the deviation between German and UK prices from 2007 to 2009 was reversed going into 2010.

Figure B5.2.5 displays prices of various models of Subarus in these markets.[3] From 2001 through 2005, prices for all three countries are for the Legacy station wagon, with a 2.0-liter engine in Germany and the United Kingdom and a 2.5-liter engine in the United States. These prices are remarkably steady in each market, but as shown in the lower right panel, when converted to a common currency, the effects of pound and dollar depreciation are evident. In 2006 and 2007, prices are for an upscale version of the Outback with 3.0 liter engine in each market; note the different price scales for these years. Although the price of this model remained stable between 2006 and 2007 in the United States, it rose considerably in Germany and the United Kingdom. The lower right panel shows that the price of this model was much higher in Europe than in the United States and that the difference in prices across markets increased in 2007. In 2009 and 2010, prices are for the Forester with a 2.0-liter diesel engine in Germany and the United Kingdom and a 2.5-liter gasoline engine in the United States. Prices were stable in Germany and the United States, with a modest increase in the United Kingdom probably reflecting a lagged and partial pass-through of the pound depreciation of 2009. Once again, the United States had the lowest prices and Germany the highest.

A high degree of pricing to market, and hence low pass-through, is evident in these figures, a result that was confirmed statistically. For the BMW and Volkswagen automobiles, the UK and US prices were regressed on exchange-rate-adjusted German prices, which generated pass-through coefficients around 0 and never more than 0.1. For the Honda Civic, the German and US prices were regressed on the exchange-rate-adjusted UK price (with a dummy for the model shift in 2006), which generated pass-through coefficients of −0.15 and 0.1, that were not significantly different from 0. The pass-through evident in these case studies is much lower than the typical estimate of 0.5 from

(box continues next page)

Box 5.2   The international automobile market *(continued)*

empirical studies across many products and countries, as discussed in appendix 5B, but it is consistent with the more recent studies of retail pricing in the automobile market (Lutz 2000, Gil-Pareja 2003).

---

1. All prices exclude value-added and sales taxes.
2. The Civic is assembled in the United Kingdom, the United States, and Japan, with minor differences in features. This gives Honda some flexibility to shift production to the cheapest location, but this flexibility is limited by the high fixed costs of opening and closing factories and retaining work forces.
3. Various models are used because Subaru did not report data to the European Commission on the same model in all years. The Legacy and Outback are assembled in Japan and in the United States, but the US production has 45 percent non-US (mainly Japanese) content. The Forester is made in Japan only.

Figure B5.2.1   US and UK exchange rates against Germany, 2001–10

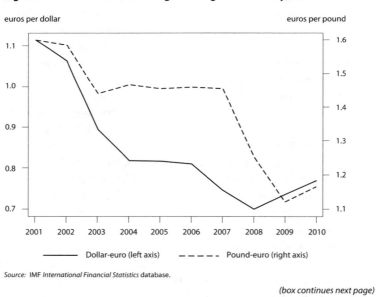

Source: IMF *International Financial Statistics* database.

(box continues next page)

biles purchased through its official dealer networks, Volkswagen can make it essentially impossible for large-scale international arbitrageurs to buy where the price is low and sell where the price is high. Volkswagen is aided in this effort by cross-country differences in language (for manuals and dashboard labels) and in regulatory standards: A Volkswagen sold in Germany may have different headlamps, bumpers, speedometer, catalytic converter, and other

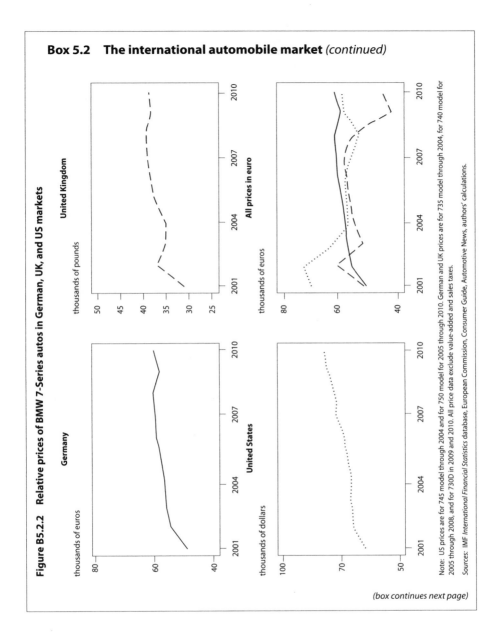

Box 5.2   The international automobile market *(continued)*

Figure B5.2.2   Relative prices of BMW 7-Series autos in German, UK, and US markets

Note: US prices are for 745 model through 2004 and for 750 model for 2005 through 2010. German and UK prices are for 735 model through 2004, for 740 model for 2005 through 2008, and for 730D in 2009 and 2010. All price data exclude value-added and sales taxes.

Sources: IMF *International Financial Statistics* database, European Commission, Consumer Guide, Automotive News, authors' calculations.

(box continues next page)

components than a Volkswagen sold in the United States, but the associated cost differences may be minimal.

Producers of many differentiated consumer products are able to indefinitely maintain different prices in different markets. This phenomenon is referred to as market segmentation. In the presence of market segmentation,

Box 5.2   The international automobile market *(continued)*

Figure B5.2.3   Relative prices of VW Passat in German, UK, and US markets

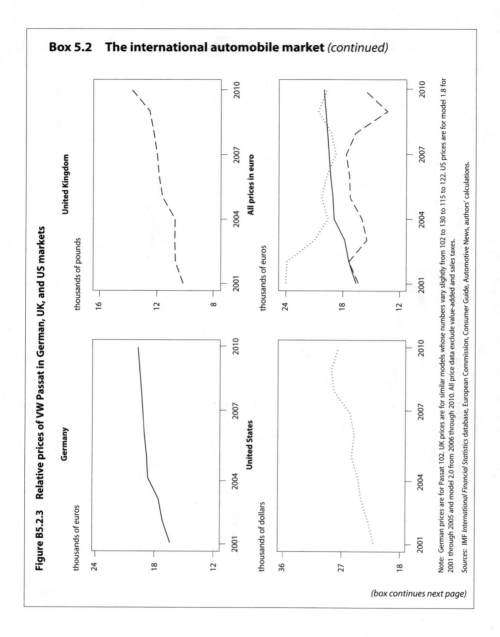

Note: German prices are for Passat 102. UK prices are for similar models whose numbers vary slightly from 102 to 130 to 115 to 122. US prices are for model 1.8 for 2001 through 2005 and model 2.0 from 2006 through 2010. All price data exclude value-added and sales taxes.

Sources: IMF *International Financial Statistics* database, European Commission, Consumer Guide, Automotive News, authors' calculations.

(box continues next page)

producers move prices in each market independently in response to competitive conditions. In general, prices will be higher in markets with less competition and in markets with wealthier consumers.

When a country's exchange rate moves, foreign producers of branded products generally adjust their prices by less than the exchange rate because they prefer to keep the ratio of their price fairly stable against the overall price

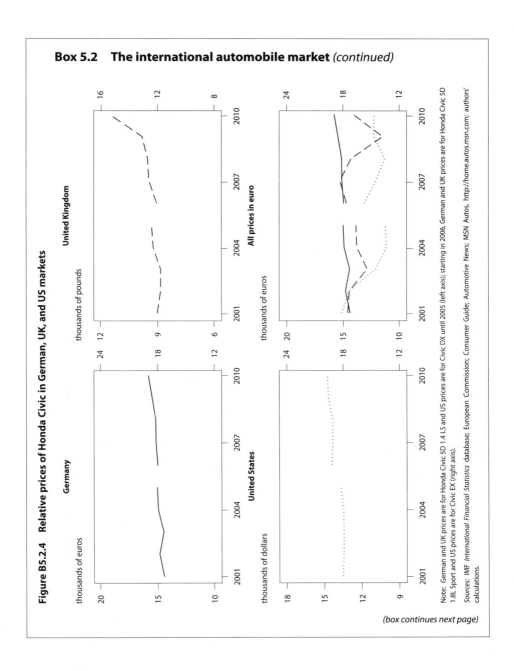

Box 5.2   The international automobile market *(continued)*

Figure B5.2.4   Relative prices of Honda Civic in German, UK, and US markets

Note: German and UK prices are for Honda Civic 5D 1.4 LS and US prices are for Civic DX until 2005 (left axis); starting in 2006, German and UK prices are for Honda Civic 5D 1.8L Sport and US prices are for Civic EX (right axis).

Sources: IMF *International Financial Statistics* database; European Commission; Consumer Guide; Automotive News; MSN Autos, http://home.autos.msn.com; authors' calculations.

(box continues next page)

level in that market. This tendency to stabilize prices in the importing country's currency is called incomplete pass-through or pricing-to-market, and it is the subject of appendix 5B. The degree of exchange rate pass-through varies widely across exporters, importers, and products. Most researchers conclude

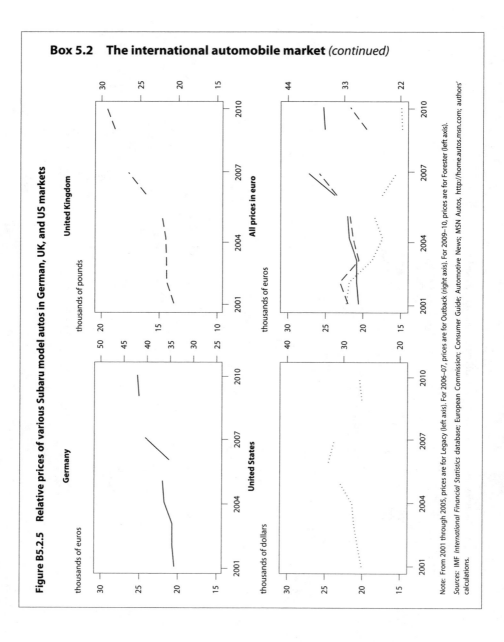

Figure B5.2.5 Relative prices of various Subaru model autos in German, UK, and US markets

that product characteristics that influence the shape of consumer demand curves and the structure of market competition both have important effects on pass-through. However, there is no widespread agreement on how to model these effects, and empirical studies generally seek to measure the degree of pass-through without trying to estimate the importance of underlying factors.

Surveying the literature as of the mid-1990s, Goldberg and Knetter (1997, 1244) conclude that "a price response equal to one-half the exchange rate change would be near the middle of the distribution of estimated responses for shipments to the United States." More recent studies find similar estimates for shipments to other countries and even lower estimates for pass-through to the United States. A number of studies find evidence that pass-through to the United States and some other countries has declined since the early 1990s. (See appendix 5B.)

Substitution across Brands

An important factor in determining how much the exchange rate affects trade prices and trade volumes is the degree to which buyers are willing to shift from local to imported brands, and vice versa, when relative prices change. The economic term for the response of sales to a change in price is the price elasticity of demand. For example, the price elasticity of demand equals 1 when a 10 percent increase in price causes a 10 percent reduction in units sold; the price elasticity equals 2 when a 10 percent increase in price causes a 20 percent reduction in units sold, and so on. As discussed in appendix 5A, estimates of price elasticities for exports and imports are wide-ranging, with typical values near or somewhat lower than 1. There are reasons to believe that price elasticities are more likely to be underestimated than overestimated, but for most economies the price elasticity between domestic and foreign goods and services is almost certainly less than 2.

Other things equal, a higher price elasticity means that a given change in prices will cause a larger response in exports or imports. This means that, with a higher price elasticity, a given depreciation of the exchange rate will cause exports to grow more, imports to shrink more, and domestic output or GDP to rise by more. However, a higher price elasticity also may be associated with a greater tendency among exporters to stabilize the prices they charge importers in their local currency and thus to pass through less of any exchange rate change. Failure to stabilize the local-currency price when the price elasticity of demand is high would result in large changes in export volume and market share. Firms may prefer to defend their market share than to stabilize their profit margin, especially if they do not expect the exchange rate movement to be permanent.[24]

In the extreme case, with complete stabilization of the local-currency price, the exchange rate has no effect on a country's import prices and thus no effect on its volume of imports. But this does not mean that the exchange rate has no effect on the economy. A depreciation of the currency will increase the profits of the country's exporters—who continue to charge the same price for their exports in terms of foreign currency—and thus increase the trade balance (or,

---

24. Krugman (1989b) conjectures that exchange rate volatility may increase the tendency of exporters to tough out adverse exchange rate movements because it increases the odds of a large rebound in the exchange rate. This would tend to reduce the price elasticity of trade.

net exports by value). The associated increase in national income may increase consumption and thus raise both output and imports.

Implications for RER Adjustment

Overall, product differentiation and price discrimination greatly diminish the pressures forcing the RER back to long-run PPP. Changes in the relative prices of home and foreign goods can persist for a very long time when these goods are not viewed as close to identical. Model simulations later in this chapter confirm that imperfect substitutability between differentiated manufactures and services, with a bias toward local products, is likely to be the most important factor behind the volatility and persistence of RERs.

Lags in the Adjustment of Trade Prices and Volumes

Adjusting the Volume of Trade

There are many reasons why trade flows may adjust slowly to a change in exchange rates: it may be impossible to recall goods already in transit; rapid adjustment may be more costly than gradual adjustment; and decision-makers at various stages of the production and consumption chains may need time to process incoming information. As discussed in appendix 5A, most estimates of these adjustment lags in trade volumes suggest that the half-life of the response to the exchange rate is about two to four quarters. By itself, this lag is not large enough to explain the much longer half-lives of RER fluctuations.

Sticky Prices

Most prices paid by consumers are not changed on a daily basis, and some are adjusted only about once a year. Workers' wages also are commonly adjusted only once a year. There are many reasons for this slow price adjustment, including the cost of printing catalogs, the managerial time required to calculate an appropriate new price, and customer resistance to frequent price changes.[25]

In a world in which consumer prices for imported goods are adjusted once a year, and at different dates for each product, the effects of an exchange rate depreciation can be expected to show up in consumer prices for imported goods gradually over a 12-month period. The effect on overall consumer prices could be delayed even further. For example, there could be a further lag if domestic producers of goods that compete with imports do not begin to adjust their prices until after consumer prices of imported goods rise. Indeed, if different firms adjust their prices on different dates, the whole process of price adjust-

---

25. When demand for a product shifts, a firm is forced to choose between incurring the costs associated either with adjusting prices or with adjusting volumes. Some firms appear to have sticky production volumes with flexible prices, whereas other firms set sticky prices and allow production or inventories to adjust in the short run.

ment could take several years, as those who adjust soon after the depreciation may not raise their prices very much in order to prevent losing sales to firms that have not yet raised their prices.

However, there are many reasons why consumer prices may adjust more quickly to a depreciation. First, price adjustments on many goods occur more frequently than once a year.[26] Second, firms may be willing to delay price adjustments and absorb small cost shocks, but they may not be able to absorb large shocks for long. Exchange rate changes of 10 or 20 percent, which are not uncommon within a year's time, are large relative to the annual changes in other business costs, and many firms are not likely to be willing or able to delay their response to such shocks. Third, firms that use imported goods or compete with importers should be able to anticipate price changes for imported goods because the exchange rate is an important and highly visible variable. Moreover, many of these firms are also exporters and thus face comparable pricing decisions in foreign markets.

Currency of Invoice

A second element of sticky prices arises from the currency a producer uses to invoice exports. If an exporter invoices in its own currency and the exchange rate depreciates while the goods are in transit, then the import price will rise by the full amount of the depreciation. If the exporter invoices in the importing country's currency, then the import price will not be affected by a depreciation that occurs while the goods are in transit. However, even in these cases, the lag in the price adjustment to a depreciation is only as long as the time it takes to ship the goods. Therefore, the currency of invoice can affect import prices for a few months at most.[27]

How Important Are Lags?

Altogether then, the adjustment lags for trade volumes and prices are not significant factors for slow equilibration of the RER over periods lasting several years or more, but they may play a role in the months just following a change in the exchange rate. This conclusion is supported by empirical research (Bergin, Glick, and Wu 2009) and by simulations of an economic model described in the next section.

---

26. Bils and Klenow (2004) find a median time between price changes (excluding temporary sales) of 5.5 months.

27. Hummels (2007, 150) states that "shipping containers from Europe to the US Midwest requires 2-3 weeks; from Europe to Asia requires 5 weeks." His estimate does not include any lag in processing an order, the transportation time from factory to port of export, and the transportation time from port of import to retail store.

Relative Importance of These Factors

The discussion in the previous three sections suggests that a preference for local products, or home bias, with only moderate substitutability of home and foreign goods is probably the most important factor behind the large swings and slow adjustment of the CPI-based RER. The existence of trade barriers and trade costs probably contributes to deviations of the RER from PPP, but even RERs based on the most tradable goods can be highly volatile and persistent. Price discrimination may contribute to large swings in the RER. Lags in the adjustment of volumes and prices have only a small effect on the behavior of the RER.

An alternative explanation for the exchange rate disconnect is that CPIs are measured incorrectly, so that swings in RERs are overstated. Box 5.3 addresses this argument and concludes that large swings in the CPI-based RER do not arise mainly because of errors in the measurement of CPIs.

The rest of this section confirms these conclusions and explores the effects of these factors on the behavior of the CPI-based RER using a mathematical model of the economy. (The model is described in detail in chapter 6.) Figure 5.13 shows how the economy responds to a large and persistent swing in the exchange rate caused by an increase in the risk premium on domestic assets. The lines in each panel display the response of each variable relative to its initial value (a value of zero means no change from initial value). The domestic currency depreciates 5 percent in the first year and then appreciates very slowly in subsequent years. The shock causes only a small temporary increase in inflation. The combination of a large nominal depreciation and a small increase in prices means that the RER depreciates substantially and then gradually returns to PPP after eight years. The drop in the RER boosts net exports. The central bank tightens monetary policy, raising both nominal and real interest rates, thus damping consumption to keep the increase in output small and to prevent inflation from rising. The responses displayed in figure 5.13 capture the exchange rate disconnect well: Both inflation and output are relatively stable despite a large and persistent swing in the RER.

The model can be changed to remove each of the structural economic factors that may be related to the exchange rate disconnect, and the same exchange rate shock can be rerun under each of the following scenarios:

- *Flexible prices.* All prices are free to adjust rapidly.
- *Full pass-through.* Exporters charge the same price abroad as they do at home so that import prices move in inverse proportion to the exchange rate.
- *All goods tradable.* There are no trade barriers or trade costs, so that all goods and services are tradable, though still subject to sticky prices and adjustment lags.
- *Tradable goods perfect substitutes.* Not all goods are tradable, but goods that are tradable are perfectly substitutable across countries.
- *All goods tradable and perfect substitutes.* This scenario is a combination of the two previous scenarios.

Box 5.3 Measurement issues

Are prices and price indices in different countries measured in such a way that RERs seem subject to large and persistent swings even though—when measured correctly—there are no such swings? Some researchers have raised this possibility, but the evidence to date does not support it.

Differences in Consumption Patterns

Consumer spending patterns are not the same across countries. For example, Italians eat more pasta than other people, and Eastern Europeans eat more potatoes.[1] When the distribution of consumer spending on different products varies across countries, some of the fluctuations in CPI-based RERs can reflect fluctuations in relative prices between different goods in the CPI basket rather than fluctuations in the exchange-rate-adjusted relative prices of similar goods. In other words, the law of one price (LOP) might hold for every good, but PPP may not hold for broad price indices when the spending shares for particular goods differ across countries.[2] For example, an increase in the world price of pasta relative to the price of potatoes would cause the Italian RER vis-à-vis Eastern Europe to rise, even when the exchange rate and all relative prices of specific goods across the two regions remain constant.

In reality, however, movements in RERs arising from different spending shares appear to be rather small. Exchange-rate-adjusted relative prices for narrow categories of goods (such as televisions or toothpaste) or even specific products (such as McDonalds Big Mac hamburgers or Volkswagen Passat autos) fluctuate nearly as much and as persistently as those at the aggregate level, suggesting that differences in consumption baskets are not a key factor.

New Goods

Dealing with the entry into the market of new goods and the exit of existing goods poses major problems for statistical agencies. It is widely believed that CPIs and import price indices fail to capture much of the true decline in prices that is associated with the introduction of new goods, as well as some of the true increase in prices associated with discontinued goods.[3] Because the number of goods rises over time, the missing price declines from the introduction of new goods probably outweigh the missing price increases from the discontinuation of existing goods, so that the net effect is to overestimate inflation.

Emi Nakamura and Jón Steinsson (2009) point out that if new imported goods are disproportionately introduced when the home currency appreciates, there

(box continues next page)

Box 5.3   Measurement issues *(continued)*

will be an underestimation of the fall in import prices associated with the currency appreciation. Analogously, if existing imported goods are disproportionately discontinued when the currency depreciates, the rise in import prices associated with the depreciation will be underestimated. These effects also apply to the CPI because many imports end up in the consumption basket. Nakamura and Steinsson (2009) estimate that these considerations lead to a small but noticeable understatement of the effect of exchange rate movements on the import price index.[4] This understatement implies that a given movement in the nominal exchange rate has a larger effect on the measured RER than on the true RER. Nakamura and Steinsson did not estimate the effect of this measurement error on the CPI-based RER, but it is almost surely less than the effect on import prices.[5] Moreover, the new goods problem cannot explain the large swings in exchange-rate-adjusted relative prices for specific consumer goods that neither entered nor exited but merely stayed in the market, as documented by studies discussed in box 5.2 and appendices 3B and 5C.

Randomness in Transaction Prices

Studies that look at highly disaggregated prices, such as daily transaction prices for specific goods at individual retail locations, find a large degree of dispersion across locations and over time (Broda and Weinstein 2008). This dispersion is comparable in magnitude to the dispersion of prices across countries. The reasons for this dispersion are not well understood. Much of it reflects temporary sales that are probably designed to lure price-sensitive buyers, and much reflects differences in retail services—chic boutique versus drab warehouse. Whatever the cause, the existence of such local dispersion helps put price dispersions across countries into a better perspective. However, it does not solve the puzzle of why movements in the nominal exchange rate are so large and why they cause movements in the CPI-based RER that are essentially the same size. As discussed in appendix 3B, in response to macroeconomic shocks, exchange-rate-adjusted prices of specific goods display persistent deviations from the LOP comparable to the deviations of RERs from PPP (Bergin, Glick, and Wu 2009).

---

1. See www.pasta.go.it/statistics.htm and www.potato2008.org/en/world/index.html.
2. This point is similar to the manner in which home bias in differentiated products induces movements in RERs. In this case, there are different spending patterns across goods whereas under home bias there are different spending patterns across brands of the same good.

(box continues next page)

3. Feenstra (1994) argues that the introduction of new goods should be viewed as reductions in prices from some unknown level that is so high that it completely chokes off all consumer demand. Discontinuations of existing goods should similarly be viewed as increases in prices to a level that chokes off all consumer demand.

4. Gagnon, Mandel, and Vigfusson (2011) argue that the understatement of the effect on import prices is very small.

5. Imports in advanced economies contain many new goods because developing economies are establishing many new export firms. Many of these imports replace domestic parts in existing consumer goods or they reflect the offshoring of production of existing goods, and so they do not reflect new goods in the CPI. Also, CPIs cover a much broader array of goods and services than goods imports, including goods that compete with imports.

Because monetary policy responds aggressively to deviations of inflation from its target, the inflation rate (not shown in figures 5.14 and 5.15) is similar across each of these scenarios. There are notable differences in the behavior of the RER and output, however.

Figure 5.14 displays the response of the RER to the exchange rate risk premium shock under the baseline model and under each of the alternative scenarios. Price flexibility has essentially no effect on the RER relative to the baseline model. Removing trade barriers and trade costs reduces the swing in the RER by a tiny amount. Full pass-through also reduces the swing in the RER by a small amount. Perfect substitutability across tradable goods reduces the swing in the RER by a large amount. And combining perfect substitutability with a removal of trade barriers and trade costs essentially eliminates the swing in the RER.

Figure 5.15 displays the response of output to the exchange rate risk premium shock under the baseline model and under each of the alternative scenarios. Price flexibility essentially eliminates the small rise in output that occurs in the baseline scenario; the line for this alternative is not visible because it is flat at 0. Removing trade barriers and costs has no effect on output relative to the baseline. Full pass-through increases the rise in output by a tiny amount. Perfect substitutability across tradable goods gives rise to a large swing in output. Combining perfect substitutability with a removal of trade barriers and trade costs also creates a large swing in output, albeit slightly less than with perfect substitutability alone.

Figures 5.14 and 5.15 confirm that imperfect substitutability of goods produced in different countries is the key factor behind large and persistent swings in RERs. In the presence of imperfect substitutability, reducing trade barriers and trade costs has only a minimal effect on swings in the RER.[28] But,

---

28. This finding may explain why figure 5.9 shows that a RER based on tradable goods moves similarly to a RER for all goods and services.

Figure 5.13   Economic response to a risk premium shock, baseline model (deviations from initial values)

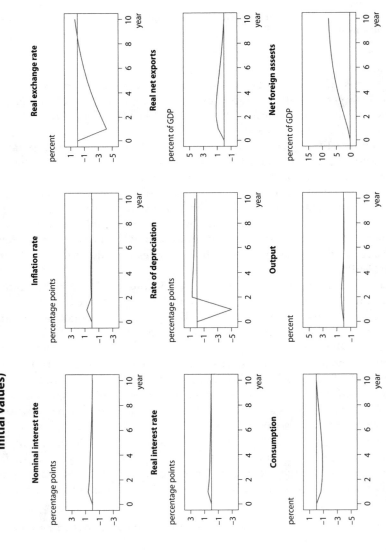

Source: Author's calculations.

Figure 5.14 Response of the real exchange rate to a risk premium shock under alternative scenarios (deviations from initial values)

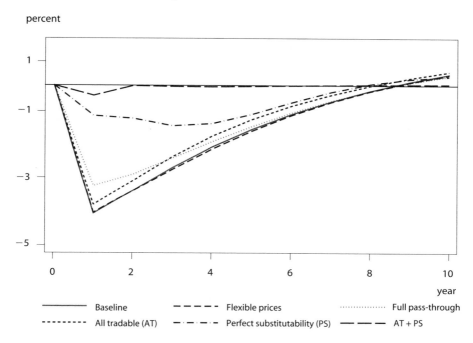

Source: Authors' calculations.

when goods are highly substitutable, reducing trade barriers and trade costs can have an important additional damping effect on swings in the RER. The effects of these factors on output are essentially the opposite of the effects on the RER: Scenarios with large swings in the RER had little movement in output, and scenarios with small movements in the RER had large movements in output. It appears that in order for a central bank to be able to stabilize output in response to a shock to the exchange rate risk premium, the RER has to move. In other words, it is the volatility of the RER that enables output to be stable.

Conclusions

Exchange rate volatility—particularly over horizons of one year or longer—is not necessarily associated with volatility of inflation or output over similar horizons. Directing monetary policy at stabilizing inflation and output is an essential condition for this exchange rate disconnect. Two other features of economies are also important. Imperfect substitutability between goods and services produced in different countries with a preference for home goods is

Figure 5.15 Response of output to a risk premium shock under alternative scenarios (deviations from initial values)

percent

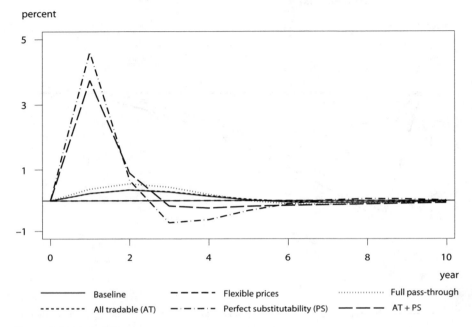

Source: Authors' calculations.

an essential underlying factor, and trade barriers and trade costs contribute under certain circumstances. In contrast, price discrimination across markets, or incomplete exchange rate pass-through, is only a minor factor, and sticky prices are unimportant.

Appendix 5A
Studies of Substitution across Tradable Goods

The Goldstein and Khan (1985) and Marquez (2002) Surveys

Two standard references on price elasticities in international trade are the surveys by Goldstein and Khan (1985) and Marquez (2002). The typical model of import demand is expressed in equation 5A.1 (all variables are in logarithms), where M stands for the volume of imports, Y for domestic output or spending, PM for the price of imports, P for a domestic price index such as the CPI, Z for other control variables, and v is a random error.

$$M_t = \mu + \rho\, Y_t - \sigma\, PM_t/P_t + \phi\, Z_t + v_t \tag{5A.1}$$

Equation 5A.1 is based on the model of Armington (1969), in which goods are differentiated by country of production. Imports respond positively to domestic output; sometimes Y stands for domestic spending but it makes little difference whether one uses output or spending. Imports respond negatively to the price of imports relative to the price of other goods in the home market. Not all studies include other variables, represented by the vector Z, but some candidate control variables include measures of trade barriers, measures of the number of varieties of imports available, and measures of cyclical elements of demand. Studies generally allow for lagged adjustment. Studies examine imports at different levels of aggregation across source countries or categories of goods. Some studies examine the analog to equation 5A.1 for exports, which depend on foreign output and the ratio of the export price to the exchange-rate-adjusted foreign price level.

Goldstein and Khan note that there is also a supply function for imports, which implies in principle that ordinary least squares (OLS) estimates of equation 5A.1 are biased. A few studies estimate import demand and supply together. Generally speaking, the price elasticity of supply appears to be much higher than the price elasticity of demand, which means that the bias from OLS estimates of equation 5A.1 may be small.[29] Some studies use instrumental variables when estimating equation 5A.1. A typical instrument for the relative import price is the real exchange rate (RER). In principle, the RER also is endogenous to trade flows, but in practice, this endogeneity is weak for most economies and sample periods.

Goldstein and Khan report estimates of the price elasticity, σ, from various studies. For aggregate imports, the central tendency is 0.5 to 1.5. For aggregate exports, the central tendency is 1 to 2. For both exports and imports, there are many estimates outside of these central tendencies. About half of the long-run response to a change in the price of imports occurs within one year.

---

29. Indeed, as shown in appendix 5B, models of import supply (that is, import price) often do not include measures of import volumes because producers appear willing to adjust volumes flexibly in response to demand.

Marquez does not catalog results for a large number of studies, but he does present results from three major studies of exports and imports in the G-7 countries: Cline (1989); Caporale and Chui (1999); and Hooper, Johnson, and Marquez (2000). The central tendencies of elasticity estimates in these three studies are somewhat lower than in Goldstein and Khan, at about 0.5 to 1 for imports and 0.5 to 1.5 for exports. Marquez does not report speeds of adjustment.

Goldstein and Khan report price elasticities for goods disaggregated at the one-digit Standard International Trade Classification (SITC) level that are comparable to those for aggregate trade. Marquez reports separate estimates for production and consumption goods as well as services. He further disaggregates production goods by one-digit end-use categories. He finds import price elasticities predominantly in the range of 0.5 to 1.5.

There is a presumption that the output (or income) elasticity, ρ, should equal 1. However, it is typically estimated to be greater than 1, and it differs noticeably across countries. There are numerous proposed explanations for these deviations from 1, including secularly declining trade barriers and transportation costs, large cyclical effects, imports as luxury goods whose demand increases with income, and the role of immigrants and multinational corporations in boosting imports. Many studies include measures of these factors in the vector, Z, of auxiliary variables. One important explanation for differences in the output elasticity across countries—advanced by Krugman (1989a) and implemented by Gagnon (2008)—is that consumers' taste for variety is important and that fast-growing economies develop more new varieties than slow-growing economies. However, the specification and value of the output elasticity is not important for the issues considered in this book, and therefore these are not explored further here.

Other Time-Series Aggregate Studies

Gagnon (1989) examines bilateral trade between Germany, Japan, the United Kingdom, and the United States. He finds price elasticities of roughly 0.5 to 1.5. Adjustment is moderately rapid, with more than half the long-run response occurring within one year.

Senhadji (1998) estimates import price elasticities for 66 advanced and developing economies. He finds an average price elasticity of about 1. Senhadji and Montenegro (1999) estimate export price elasticities for 53 advanced and developing economies. They find an average price elasticity of about 1. In both of these studies, adjustment is moderately slow, with slightly less than half the long-run response occurring within one year.

Adler and Hufbauer (2009) survey studies of US export and import price elasticities conducted since 2000. They find a wide range of estimates with a central tendency of 0.5 to 1 for imports and 0.5 to 1.5 for exports.

Other Approaches

Studies that estimate the price elasticity of demand between similar goods produced in different countries obtain a wide range of results, but typically find higher elasticities than the studies cited above. Harrigan (1993) finds price elasticities of demand of 5 to 12 at the three-digit industry level in the Organization for Economic Cooperation and Development (OECD) countries. Feenstra (1994) examines six categories of US manufactured imports at the finest level of disaggregation available and obtains price elasticities of 3 to 8. Broda and Weinstein (2006) extend Feenstra's analysis to all categories of US imports and obtain a median estimated price elasticity of about 3. This result is not sensitive to estimating at the finest level of trade disaggregation or the relatively more aggregated three-digit SITC level. Other studies of disaggregated trade that find price elasticities of 3 or more include Eaton and Kortum (2002) and Simonovska and Waugh (2011).

Lai and Trefler (2002) show that these high price elasticities do not arise solely in studies of disaggregated products. They examine bilateral trade in aggregate manufactured goods among 36 advanced and developing economies and find a mean price elasticity of 5.

Ruhl (2008) suggests that the difference between high and low elasticity estimates may have to do with the perceived permanence of the price changes. Cross-sectional regressions tend to focus on long-lasting price differences, and they obtain high elasticities, whereas time-series regressions may be capturing short-run responses to price differences that are perceived as temporary. Ruhl focuses in particular on export supply behavior, noting that some producers will enter a market only if the price change is perceived to be permanent.[30] His study does not include any empirical tests. A potential problem for his theory is that exchange rate changes are highly persistent, and most time-series estimates of elasticities do allow for lagged adjustment.

Feenstra, Obstfeld, and Russ (2010) argue that the difference between studies that find high price elasticities and those that find low price elasticities is that the former examine the elasticity between different foreign suppliers whereas the latter examine the elasticity between domestic and foreign suppliers. To estimate both types of elasticities, they match up bilateral trade data with US production data at the finest level of disaggregation. Due to changes in classification over time and differences in the way trade and production are categorized, their sample does not cover all manufactured goods. For the 113 industries they do cover, they show that the median price elasticity across foreign suppliers is 4.4 and the median price elasticity between domestic and foreign suppliers is 1.

The findings of Feenstra, Obstfeld, and Russ (2010) potentially may explain the results reported in Goldstein and Khan (1985) and Adler and

---

30. Ruhl's model assumes that most empirical estimates of price elasticities capture a combined effect of demand and supply responses.

Hufbauer (2009) that export price elasticities tend to be higher than import price elasticities. When a country's currency depreciates, all of its imports become more expensive, and the only relevant price elasticity is the small elasticity between domestic and foreign producers. But there are two elasticities relevant for its exports: a small elasticity as foreign consumers substitute between their local products and the now-cheaper exports and a large elasticity as foreign consumers substitute between products from third countries and the now-cheaper exports.

Appendix 5B
Studies of Exchange Rate Effects on Trade Prices

Many economists have long suspected that the link between exchange rates and prices of exports and imports is the key element in explaining the exchange rate disconnect. This led to an explosion of research in this area over the past 30 years.

The Goldberg and Knetter (1997) Survey Article

In an influential article, Goldberg and Knetter (1997) survey studies from the mid-1970s to the mid-1990s on the connections between exchange rates and prices. They group the empirical papers into three categories: (1) studies of the law of one price (LOP) for specific categories of goods in different countries; (2) studies of exchange rate pass-through (ERPT) into import or export prices; and (3) studies of pricing-to-market (PTM) of export prices to different destinations. Appendix 3B reviewed the literature on purchasing power parity (PPP), beginning with the survey article by Rogoff (1996) that essentially encompasses the LOP section in Goldberg and Knetter. This appendix focuses on the other two categories: ERPT and PTM.

In principle, ERPT = 1 − PTM when ERPT estimates include a control for the exporter's marginal cost. In practice, models of PTM have a more flexible, and presumably superior, approach to controlling for marginal cost by using information from exports of the same good to different destinations.

Exchange Rate Pass-Through

In the 1970s, standard textbook models assumed that the average price of each country's exports was the same as the average domestic price of its output. With the onset of floating exchange rates, researchers began to test this hypothesis. Equation 5B.1 is the generic regression model used in these studies:

$$PM_t = \alpha + \delta X_t + \gamma (1/E_t) + \lambda Z_t + u_t \tag{5B.1}$$

where all variables are in logarithms, PM is the import price in the importer's currency, X is a control for cost in the exporter's currency, E is the exchange rate (which is inverted because an appreciation of the home currency tends to lower the import price), Z denotes other control variables (for example, on the state of the business cycle), and u is a random error.[31] These studies cover different countries and time periods. Most allow for lags in the effects of the independent variables. They use different measures for costs and other controls, and they were conducted at different levels of aggregation across types of traded

---

31. As a model of import supply, the control variables should include import volumes but studies generally find little role for import volumes in equation 5B.1. This result is consistent with oligopolistic markup pricing in which import volumes have little effect on marginal cost.

goods. Studies of import price pass-through typically use weighted averages of foreign costs and exchange rates (X and E) as well as purely domestic control variables (Z). Other studies focus on export price pass-through using a domestic cost control for the exporting country (X) and weighted averages of exchange rates and other controls in the importing countries (E and Z).

The coefficient γ in equation 5B.1 measures ERPT; a value of 1 denotes complete ERPT, and a value of 0 denotes the lack of ERPT.[32] According to Goldberg and Knetter, estimates of ERPT (mainly on US imports) are centered about 0.6, with essentially all of the adjustment occurring within two or three quarters.

Pricing-to-Market

In the face of strong evidence for less than complete ERPT, researchers in the 1980s debated whether incomplete ERPT necessarily implies that producers were charging different prices in the export market than in the home market. The presumption of most researchers was that incomplete ERPT means that producers charge a different price in the export market than at home, but most studies do not test this hypothesis directly, in large part because of the difficulty of matching up trade prices and domestic prices of the same good at the wholesale level. Some researchers conjecture that incomplete ERPT might reflect a common effect of exchange rates on the prices of traded goods in all markets.

The inclusion in equation 5B.1 of cost controls (or prices of similar goods in the producer's home market) is meant to control for common effects on the prices of traded goods across markets, including those arising from the exchange rate. But these price or cost controls typically measure different baskets of goods than the import prices, or they more closely capture average costs than marginal costs. In theory, prices should be linked to marginal costs. In competitive markets, price equals marginal cost. In oligopolistic markets, price equals a markup over marginal cost, where the markup depends on the firm's perceived elasticity of demand.

There are at least two reasons why exchange rates might affect marginal cost. First, an appreciation of the exporter's currency lowers the cost of imported inputs. This may be especially important if export industries use imported inputs more intensively than other industries, as appears to be the case for some countries.[33] Second, an appreciation of the exporter's currency may reduce total demand for the export good and thus reduce marginal cost if production costs are increasing in output.

A new empirical literature, pioneered by Knetter (1989), uses the following

---

32. For studies based on export prices in the exporter's currency, $\gamma = 0$ denotes complete ERPT and $\gamma = 1$ denotes no ERPT, when the exporter's currency is defined as the home currency.

33. High import content of exported manufactures is characteristic of Mexico and many developing Asian economies.

regression equation to look at prices charged in different markets while controlling for unobserved marginal costs:

$$PX_{it} = \alpha_i + \theta_t + \beta\,(1/E_{it}) + u_{it} \qquad (5B.2)$$

Where PX_{it} is the price in exporter currency of exports to destination i in period t, α_i is a set of destination effects, θ_t is a set of time effects, E_{it} is the bilateral exchange rate between the exporter and destination i, and u_{it} is a random error. As in equation 5B.1, the exchange rate is inverted so that an appreciation of the exporter's currency causes it to reduce the price in terms of its own currency even as it may be increasing the price in terms of the importer's currency (i.e., when $0 < \beta < 1$). The Greek letters denote parameters to be estimated. Equation 5B.2 is implemented at the finest possible level of disaggregation in an attempt to measure prices of essentially the same good at the port of export bound for different destinations. Differences in these prices are direct evidence of price discrimination in international trade and thus of segmented markets between countries.

The α_i coefficients are measures of differences across countries in the average price charged. To some extent, the α_i coefficients can be taken as evidence of price discrimination and market segmentation. However, even at the finest disaggregation available (Knetter uses seven-digit SITC industry categories), there may be differences in product quality, and so these coefficients may reflect different quality levels shipped to different destinations.

The θ_t coefficients capture common movements in prices charged to all destinations. If price equals marginal cost (or a fixed markup over marginal cost), and marginal cost movements are the same for all destinations, then price movements should be the same for all destinations. In that case, the θ_t coefficients would capture all the variation in export prices and PTM, as estimated by β, would be zero.

In practice, estimates of PTM are often highly significantly different from zero, providing strong evidence that export prices respond to exchange rate movements in each destination market independently of the other markets. In other words, for many traded goods, national markets are segmented from each other and producers seek to stabilize prices in the currencies of each market. According to Goldberg and Knetter, there is a very wide range of estimated values of PTM, and the differences seem to arise more from differences in the industry examined than the country of the exporter or the destination market. The center of the PTM distribution is roughly 0.5, implying that exporters offset about half the effect of exchange rate movements on the prices charged in local currency in each destination market. Moreover, the rough equality of the PTM estimates and the estimates of 1 − ERPT implies that PTM is the overwhelming source of incomplete ERPT and that exchange rate effects on marginal costs are generally small.

Exchange Rate Pass-Through Studies since 1997

Aggregate Trade Data

Gottfries (2002) finds ERPT of about 0.4 for Swedish manufactured exports over the period 1972–96. Using price data for total merchandise exports from 1980 through 2004, Vigfusson, Sheets, and Gagnon (2009) find ERPT of 0.96 for Germany, 0.84 for the United States, 0.76 for the Asian newly industrialized economies as a group, 0.71 for Canada, 0.69 for the United Kingdom, and 0.53 for Japan.[34] They find substantially lower estimates of ERPT—about 0.2 to 0.3—on bilateral exports from these regions to the United States. Brissimis and Kosma (2007) estimate ERPT of 0.27 by Japanese exporters to the United States from 1975 through 2001.

Campa and Goldberg (2005) estimate ERPT for total goods imports of 23 OECD countries over the period 1975–2003. They find estimates ranging from nearly 0 in Austria and Ireland to about 1 in Japan and Portugal. The average ERPT is 0.64 and ERPT for US imports is 0.42. They show that countries with higher rates of inflation and countries with more volatile exchange rates tend to have higher estimates of ERPT into their import prices. Barhoumi (2006) studies ERPT into goods import prices in 24 developing economies over the period 1980–2003. He finds estimates ranging from about 0.3 to more than 1.0 (though not statistically significantly greater than 1.0). He finds that ERPT into import prices is greater in countries with fixed exchange rate regimes than with floating exchange rates, perhaps because exchange rate changes are viewed as more permanent in the former group. ERPT also is higher in countries with higher (and more volatile) inflation and in countries with lower trade barriers. Bussiere and Peltonen (2008) examine goods export and import prices for 41 countries, including 28 developing countries, over the period 1980–2006 (some countries have missing data for part of this period). Their ERPT estimates for imports range from about 0 to 0.7. When constrained to be the same across all countries, ERPT is estimated at 0.42. See table 5B.1.

Industry-Level Studies

Yang (1998) studies ERPT in four-digit Standard Industrial Classification (SIC) categories of US imports and exports over the period 1982–92. For imports, he finds estimates ranging from less than 0 to almost 1, with a median well below 0.5. For exports, ERPT almost never is estimated below 0.5. In many categories, the ERPT in US imports is significantly lower than the ERPT in US exports, a result at odds with the finding cited by Goldberg and Knetter (1997) that the ERPT behavior of US exporters is generally not significantly different from that of foreign exporters within the same industry.[35] Feinberg (1996) finds ERPT of

---

34. The Asian newly industrialized economies are Hong Kong, Korea, Singapore, and Taiwan.

35. The Goldberg and Knetter finding is based on a different sample period and a smaller and more disaggregated selection of industries than that studied by Yang.

Table 5B.1 Selected exchange rate pass-through estimates, aggregate data

Source	Years	Countries	Imports or exports	Level	Estimates
Goldberg and Knetter (1997)	Various during 1970s–1990s	Various, mainly United States	Mainly import	Various	Centered on 0.6
Gottfries (2002)	1972–96	Sweden	Export	Manufactures	0.4
Campa and Goldberg (2005)	1975–2003	OECD	Import	Total goods, manufactures	0 to 1 average 0.6
Barhoumi (2006)	1980–2003	24 developing economies	Import	Total goods	0.3 to 2.1 average 0.8
Brissimis and Kosma (2007)	1975–2001	Japan	Exports to United States	Total goods	0.27
Vigfusson, Sheets, and Gagnon (2009)	1980–2004	G-7 + Asian NIEs	Export	Total goods	0.5 to 1, total 0.2 to 0.3, to United States only
Bussiere and Peltonen (2008)	1980–2006	41 OECD members + developing economies	Import and export	Total goods	0 to 0.7 0.42 (joint)[a]

OECD = Organization for Economic Cooperation and Development; G-7 = Group of Seven highly industrialized economies; Asian NIEs = Asian newly industrialized economies (Hong Kong, Singapore, Korea, and Taiwan); PPP = purchasing power parity

a. Refers to estimate constrained to be equal across countries.

about 0.25 to 0.5 for US imports in 26 manufacturing industries from 1978 through 1987. Lee (1997) finds ERPT of about 0.4 to 0.9 for Korean imports in 24 manufacturing industries from 1980 through 1990. Olivei (2002) finds average ERPT of 0.4 in 34 US manufacturing industries from 1981 through 1999. Pollard and Coughlin (2003) find median ERPT estimates of about 0.4 for 20 three-digit US manufacturing industries between 1978 and 2000.

Campa and Goldberg (2005) estimate ERPT in OECD countries for five categories of goods imports: food, energy, raw materials, manufactured goods, and nonmanufactured goods. Average ERPT is lowest for manufactured goods (0.62) and highest for raw materials (0.85). Focusing on euro-area countries from 1989 through 2001, Campa and Minguez (2006) find ERPT estimates for 13 industries range from 0.62 for vehicles to 1.02 for mineral fuels. In a relatively short sample (2000–2007) Maria-Dolores (2010) estimates ERPT for nine industries in the new member states of the European Union ranging from 0.13 in basic manufactures to 1.57 in mineral fuels.

In a study of the US photographic film market, Kadiyali (1997) finds very low and somewhat asymmetric ERPT of 0.08 when the dollar was appreciating (1980–84) and 0.18 when the dollar was depreciating (1985–90). The market was essentially a duopoly in which the domestic producer, Kodak, had a dominant share, and Fuji, the largest foreign producer, was a recent entrant. Interestingly, Kadiyali notes that Fuji moved production to the United States in the mid-1990s when the yen was very strong, probably to take advantage of lower production costs in the United States at that time.

Bernhofen and Xu (2000) examine ERPT in the US petrochemical market. They have unusually detailed measures of marginal cost based on engineering studies of German and Japanese petrochemical producers. They find that ERPT = 1 for German exporters and ERPT=0.6 for Japanese exporters over the period 1982–93. See table 5B.2.

The Automobile Market

Many researchers have studied ERPT and PTM in the automobile industry. Feenstra, Gagnon, and Knetter (1996) study ERPT by producers in the United States, Germany, France, and Sweden to 12 destination markets over the period 1972–87. They find median ERPT of about 0.5, with higher ERPT from Germany and the United States and lower ERPT from France. By destination market they find that ERPT is lowest to Norway and the United States, highest to Israel, and also relatively high to Finland, Austria, and Switzerland.

Gron and Swenson (1996) find ERPT of 0.5 to 0.65 for US imports of nonluxury Japanese automobiles between 1984 and 1993. They find that ERPT on luxury autos is higher by about 0.2 to 0.3.[36] They also find that the pass-through of cost shocks (including exchange rate shocks) is lower for those

---

36. Gagnon and Knetter (1995) also find higher ERPT on the most expensive categories of autos.

Table 5B.2   Selected exchange rate pass-through estimates, industry-level data

Source	Years	Countries	Import or export	Level	Estimates
Feinberg (1996)	1978–87	United States	Import	26 4-digit SIC manufactures	0 to 0.5
Lee (1997)	1980–90	Korea	Import	24 3- and 4-digit SITC manufactures	Average 0.6
Yang (1998)	1982–92	United States	Both	103 2-, 3-, and 4-digit SIC manufactures	Median 0.2 import Median 0.9 export
Pollard and Coughlin (2003)	1978–2000	United States	Import	9 2-digit and 20 3-digit ISIC manufactures	Average 0.3 2-digit Average 0.4 3-digit
Campa and Goldberg (2005)	1975–2003	OECD	Import	5 1-digit OECD goods	0.6 to 0.9
Campa and Minguez (2006)	1989–2001	Euro area	Import	13 1- and 2-digit SITC goods	0.6 to 1.0
Maria-Dolores (2010)	2000–07	EU accession	Import	9 1-digit SITC goods	0.1 to 1.6
Kadiyali (1997)	1980–90	United States	Import	Photo film retail prices	0.1, 1980–84 0.2, 1985–90
Bernhofen and Xu (2000)	1982–93	United States	Import	Petrochemicals	1, Germany 0.6, Japan

OECD = Organization for Economic Cooperation and Development; SIC = Standard Industrial Classification; SITC = Standard International Trade Classification; ISIC = International Standard Industrial Classification

Note: EU accession refers to the 10 countries that joined the European Union in 2004 (Cyprus, Czech Republic, Estonia, Hungary, Latvia, Lithuania, Malta, Poland, Slovakia, and Slovenia).

models that are produced both in Japan and in the United States, presumably reflecting the ability to shift production to the lower-cost location.

Goldberg and Verboven (1998) examine retail automobile prices (net of tax) in Europe from 1980 through 1993. They find "large and persistent differences across countries," including differences associated with stabilizing prices in local currencies when exchange rates move. By examining prices of the same models in different markets, they are able to control for marginal cost shocks at the producer level, as in Knetter's PTM model. However, their use of retail prices introduces an additional cost margin that may differ across countries and over time. This margin is denominated in local (importer) currency and includes dealer costs, advertising, and transportation. They estimate ERPT to retail prices of just over 0.5. Their structural model attributes two-thirds of the incomplete ERPT to fixed costs in local currency and one-third to markup adjustment (PTM). Goldberg and Verboven defend their estimate of the importance of local currency costs by noting that "industry wisdom is that local costs are up to 35% of the value of a car." If this is true, local currency costs are a much higher share of auto prices in Europe than in the United States, where such costs are about 10% of the retail price.[37]

Using similar data but a later sample (1993–98), Lutz (2000) finds ERPT of only 0 to 0.2 in European retail automobile prices. Although there are several methodological differences between Goldberg and Verboven (1998) and Lutz (2000), perhaps the most important factor behind the lower ERPT in the Lutz paper is that inflation was much lower and less variable during 1993–98 than during 1980–93. As discussed above, other studies find that ERPT to import prices is lower for countries with lower (and less variable) inflation rates. Gil-Pareja (2003) also examines retail prices in Europe from 1993 through 1998 and finds ERPT of 0.1 to 0.2. He finds no important differences in ERPT arising from the currency in which a producer invoices auto exports. In part, low ERPT into retail prices may arise from local currency costs, but the much lower ERPT estimates in Lutz and Gil-Pareja compared with Goldberg and Verboven imply a much greater role for PTM by producers. Box 5.2 reports that low pass-through continues to characterize the automobile market in the 10 years after these studies.

Gross and Schmitt (2000) examine import unit values of small and medium autos for Switzerland from 1977 through 1994. Because import

---

37. According to the Edmunds.com website (accessed 4 May 2010) the dealer markup plus freight costs ranged from 6 to 12 percent of the manufacturer's suggested retail price plus freight for the following car models, with an average value of 9 percent: BMW 535i, Buick Enclave CXL AWD, Chevrolet Malibu, Chrysler PT Cruiser, Honda Accord EX-L V6, Lincoln Navigator L 4WD, Nissan Altima 2.5 sedan, Subaru Legacy sedan, Toyota Highlander Ltd AWD, and Volkswagen Golf 4D Hatchback 2.5L. National advertising is another local currency cost, judged to be about 1 or 2 percent of retail sales. No manufacturer incentives are reported on this date for any of these models, but at times such incentives may represent an increase in the margin between suggested retail and manufacturer price of 2 to 5 percentage points. Many of these incentives are passed on to consumers in lower retail transactions prices.

unit values do not include any local costs, they are a more direct measure of producer price adjustment. However, Gross and Schmitt use broad unit labor costs to control for marginal cost rather than estimating marginal cost from prices of the same models in different destinations. They find ERPT of essentially 0 for small autos and between 0 and 0.5 for medium autos, depending on the country of the exporter.

Di Mauro et al. (2011) find moderate to high values of ERPT in French and German auto exports from 1993 through 2007. They do not examine retail prices, and they do not report the functional form of their regressions or the destination markets. See table 5B.3.

Pricing-to-Market Studies since 1997[38]

Alexius and Vredin (1999) use the multimarket PTM framework to study export prices of 18 Swedish industries between 1980 and 1994. They find a significantly positive correlation between the ratio of export prices across pairs of foreign markets and the exchange rate between the same two markets, consistent with PTM, in 55 percent of cases. They also find that unemployment rates in the destination markets often have a significant effect on export prices.

Determinants of PTM

Drawing on earlier studies of industrial organization, Goldberg and Knetter (1997, 1245) state that price discrimination across markets requires both market power by sellers and segmented markets. Market power exists when a firm can sell its products above their marginal cost. Segmented markets exist when "the location of the buyers and sellers influences the terms of the transaction in a substantial way (i.e., by more than the marginal cost of physically moving the good from one location to another)."

Segmented international markets are common with branded differentiated products. They are supported in some cases by regulations that prohibit consumers or third parties from importing certain products. They are also supported by differences in safety or environmental regulations or customer tastes that require producers to build slightly different products for each destination market; usually these differences involve only minimal costs. In addition, producers may provide warranties on their products that are valid only on products purchased through authorized distributors.

Some studies analyze the degree of market segmentation indirectly, based on either differences in the levels of prices across locations or the volatility of such differences. Engel and Rogers (1996) famously find that distance is posi-

---

38. As discussed above, Goldberg and Verboven (1998), Lutz (2000), and Gil-Pareja (2003) use the multimarket PTM framework to control for common costs at the producer level, but they apply their analysis to retail prices, which include unobserved local currency costs.

Table 5B.3 Selected exchange rate pass-through estimates, auto industry

Source	Years	Countries	Import or export	Notes	Estimates
Feenstra, Gagnon, and Knetter (1996)	1972–87	United States, Germany, France, Sweden	Export	To 11 OECD destinations and Israel	Median 0.5
Gron and Swenson (1996)	1984–93	Japan	Export	To US	0.5 to 0.65 + 0.2 extra for luxury cars
Goldberg and Verboven (1998)	1980–93	European Union	Import	0.5 retail	0.85
Lutz (2000)	1993–98	European Union	Import	0 to 0.2 retail	Retail only
Gil-Pareja (2003)	1993–98	European Union	Import	0.1 to 0.2 retail	Retail only
Gross and Schmitt (2000)	1977–94	Switzerland	Import		0, small car 0 to 0.5, medium car
Di Mauro, Formai, Marquez, and Osbat (2011)	1993–2007	France, Germany	Export		0.4 to 0.9

OECD = Organization for Economic Cooperation and Development

tively related to market segmentation, but that the border between the United States and Canada creates a degree of market segmentation equivalent to a distance of 75,000 miles! Parsley and Wei (2001) find that distance, shipping costs, and exchange rate volatility can explain a significant amount of market segmentation across countries.

The relationship between market power and the degree of PTM is ambiguous. For homogeneous products and integrated markets, PTM = 0, because prices are the same in all markets. As discussed above, industry studies typically find PTM is close to 0 (or ERPT close to 1 from the point of view of individual country imports) for homogeneous commodities such as petroleum and other raw materials, consistent with integrated world markets.

For differentiated goods, Feenstra, Gagnon, and Knetter (1996) model pricing behavior of a group of exporters who face an exchange rate shock that is not faced by other sellers in a given market. They show that for broad classes of consumer demand curves, PTM = 0.5 when market share is 0 and PTM = 0 when market share is 1.[39] As market share rises above 0, PTM may either rise or fall initially, but eventually it must fall as market share approaches 1. One class of demand curve that is ruled out in the preceding analysis is the constant elasticity of substitution (CES) demand curve. Feenstra, Gagnon, and Knetter (1996) show that for CES demand, PTM starts at 0 for market share of 0, initially rises with rising market share, and then falls as market share approaches 1. As discussed above, they estimate PTM as a function of the market share of each of four exporting countries to each of 12 destination markets. They find that PTM initially rises and peaks when the exporting country has a market share of 0.4. The average level of PTM differs across source-destination pairs. For the median pair, estimated PTM starts at 0.3 when market share is 0, peaks at 0.7, and falls to −0.2 (but not significantly different from 0.0) when market share is 1.

Some recent studies focus on the effects of differences in product variety and productivity across exporters. Auer and Chaney (2009) develop a theoretical model in which producers of lower-quality goods price to market more than producers of higher-quality goods, but they find "only weak empirical evidence in support" of their theory. Berman, Martin, and Mayer (2010) develop a model with monopolistic competition (arising from product varieties) and distribution costs in the importing market. They show that high-productivity (low-cost) suppliers should price to market more than low-productivity suppliers. They confirm this prediction for French exports from 1995 through 2005.

Other studies take a more purely empirical approach, focusing on ERPT in a single market or from a single exporting country rather than PTM across markets. Feinberg (1996) finds that estimated ERPT in imports is decreasing with the four-firm concentration ratio across 26 manufacturing industries in the United States. Lee (1997) finds a similar result for imports in 24 Korean

---

39. In this example, market share refers to the group of exporters subject to the same exchange rate shock. It is assumed that no single exporter has a substantial market share.

manufacturing industries from 1980 through 1990. On the other hand, Brissimis and Kosma (2007) find only weak evidence that market share affects ERPT by Japanese exporters to the United States between 1975 and 2001 at either the aggregate or (selected) three-digit SITC industry level. Olivei (2002) finds that changes in the import share by industry between the 1980s and 1990s are negatively related to ERPT. This result is consistent with Feenstra, Gagnon, and Knetter (1996) as long as imports have less than a 40 percent share of the market.

Price Adjustment and Currency of Invoicing

All of the ERPT and PTM estimates discussed above are long-run or static estimates. Many of the studies estimate dynamic adjustment of ERPT and PTM. In almost all cases, adjustment lags are short, typically no more than one or two quarters after the quarter in which the exchange rate moves. Some studies note that the ratio between short-run and long-run ERPT provides evidence on whether the exporter's or importer's currency is the dominant currency of invoicing. For example, Gagnon and Knetter (1995) note that short-run ERPT is lower than long-run ERPT for Japanese auto exports to the United States, consistent with invoicing in dollars. But short-run ERPT is greater than long-run ERPT for Japanese auto exports to some other destinations, consistent with invoicing in yen. The general tenor of the findings of this and other studies is that exporters tend to invoice in their own currencies except for exports to the United States and except for exporters in countries with high and variable inflation rates.

Gopinath, Itshoki, and Rigobon (2007) find that US imports invoiced in dollars (over the period 1994–2005) have long-run ERPT of 0.25, whereas US imports invoiced in foreign currency have long-run ERPT of 0.95. (Most US imports are invoiced in dollars.) Gopinath and Itshoki (2008) find that ERPT is much higher for goods with frequent price adjustment than for goods with infrequent price adjustment. This finding is consistent with previous results that ERPT is higher for primary commodities, whose prices tend to adjust more frequently than differentiated manufactures. However, Gopinath and Itshoki show that this holds true even within differentiated manufactures.

Is ERPT Declining (or PTM Increasing)?

Campa and Goldberg (2005) find mild evidence of declining rates of ERPT in their 1975–2003 sample of OECD countries. They conclude that most of the decline in ERPT estimates can be attributed to declines in the shares of energy and raw materials in imports, as these categories have the highest rates of ERPT.

However, for US imports, Olivei (2002) and Marazzi and Sheets (2007) show that the decline in ERPT is substantial, even within the manufacturing sector. Olivei finds that average ERPT in 34 manufacturing industries declined from 0.5 in the 1980s to 0.22 in the 1990s. Marazzi and Sheets obtain similar results for US finished goods imports, and the decline appears to have persisted into the 2000s. The Marazzi and Sheets result is robust to a wide range of alternative specifications. Ihrig, Marazzi, and Rothenberg (2006) find statistically significant declines after 1990 in ERPT to nonenergy import prices in France, Japan, and the United States. In their second sample period (1990–2004) they find ERPT in nonenergy goods import prices of 0.16 for France, 0.29 for Germany, 0.32 for the United States, 0.47 for Italy, 0.59 for the United Kingdom, 0.61 for Japan, and 0.89 for Canada. Vigfusson, Sheets, and Gagnon (2009) find declining rates of export ERPT in Canada and the Asian newly industrialized economies.

As discussed above, studies of the automobile market that focus on the 1990s find lower ERPT than studies that focus on earlier years, except for the study by Di Mauro et al. (2011). Box 5.2 finds a low level of ERPT in retail auto sales in the 2000s.

Taylor (2000) conjectures that ERPT may decline when current and expected inflation declines. Campa and Goldberg (2005) and Olivei (2002) test this hypothesis and find little or no support for it as an explanation of the decline in ERPT. Shintani, Terada-Hagiwara, and Yabu (2009) show that short-run ERPT in US imports declined with the fall in average US inflation in the 1990s, but then rose as inflation picked up somewhat in the 2000s. However, their results do not address behavior of long-run ERPT because they assume it always equals 1.

Marazzi and Sheets (2007) conjecture that the growth of Chinese imports to the United States during a period when the Chinese currency was closely tied to the dollar may have led to reduced ERPT because other exporters to the United States felt compelled to match the (constant) price of Chinese exports. Bergin and Feenstra (2007) develop a structural model in which the presence of fixed-exchange-rate exporters reduces the ERPT of floating-exchange-rate exporters. They estimate this model over the period 1993 to 2006 and find that it can explain about half the observed decline in ERPT in US imports.

Gust, Leduc, and Vigfusson (2010a) develop a model in which globalization driven by lower communication and trade costs increases the competitiveness of the local market and thus reduces ERPT. This result applies when the exchange rate movement affects a minority of suppliers to the market in question. The logic of the model implies that globalization should increase ERPT when a majority of market suppliers is affected by the exchange rate movement. They find that about one-third of the decline in ERPT in US imports can be attributed to lower costs of trade. Gust, Leduc, and Vigfusson (2010b) show that the preceding effect arises through increases in exports by existing exporters and not from an increase in the number of exporters.

Appendix 5C
Studies of Exchange Rate Effects on Consumer Prices

Appendix 3B examined the long-run behavior of the real exchange rate (RER). This appendix looks at the components of the RER. What effect does the nominal exchange rate have on prices of specific consumer goods and the domestic consumer price index (CPI)?

Estimated ERPT in Aggregate Data

Using an eight-variable vector auto-regression (VAR) model, McCarthy (2000) shows that the CPI response to an exchange rate shock is very small and never significantly different from zero for nine OECD countries from 1976 through 1998. Using a seven-variable VAR model, Choudhri, Faruqee, and Hakura (2003) find that a 1 percent exchange rate depreciation raises the CPI about 0.2 percent after 10 quarters on average across the non-US G-7 countries over the period 1979–2001. This estimate is statistically significant at the 10 percent level. Gagnon and Ihrig (2004) find that a 1 percent exchange rate depreciation raises the CPI about 0.2 percent in the long run on average across the OECD countries over the period 1971–2003.

Are Changes in ERPT Related to Changes in Monetary Policy?

Goldfajn and Werlang (2000) examine episodes of large depreciations in seven emerging markets and five industrial countries in the 1990s. In each case, they find that ERPT to consumer prices was less than predicted by a model using data mainly from before the depreciation. One interpretation of these results is that the reduction in ERPT reflects increased monetary policy credibility. Ito and Sato (2006) find that rates of ERPT to consumer prices in countries affected by the Asian crisis of 1997–98 were lower than expected based on past behavior except for Indonesia. They attribute these outcomes to increases in anti-inflationary policy credibility in Asian developing economies except in Indonesia.

Taylor (2000) suggests that a low-inflation environment is consistent with lower ERPT to consumer prices because firms perceive cost shocks as less persistent. However, one problem with this hypothesis is that the persistence of exchange rates has not declined with the shift to lower inflation.

For 20 OECD countries, Gagnon and Ihrig (2004) find that ERPT to consumer prices is positively related to the level and variability of CPI inflation. They link this finding to changes in monetary policy that more aggressively target inflation and thus directly reduce ERPT into CPIs. In the sample periods with more stable CPI inflation (typically after the mid-1980s), ERPT to consumer prices averages only 0.05.

For 71 industrial and developing countries between 1979 and 2001, Choudhri and Hakura (2006) find that ERPT is about 0.15 in countries with low average CPI inflation rates, 0.35 in countries with moderate rates of inflation, and 0.55 in countries with high rates of inflation. For 76 countries from 1990 through 2001, Frankel, Parsley, and Wei (2005) find that ERPT to consumer prices is higher in developing countries than in industrial countries, but that it has declined substantially in developing countries and that this decline appears related in part to the decline in trend inflation.

Campa and Goldberg (2006) note that imported inputs of intermediate materials increased in almost all OECD countries between 1995 and 2000 and that this development should raise ERPT to consumer prices, other things equal. However, they do not conduct a direct test of ERPT.

Reinhart, Rogoff, and Savastano (2003) find that ERPT to consumer prices in developing economies is about 0.2 in nondollarized economies, rising to about 0.7 in highly dollarized economies. (Dollarization is defined by the fraction of financial assets and liabilities of households and firms that are denominated in a foreign currency.)

Microeconomic Studies

Gagnon (2006) shows that low ERPT associated with a low inflation environment arises at least in part from the countervailing movement of profit margins in nontradable industries. In the United Kingdom after the 1992 depreciation, profit margins of the distribution sector (including retail stores) shrank as they were not able to fully pass-through higher import prices into higher retail prices. However, Berger et al. (2009) do not find similar evidence of retail margin compression in US data.[40]

Goldberg and Hellerstein (2007) analyze the effect of exchange rate changes on the retail price of beer in a Chicago supermarket chain from 1991 through 1995. They find ERPT into consumer prices of only 0.07. They attribute the incomplete pass-through to the following factors: local-currency (i.e., nontraded) costs, 54 percent; markup adjustment, 34 percent; and price adjustment costs, 12 percent. Nakamura and Zerom (2009) analyze ERPT into nationwide retail prices of ground coffee from 2000 through 2004. They find ERPT into consumer prices of 0.25. They attribute the incomplete pass-through to the following factors: local-currency costs, 59 percent; markup adjustment, 33 percent; unexplained, 8 percent. They find no role for price adjustment costs.

A number of studies examine the retail automobile market, and these are described in appendix 5B and box 5.2. Most of these studies, especially the more recent ones, find very low ERPT in auto prices.

---

40. The Berger et al. margins are for total domestic value added, whereas the Gagnon results are for operating surplus and thus do not include labor compensation or indirect taxes. Gagnon finds little effect of exchange rates on labor compensation, which is the largest component of domestic value added and which may explain why Berger et al. do not find an effect on value added.

6

Monetary Policy with Fixed and Floating Exchange Rates

Experience is simply the name we give our mistakes.
—Oscar Wilde

Chapter 5 demonstrated that large exchange rate fluctuations often have little effect on inflation or economic output. This chapter goes further and shows that inflation and output are more stable with a floating exchange rate than with a fixed exchange rate provided that the central bank is able to conduct monetary policy appropriately.

The standard textbook model shows that monetary policy can stabilize the economy from shocks—but only if the exchange rate is flexible. This result holds up in a more advanced economic model and is supported by the weight of empirical research. Quantifying the stabilization benefits of sound monetary policy with a floating exchange rate is challenging, but it seems likely that these benefits exceed the transaction and other costs of floating exchange rates.

These conclusions are supported by specific historical episodes of exchange rate pressures and monetary policy. This chapter demonstrates that holding on to a fixed exchange rate often leads to excessively loose or tight monetary policy, which destabilizes inflation and output. The chapter also examines, on the other hand, some of the many instances in which appropriate monetary policy has succeeded in stabilizing inflation and output despite large exchange rate movements, even in relatively small open economies.

The Textbook Model

Economic textbooks teach that monetary policy is more potent under a floating exchange rate than under a fixed exchange rate, especially when capital is mobile across countries (Krugman and Obstfeld 2000; Caves, Frankel, and Jones 2007; Feenstra and Taylor 2008). In principle, a floating exchange rate gives the central bank the freedom to use monetary policy to stabilize the

Figure 6.1 Response to a negative spending shock in a small open economy with a floating exchange rate

interest rate

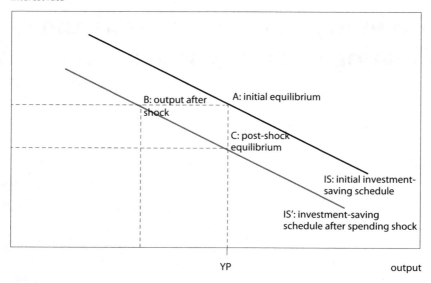

YP = potential output

Source: Authors' illustration.

economy against a variety of domestic and foreign shocks. Under a fixed exchange rate, the central bank is committed to maintaining the exchange rate and is not free to respond to other shocks besides shocks to the exchange rate. Textbooks also teach that if the central bank is itself a destabilizing force in the economy, then tying its hands by forcing it to peg the exchange rate may make the economy more stable.

Response to a Spending Shock

Figure 6.1 displays a typical textbook model of short-run monetary stabilization in a small open economy with a floating exchange rate. The vertical axis displays the policy interest rate. The horizontal axis displays economic output. The downward sloping line labeled IS is the investment-saving schedule. The IS schedule captures the way in which consumption and investment spending respond to the interest rate.[1] The IS schedule slopes downward because a

---

1. The label IS is standard in textbooks. Perhaps the IS schedule should be called the IC schedule, for investment and consumption. Nevertheless, consumption equals income (or output) minus saving, which provides the connection to the saving in the IS label.

decline in the interest rate encourages more consumption and investment and thus more output. Lower interest rates encourage businesses to invest in factories and machines. Lower interest rates also encourage households to borrow, especially to buy cars and build houses. Lower interest rates also increase exports because they cause the currency to depreciate, as shown in chapter 3.[2] Point A represents the initial equilibrium of the economy, with output equal to potential output, or YP.[3]

A shock to total spending is a shift in the IS schedule. Figure 6.1 shows a negative shock to spending, which means that at the original interest rate, businesses, households, and foreigners reduce their total spending. Such a shock might occur because of a tax increase or because people become less optimistic about the future. The IS schedule shifts left to IS' and output falls toward point B. With a floating exchange rate, the central bank is free to lower the interest rate as far as necessary to keep output at potential. As the interest rate declines, the economy moves to the right along the IS' schedule and spending increases. The post-shock equilibrium is point C.

Figure 6.2 displays a negative shock to the same small open economy with a fixed exchange rate, starting from equilibrium with output at potential, YP, and the domestic interest rate equal to the interest rate in the rest of the world, i*. When the negative spending shock hits, the central bank is not free to lower the interest rate, because that would depreciate the exchange rate. As long as the exchange rate is expected to remain fixed, the domestic interest rate must equal the foreign interest rate.[4] Now the post-shock equilibrium is at point B.

Point B is only a short-run equilibrium, however, because output is below potential. One of the shortcomings of the simple textbook model, as displayed in figure 6.2, is that it does not explain the process of long-run convergence. With output below potential, domestic inflation starts to fall below inflation in the rest of the world. Lower inflation gradually lowers the real exchange rate (RER), which makes domestic goods less expensive to foreigners and foreign goods more expensive to domestic residents. This relative price movement increases exports and reduces imports, shifting spending and the entire IS schedule gradually back to the right until output returns to potential. The forces that push the IS schedule back to the right are too complicated to be shown in a simple diagram like figure 6.2.

---

2. The effect of a lower interest rate on *net* exports is ambiguous because higher consumption and investment tend to increase imports.

3. Potential output is the level of output the economy can produce in equilibrium without any inflationary or deflationary pressures.

4. This country is small relative to the rest of the world and cannot affect the foreign interest rate. The situation is more complicated, though similar in all important aspects, when the country is large relative to the rest of the world.

Figure 6.2 Response to a negative spending shock in a small open economy with a fixed exchange rate

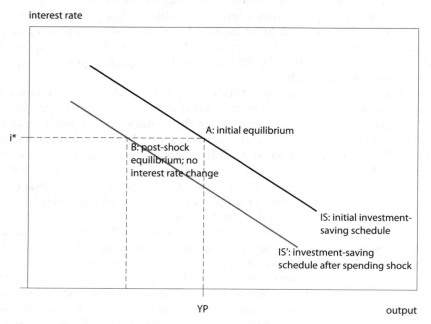

interest rate

i*

A: initial equilibrium

B: post-shock equilibrium; no interest rate change

IS: initial investment-saving schedule

IS': investment-saving schedule after spending shock

YP

output

i* = world interest rate
YP = potential output

Source: Authors' illustration.

Response to a Monetary Shock

Figure 6.3 displays the small open economy's response to a monetary shock. With a floating exchange rate, the central bank is free to lower the interest rate from the world rate, i*, to i'. This lower interest rate increases domestic spending and depreciates the exchange rate, which increases foreign spending on domestic exports. These responses are not shocks to the IS schedule; rather, they reflect a movement out along the IS schedule to point B. Point B is only a short-run equilibrium, however, because output is now above potential. Like figure 6.2, figure 6.3 does not show how the economy adjusts over time. In the long run, the central bank must raise the interest rate back to the world rate or else inflation will continue to accelerate indefinitely.

With a fixed exchange rate, the central bank is not free to lower the interest rate, but the central bank in the anchor country (assumed to be much larger than the home country) is free to lower the interest rate (in this case, i*). After a foreign monetary shock, i* falls, and the effect on spending in the domestic economy is similar to that shown in figure 6.3. Once again, point B is only a temporary equilibrium.

Figure 6.3   Response to a monetary shock in a small open economy with a floating exchange rate

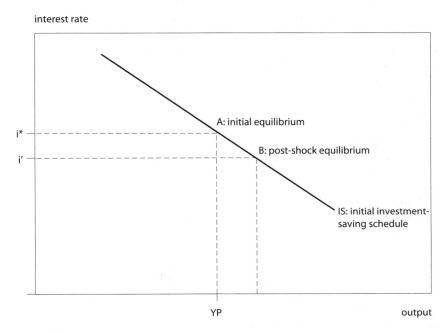

interest rate

A: initial equilibrium

B: post-shock equilibrium

i*

i′

IS: initial investment-
saving schedule

YP

output

i* = world interest rate
i′ = post-shock interest rate
YP = potential output

Source: Authors' illustration.

A Modern Economic Model

The insights of the simple textbook model generally hold up in more detailed economic models, including those used for policy analysis at central banks. These models are mathematical representations of how households and businesses respond to various economic conditions, including government policies and global shocks. Such models typically feature dynamic adjustment from the short run to the long run for output, inflation, exchange rates, trade flows, and more. Even in these more complex models, however, monetary policy has considerable capacity to stabilize inflation and output when the exchange rate is floating but greatly reduced capacity when the exchange rate is fixed. Of course, there is no guarantee that the central bank will pursue a stabilizing monetary policy. But, as discussed in chapter 5, advanced economies and some developing economies have had a high degree of stability in inflation and output in recent decades, and many economists credit this to improvements in monetary policy.

The rest of this section uses a small version of a cutting-edge economic model to show how the economy behaves when the central bank pursues a stabilizing monetary policy, both with a fixed exchange rate and with a floating exchange rate. The model includes economic features discussed in previous chapters, such as the uncovered interest rate parity (UIRP) model of exchange rates augmented with a portfolio balance risk premium, home bias in tradable goods, imperfect substitution of tradable goods, nontradable goods, sticky prices, and price discrimination across markets. Appendix 6A provides details of the model. The model's parameters are those commonly used by other researchers, but none of the conclusions would be affected by alternative choices of parameters within the range of most existing studies. Appendix 6A also discusses recent academic research in monetary stabilization policy in a multicountry setting.

Expectations are critical to financial markets, including the foreign exchange market, as was discussed in chapter 3. An important feature of the model is the assumption of "rational expectations," which means that if there are no further economic shocks, agents expect the future to be what the model predicts. An alternative assumption is "lagged expectations," which means that agents set their expectations based on extrapolations of past behavior, which often simplifies the mathematics of the model. The basic result of the model used here—namely, that monetary policy can stabilize the economy better with a floating exchange rate than with a fixed exchange rate—also holds true in most models using lagged expectations.

Another important feature of the model is that it assumes that prices are sticky in the short run. This assumption is supported by a wealth of economic research, including many papers cited in appendix 6A. If prices were completely flexible, there would be no room for monetary policy to stabilize economic output or employment—but even then a floating exchange rate would be preferable to a fixed rate because it would enable the central bank to insulate the economy from inflationary and deflationary shocks elsewhere in the world.

The model is calibrated to portray a small country that is open to international trade, such as Sweden or New Zealand.[5] This calibration helps to refute a common assertion that only large countries can have independent monetary policies. If a small open economy can use monetary policy effectively to stabilize inflation and output, then there is no question that a large country can also do the same.[6]

The model includes both tradable and nontradable goods; these goods are assumed to be poor substitutes for each other. In the long run, the tradable and nontradable sectors can grow or shrink in response to demand for their products, but this process takes many years. In the short run, productive capacity in

---

5. "Small" is used to indicate that policies and shocks in the country do not have a material influence on economic conditions in the rest of the world taken as a whole.

6. As appendix 6A mentions, the results indeed hold true in a large-country version of the model.

each sector is fixed. Tradable goods produced at home are moderate—but far from perfect—substitutes for those produced abroad. Trade responds quickly to changes in spending and slowly to changes in relative prices. About half of the trade response to a change in relative prices occurs within two years. Exporters pass-through half of any change in the exchange rate into the price they charge foreign buyers in terms of foreign currency; this is close to the median of most pass-through estimates, as discussed in appendix 5B. Domestic prices of domestically produced goods are forward-looking but sticky.

Monetary policy operates either through the interest rate or the exchange rate. With an interest rate policy, the exchange rate is allowed to float and the central bank is assumed to set the interest rate according to the rule first popularized by John Taylor (1993).[7] Monetary policy rules, under which the interest rate rises when inflation rises or when output rises above potential, are a common way to represent monetary policy that is aimed at stabilizing output and inflation. Some argue that the use of such rules by central banks has contributed to improved economic outcomes (Clarida, Galí, and Gertler 1998). With an exchange rate policy, the central bank is assumed to peg the exchange rate relative to currency levels in the rest of the world and the interest rate is determined by financial arbitrage. Financial arbitrage is given by UIRP plus a risk premium based on portfolio balance. The portfolio balance effect is not large; a risk premium of 1 percentage point is sufficient to induce foreign investors to hold domestic bonds equivalent to 25 percent of domestic output.

Economic Shocks in the Model

Economic models typically are used to predict how economic variables will respond to exogenous forces or government policies. Changes in these forces or policies are called shocks. This model is used to predict responses to six shocks.

- *Temporary shock to monetary policy.* This is a reduction in the interest rate or a depreciation of the exchange rate. The main reason for showing the effect of a monetary shock is to understand how monetary policy can offset the effects of other shocks on the economy.

- *Temporary shock to the exchange rate risk premium.* The risk premium shock is the primary driver of exchange rate volatility. Its effects are explored in chapter 5 (see figures 5.13 through 5.15).

- *Temporary shock to consumption (aggregate demand).* The consumption shock reflects an increase in the fraction of household income that is consumed,

---

7. The Taylor rule states that the real short-term interest rate should equal the equilibrium, or long-run, real rate plus a response to two factors: (1) the deviation of inflation from its target and (2) the deviation of output (or employment) from potential.

other things equal.[8] Because there are no separate government or investment sectors in this model, a consumption shock is equivalent to a fiscal shock or an investment shock.[9] Ordinarily, fiscal policy is another tool that can be used for macroeconomic stabilization, but when fiscal policy is used in a destabilizing manner, central banks are forced to respond. (Chapter 7 discusses fiscal policy.) Consumption, investment, and fiscal shocks are all types of spending shocks; merging them into one sector simplifies the model without losing any key insights for exchange rates and trade.

- *Temporary shock to export demand.* The export shock is an unexpected increase in export sales. It could reflect a change in foreign tastes, a reduction in foreign trade barriers, or an increase in foreign spending, perhaps owing to stimulative economic policies in the rest of the world. Thus, the export shock captures the spillover to the domestic economy of policies and developments in the rest of the world. It could also reflect a new source of exports such as the development of an oil field or a mineral deposit.

- *Permanent shock to productivity in either tradables or nontradables.* Total labor in the economy is fixed, but it moves slowly between tradables and nontradables to keep the ratio of prices between the two sectors equal to the ratio of labor input required.[10] In this model, an inflationary shock, such as upward pressure on wages, is equivalent to a temporary negative shock to productivity in both sectors. The model also tracks the response to shocks to each sector individually.

  - *Permanent shock to productivity in tradables.* This is an increase in the production of tradables for a given labor input.

  - *Permanent shock to productivity in nontradables.* This is an increase in the production of nontradables for a given labor input.

How Monetary Policy Works

Figure 6.4 displays the behavior of key macroeconomic variables in response to a temporary easing of monetary policy with a floating exchange rate.[11] As in figures 5.13 through 5.15, the lines in each panel show the deviation of each variable from its pre-shock value over a period of 10 years. Here, the shock

---

8. One thing that does not remain equal is the real interest rate.

9. In this model, the household sector can be interpreted as a combined business, household, and government sector that earns all the revenue from output.

10. This behavior reflects an implicit assumption that wages in both sectors are equal, at least in the long run.

11. A one-period residual of −2 is added to the Taylor rule. This residual would reduce the nominal interest rate 2 percentage points in the first period if output and inflation were held constant. Because output and inflation do increase somewhat in the first period, the nominal interest rate declines less than 2 percentage points.

Figure 6.4 Response to a temporary monetary easing with a floating exchange rate (deviations from initial values)

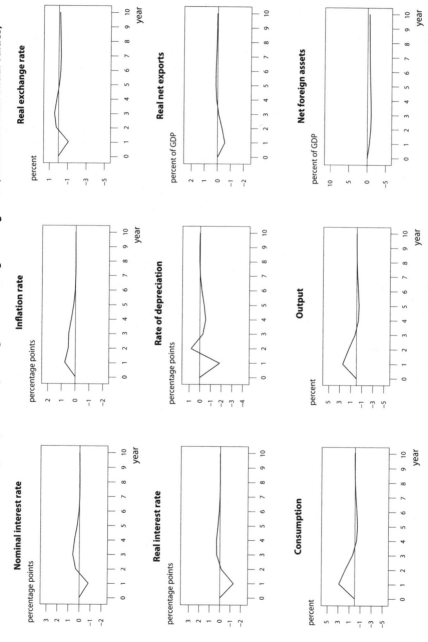

Source: Authors' calculations.

171

begins in year 1. The real interest rate falls considerably at first and then rises slightly above its original value for a few years. The lower real interest rate boosts consumption directly and causes the exchange rate to fall. Higher consumption immediately boosts imports and output. The RER declines briefly but has little effect on exports and imports because the decline is small and temporary. The increase in imports causes net exports to decline. Pushing output above potential causes inflation to rise. All of these effects are temporary.[12] On balance, the primary channel by which monetary policy affects the economy is through the real interest rate, which in turn affects consumption (spending).

The monetary shock creates a strong negative correlation between exchange rates and prices. Inflation rises at the same time that the exchange rate depreciates. The increase in the long-run expected price level is the main reason the nominal exchange rate depreciates, but a temporarily lower real interest rate also contributes to the depreciation. This negative correlation is consistent with the popular view that exchange rate depreciation and inflation go hand in hand. As discussed in chapter 5 and later in this chapter, this strong negative correlation between inflation and the exchange rate does not hold true for other economic shocks. Thus, the popular view appears to be influenced by past episodes in which monetary policy was the main shock destabilizing the economy.

Figure 6.5 displays the effects of a monetary policy easing with a fixed exchange rate. The central bank devalues the exchange rate by the same amount over time as the long-run depreciation in the floating rate simulation of a monetary policy easing (figure 6.4). The initial effects on all the real variables are similar to those with a floating exchange rate, but the subsequent oscillations are more noticeable.[13] Note that the negative correlation between inflation and the change in the nominal exchange rate is roughly as strong with a fixed exchange rate as with a floating exchange. Again this suggests that the popular view that inflation and devaluation are connected derives from previous monetary policy shocks. As with a floating exchange rate, all of these effects are temporary, and there is little difference between any of the variables in the two scenarios after 10 years.

A Shock to the Risk Premium

Chapter 5 examined the economic effects of a shock to the risk premium in the foreign exchange market with a floating exchange rate. Figure 5.13 showed that a monetary policy based on a Taylor-style rule is able to deliver substantial stability in inflation and output. If the same risk premium shock were to hit an economy with a fixed exchange rate, there would be a considerable destabilization of inflation and output as the central bank would be forced to move

---

12. The levels of prices and the nominal exchange rate (not shown) are permanently higher, but their rates of change and the RER both return to their initial values.

13. In principle, it is possible to design a path of devaluation that would damp these oscillations.

Figure 6.5   Response to a temporary monetary easing with a fixed exchange rate (deviations from initial values)

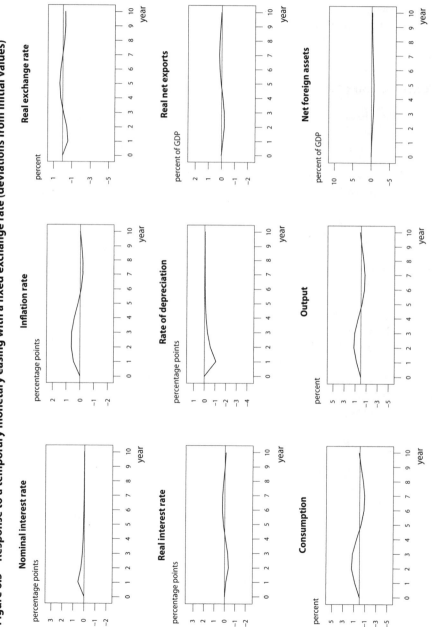

Source: Authors' calculations.

the interest rate to offset the risk premium rather than to hold output and inflation stable.

However, one of the key benefits of a fixed exchange rate regime is that it greatly reduces risk premium shocks. Therefore, it is not very useful to compare the stabilization properties of fixed versus floating exchange rates in the face of risk premium shocks. Both regimes protect the economy well from such shocks: A floating rate regime does so through the offsetting effects of interest rates, and a fixed rate regime does so by preventing fluctuations in risk premiums.

Consumption (Aggregate Demand) Shock

Figure 6.6 displays the effects of a temporary but persistent increase in consumption.[14] The solid line is the response with a floating exchange rate. Consumption (not shown) initially rises, causing output to increase and net exports (not shown) to decrease. The central bank pushes up the interest rate and the real exchange rate (RER) also rises. The trade deficit pushes down net foreign assets (NFA, not shown) gradually over time, thus causing consumption to fall slightly below its original value for a few years.[15] The correlation between inflation and the change in the exchange rate is positive in year 1 and then negative after year 2; on average there is little correlation, unlike for the monetary shock. The higher inflation occurs because the initial increase in consumption pushes output above potential. All of these effects gradually unwind as the shock fades away.

The dashed line in figure 6.6 displays the effects of the same consumption shock with a fixed exchange rate. Because the central bank must maintain a fixed exchange rate, it is not free to raise the interest rate, and consumption and output increase a bit more than under a floating rate. Because the central bank is not free to stabilize the economy, the variables oscillate a bit more than with a floating exchange rate, but the difference in outcomes between fixed and floating are mostly eliminated after 10 years. The volatility of output and inflation are modestly higher with a fixed exchange rate than with a floating rate.

Export Demand

Figure 6.7 displays the effects of a temporary but persistent increase in demand for exports. Again, the solid line shows the response with a floating exchange rate, and the dashed line shows the response with a fixed exchange rate. Under a floating rate, this shock slightly increases net exports and output, but it also

---

14. The shock is assumed to diminish over time at a rate of 10 percent per year.

15. It may seem strange that the effect of an increase in desired consumption is to lower future consumption, but higher current consumption means lower saving, lower saving leads to lower future income, and lower future income means lower future consumption. In this shock, income declines relative to output because domestic residents must pay interest on their foreign borrowing.

Figure 6.6 Response to a temporary consumption shock with a floating exchange rate and a fixed exchange rate (deviations from initial values)

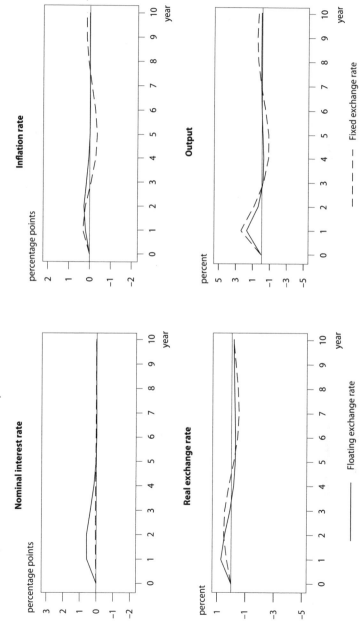

Figure 6.7   Response to a temporary export demand shock with a floating exchange rate and a fixed exchange rate (deviations from initial values)

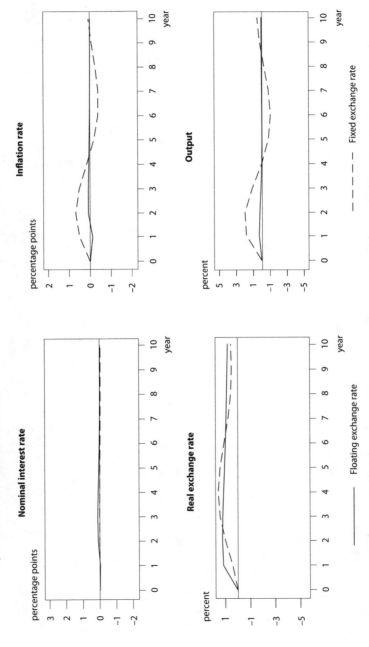

Source: Authors' calculations.

causes the interest rate to rise slightly and the RER to appreciate significantly. The higher interest rate chokes off consumption (not shown), thus damping the effect on output. All effects are quite small except the RER appreciation.

With a fixed exchange rate, the nominal exchange rate cannot move to offset the shock, and more of the increase in the RER occurs through higher inflation. With the nominal interest rate tied down by the fixed exchange rate, higher inflation reduces the real interest rate, boosting consumption (not shown) and output. The swings in all of these variables are greater under a fixed exchange rate than under a floating exchange rate. This is a shock that a floating exchange rate is particularly well suited to stabilize by translating the extra foreign demand immediately into a higher RER.

Productivity Shocks

Figure 6.8 shows the effects of a permanent increase in the productivity of tradable goods. With a floating exchange rate, output rises quickly and permanently. The interest rate falls, and inflation is not much affected. The RER rises permanently, consistent with the Harrod-Balassa-Samuelson (HBS) effect, because the price of nontradable goods rises permanently relative to the price of tradable goods. With a fixed exchange rate, the long-run effects are identical, but output and inflation oscillate slightly more in the medium run.

Figure 6.9 shows the effects of a permanent increase in the productivity of nontradable goods. As for tradable goods, with a floating exchange rate, output rises quickly and permanently. The effect on the RER is larger and opposite that of the tradables shock—effectively an inverse HBS effect—because the price of nontradable goods falls permanently relative to the price of tradable goods. Again, with a fixed exchange rate, all these effects are identical in the long run to those for a floating rate, but the medium-run oscillations are greater.

Overall Policy Lessons

Table 6.1 summarizes the volatility of inflation, output, the RER, and the rate of nominal depreciation in figures 6.6 through 6.9. Here volatility is measured as the mean absolute deviation of each variable from its long-run value.[16] The first section of the table shows that output is more stable with a floating exchange rate than with a fixed exchange rate. The second section of the table shows that inflation is more stable with a floating exchange rate than with a fixed exchange rate. These results demonstrate the benefits of allowing the central bank to aim policy directly at stabilizing output and inflation.[17]

---

16. For most variables, this is just the average for years 1 through 10 of the absolute values of the lines in the figures. For output and the RER in the permanent productivity shocks, it is the average of the absolute deviations from the long-run value, which differs from zero.

17. As shown in figure 5.13, monetary policy is capable of delivering stable inflation and output in the face of a risk premium shock. But, it does not make sense to compare volatilities across fixed

Figure 6.8   Response to a permanent increase in productivity of tradable goods with a floating exchange rate and a fixed exchange rate (deviations from initial values)

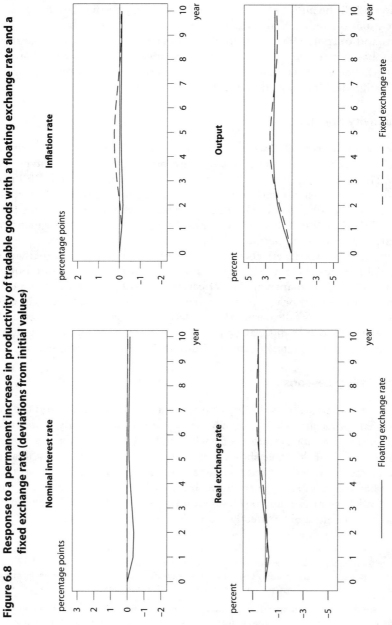

Source: Authors' calculations.

Figure 6.9 Response to a permanent increase in productivity of nontradable goods with a floating exchange rate and a fixed exchange rate (deviations from initial values)

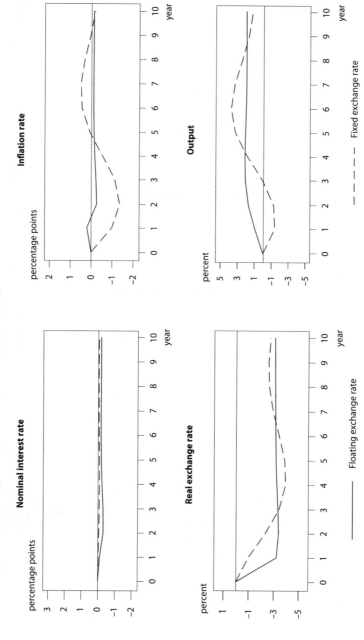

Source: Authors' calculations.

Table 6.1   Exchange rate volatility in response to economic shocks for floating and fixed regimes (mean absolute deviation in percent)

Shock	Floating exchange rate	Fixed exchange rate
Output		
Monetary	0.5	0.6
Consumption	0.1	0.3
Exports	0.1	0.9
Tradables	0.2	0.4
Nontradables	0.2	1.5
Inflation		
Monetary	0.2	0.3
Consumption	0.04	0.1
Exports	0.04	0.3
Tradables	0.03	0.1
Nontradables	0.1	0.6
Real exchange rate (RER)		
Monetary	0.3	0.3
Consumption	0.1	0.2
Exports	1.2	1.1
Tradables	0.5	0.5
Nontradables	0.2	0.7
Nominal exchange rate depreciation		
Monetary	0.4	0.2
Consumption	0.1	0.0
Exports	0.2	0.0
Tradables	0.1	0.0
Nontradables	0.4	0.0

Note: Mean absolute deviations are calculated relative to equilibrium, or steady-state, values.

Source: Authors' calculations based on simulations in figures 6.4 through 6.9.

As shown in the third section of table 6.1, the RER is not necessarily more volatile with a floating exchange rate—it is slightly more volatile in response to the export shock, but it is less volatile in response to the consumption and nontradables productivity shocks. The final section of the table shows that the nominal exchange rate is much more volatile with a floating exchange rate. With a floating exchange rate, movements in the RER occur mainly through the nominal exchange rate. With a fixed exchange rate, RER movements occur mainly through inflation. Overall, in response to these shocks, a fixed exchange rate does not deliver a significantly more stable RER than a floating

---

and floating exchange rates in response to a risk premium shock because one of the key benefits of a firmly fixed exchange rate is a reduction in the volatility of the risk premium.

rate. A fixed exchange rate stabilizes the RER only to the extent that it damps risk premium shocks. The fact that the RER is much more stable in a fixed exchange rate regime, as shown in figure 3.9, is evidence of the importance of risk premium shocks in flexible exchange rate regimes.

Taken together, the simulations in figures 5.13 through 5.15 and figures 6.4 through 6.9 show that a credible fixed exchange rate is only partially successful at damping swings in the RER, and that this success is bought at the expense of a significant destabilization of inflation and output.

Empirical Research on Monetary Policy Stabilization

The preceding sections demonstrated the potential for superior outcomes for stabilization of inflation and output with a floating exchange rate in the context of the economic model. Do these model-based results carry into the real world?

Kuttner and Posen (2001) argue that better monetary policy does deliver better outcomes with a floating exchange rate in a sample of advanced and developing economies. However, most studies of economic performance with fixed and floating exchange rates have not distinguished between good and bad monetary frameworks. As a consequence it may be useful to focus on the subset of results for advanced economies only, because almost all advanced economies with floating exchange rates have had relatively good monetary policy in recent decades. One study (Rogoff et al. 2003, 6) finds that, in advanced economies, "free floats have, on average, registered faster growth than other regimes...without incurring higher inflation." Another study (Ghosh, Ostry, and Tsangarides 2010) finds no consistent effect of exchange rate regime on either inflation or economic growth in advanced economies, but it does report that output growth is more volatile under a fixed exchange rate.

A number of studies explore whether the increased stability of inflation and output in the advanced economies is the result of improved monetary policies since the 1980s. (These studies did not focus on the issue of exchange rate volatility or exchange rate regime.) It is widely agreed that changes in monetary policy are the main reason that inflation has become more stable, but there is less agreement about whether monetary policy is responsible for the increased stability of output. The range of views on this issue is well characterized in a paper presented by James Stock and Mark Watson (2003) at the Federal Reserve's annual Jackson Hole symposium and in the discussion that followed the paper, which is published along with it. Stock and Watson accept the predominant role of monetary policy in stabilizing inflation, but they argue that other factors are more important in stabilizing output, including smaller economic shocks. The discussants overwhelmingly disagreed with the conclusion that monetary policy plays only a minor role in stabilizing output. Some suggested that the apparent reduction in the size of economic shocks may in fact have been caused by improved monetary policy. Others argued that the way in which Stock and Watson measure the improvement in monetary policy is very restrictive and fails to capture some improvements that occurred. Arminio Fraga, then-governor of the central bank of Brazil, noted that improvements in economic stabilization were even more dramatic in some developing economies that were not included in the Stock and Watson paper, and that the role of monetary policy in delivering these improvements was even more obvious in these economies than in the advanced economies (Stock and Watson 2003, 71).

One factor behind increased monetary stabilization may be a reduction in the effect of exchange rates on consumer price index (CPI) inflation. Appendix 5C discussed a number of studies that examine this issue. Gagnon and Ihrig (2004) show that a reduction in the effect of exchange rates on inflation in advanced economies is correlated with a change in monetary policy toward greater stabilization of inflation.

Gagnon (2010) studies the role of monetary policy in stabilizing inflation and output in the presence of large movements in exchange rates. He shows that large and sudden currency depreciations do not destabilize inflation or output unless they were caused by inflationary monetary policy. Moreover, no large depreciation in an advanced economy since 1985 has been caused by inflationary monetary policy. Thus, it seems that the improvements in economic outcomes from better monetary policy are durable even in the face of large exchange rate shocks.

The Great Recession

As discussed briefly in chapter 5, it is too soon to tell whether the deep global recession of 2009 marks the end of the Great Moderation in terms of the stability of economic output. However, the stability of inflation in the advanced economies after the Great Recession and the fact that the largest financial shock since the Great Depression did not cause a second depression are hopeful indicators that improved monetary outcomes may be here to stay. Even so, rising inflation in some developing economies in the wake of the Great Recession is posing a challenge to monetary policy in those economies (issues facing the developing economies are discussed in chapter 8).

Some Updated Evidence

Table 6.2 presents new evidence on the benefits of floating exchange rates in advanced economies and in some Eastern European countries that are new members of the European Union. The table covers 11 years, from 2000 through 2010. This sample focuses on the period since the launch of European Economic and Monetary Union (EMU) and includes the Great Recession and its aftermath. Each row of the table presents the average outcome for a specific group of countries. The first row covers the original members of the euro area plus Denmark and Greece, which have had fixed exchange rates to the euro since its inception. The second row displays data for the euro area as an aggregate rather than as an average of the experiences of individual members. The

Table 6.2   Economic volatility with fixed and floating exchange rates, 2000–2010 (standard deviation of annual data, percent)

	Nominal GDP growth rate	CPI inflation rate	Output gap (GDP)
Original members of euro area plus Denmark and Greece, 13 total	3.4	1.0	2.2
Euro area aggregate data	2.4	0.7	1.7
Advanced economies with floating exchange rates, 9 total[a]	2.6	0.8	1.9
Eastern Europe, continuously pegged to euro[b]	9.6	3.4	n.a.
Eastern Europe, continuously floating[c]	3.1	2.2	n.a.

n.a. = not available; CPI = consumer price index

a. Australia, Canada, Japan, New Zealand, Norway, Sweden, Switzerland, United Kingdom, United States. Norway is not included for nominal GDP growth owing to the large effect of volatile oil prices on nominal GDP in Norway.
b. Bulgaria, Estonia, Latvia, and Lithuania.
c. Czech Republic and Poland.

Source: IMF World Economic Outlook database, April 2011, and authors' calculations.

third row covers advanced economies with floating exchange rates. The fourth row covers new EU members in Eastern Europe that have had a fixed exchange rate to the euro continuously since 2000. The fifth row covers new EU members in Eastern Europe that have had a floating exchange rate continuously since 2000. Other new EU members in Eastern Europe have switched exchange rate regimes over the past 11 years.

The stabilization metrics assessed include the inflation rate and the output gap; the latter is an estimate of the deviation of output from potential that is provided by the International Monetary Fund (IMF). As noted in chapter 2, stabilization of inflation and output are the most common goals assigned to monetary policy. Because the output gap is estimated with considerable uncertainty and is not available for all countries, another stabilization metric is included—the growth rate of nominal GDP—which is roughly equal to the sum of inflation and the growth rate of real output. Nominal GDP growth thus merges both inflation and output objectives into a single statistic. Some economists urge central banks to target nominal GDP growth as a simpler alternative to targeting both inflation and output. Without taking a stance on the merits of nominal GDP targeting, it does serve as a convenient summary measure of the success of monetary stabilization.

The first column displays the standard deviation of the annual growth rate of nominal GDP. The average standard deviation of nominal GDP growth in the advanced economies with a fixed exchange rate (to the euro) is 3.4 percent, whereas the standard deviation of nominal GDP growth for the euro area as a whole is only 2.4 percent. Both inflation (second column) and the estimated output gap (third column) are more stable for the euro area as a whole than for its individual members. These results reflect the dilemma of monetary policy in a currency union. The central bank must set its policy to achieve the best outcome for the currency area as a whole, even if individual members experience greater volatility than they would with independent monetary policy. It is widely acknowledged that euro-area monetary policy was too loose in the mid-2000s for the peripheral economies of Greece, Ireland, Portugal, and Spain, and at the same time it was too tight for Germany. In the past couple of years, the reverse appears to be true.

Turning to the third row, the experience of other advanced economies with floating exchange rates is comparable, though perhaps a tiny bit worse, than that of the euro area as a whole. Yet these economies experienced better results on average than the individual members of the euro area. The average standard deviation of nominal GDP growth in the countries with a floating exchange rate is 2.6 percent, 0.9 percentage points less than the average standard deviation of countries in the euro area.[18] Both inflation (second column) and the estimated output gap (third column) are more stable in countries with a floating exchange rate. The differences between these average outcomes are not statistically significant, but they are economically important.

Differences in outcomes in Eastern Europe are even more striking. Both nominal GDP growth and inflation are far more volatile in the countries with a fixed exchange rate. (Output gap estimates are not available for these countries.) Despite the small sample, the differences across exchange rate regime are statistically significant.

The large gains in economic stabilization from a floating exchange rate implied by the last two rows of the table are not uniquely limited to these few countries and years. As discussed in the next section, fluctuations of inflation and output caused by excessive central bank focus on exchange rate stability have been as much as 5 percentage points or so in a number of prominent episodes. These are extreme cases, but it is plausible that a flexible exchange rate with sound monetary policy may deliver reductions in the standard deviations of inflation and output on the order of a percentage point or more on average. Moreover, these improvements would surely be greater if the alternative benchmark were a global fixed exchange rate because that would imply a common monetary policy across economies that had even more diverse circumstances than exist within the current, more limited, fixed-rate areas.

---

18. The United States has a large and diverse economy, comparable in size to that of the euro area. The standard deviation of US nominal GDP over this period was 2.5 percent. Within the United States there is modest evidence of a cost of currency union from imperfect macroeconomic stabilization. The standard deviation for eight US regions was 2.7 percent and the standard deviation for the 50 states plus the District of Columbia was 3.0 percent. (Source: authors' calculations based on state and regional data from the US Bureau of Economic Analysis website.)

Quantifying the Benefits

The evidence is clear that inflation and output are more stable with a floating exchange rate and sound monetary policy than with a fixed exchange rate. But how much is this extra stability worth to households in the economy?

Two recent studies (Bergin, Shin, and Tchakarov 2006; Galí 2008) estimate that the gains from a floating exchange rate relative to a fixed exchange rate (assuming that monetary policy follows a Taylor rule) are quite small—less than 0.1 percent of output for a range of assumptions about the structure of the economy. In other words, the average household in an economy with a fixed exchange rate would give up no more than 0.1 percent of its income to gain the extra stability from a floating exchange rate with sound monetary policy. However, this estimate is surely too small for several reasons:

- Both studies consider only the benefits of stabilizing against shocks to the productivity of tradable goods, and the implied reductions in the standard deviations of output and inflation were much smaller than those shown in table 6.2. There are many other shocks in the real world. Adding in a full range of shocks would increase the benefits of stabilization policy.

- Both studies are based on "representative agent" models in which all households are affected equally by economic cycles.[19] If some households are affected disproportionately, and if the cost of very bad outcomes is valued especially highly, the true benefits of stabilization are greater than implied by a representative agent model.

- Both studies assume that households enjoy reduced working hours (and unemployment) as welcome vacations rather than stressful periods of uncertainty.

- Both studies ignore any direct cost of inflation volatility. They assume all costs operate through changes in household consumption and working hours.

After making allowance for these additional costs of economic instability, the overall benefits to societies from floating exchange rates may well be valued at close to 1 percent of output. This may seem like a small benefit, but at a global level it represents about $700 billion per year as of 2011.

---

19. The representative agent framework is sometimes defended by appealing to so-called complete markets in which households with different preferences or endowments can insure themselves against shocks that are especially harmful to them. However, in the real world, households have only limited access to insurance against harmful outcomes.

Case Studies of Monetary Policy and Exchange Rate Fluctuations

This section illustrates the key results of the previous sections using 11 case studies of monetary policymaking in the presence of important pressures on the exchange rate. How do central banks achieve stability of inflation and output when exchange rates are volatile? Must they give up exchange rate stability to achieve inflation and output stability, or vice versa?

Each case study includes assessment of a short-term interest rate, the level of the nominal effective exchange rate (NEER), and the four-quarter growth rate of nominal GDP.[20] A rough guide to the stance of monetary policy is the difference between the interest rate and the nominal GDP growth rate. Loosely speaking, an interest rate above the growth rate implies contractionary monetary policy, and an interest rate below the growth rate implies expansionary monetary policy. As discussed above, nominal GDP growth is roughly the sum of inflation and the growth rate of output. If a central bank succeeds in stabilizing inflation and output, it will also stabilize nominal GDP growth.

Italy during the 1970s: Classic Inflationary Depreciation

Figure 6.10 shows that the policy interest rate in Italy was lower than the growth rate of nominal GDP continuously from 1974 through 1980. In 1975, the authorities lowered the interest rate and boosted the fiscal deficit to 10 percent of GDP in response to the global recession.[21] These aggressively stimulative policies—in the face of double-digit inflation—spooked financial markets and brought about a sharp depreciation of the lira in January 1976. Nominal GDP growth had already begun to turn up before the currency depreciated. Belatedly, the central bank raised the interest rate in response to the surge of inflation, but the increase was not sufficient to actually tighten the stance of monetary policy, and inflation (and nominal GDP growth) roared on, albeit with considerable volatility.

The United States, 1981–85: Allowing the Dollar to Rise

Figure 6.11 displays key macroeconomic variables during the Reagan administration in the United States. The high interest rate in 1981 was a continuation of the strong anti-inflationary policy launched by the Federal Reserve under Chairman Paul Volcker in late 1979. Tight monetary policy caused the sharp recession of 1982, which is evident in nominal GDP growth that year. Volcker

---

20. The interest rate and GDP are from the IMF's *International Financial Statistics* database. The interest rate is a three-month Treasury bill or three-month interbank rate. The NEER is from the Bank for International Settlements website.

21. Fiscal data are from the Organization for Economic Cooperation and Development (OECD) *Economic Outlook* database.

Figure 6.10   Italy during the 1970s: Classic inflationary depreciation

percent   index, 2005 = 100

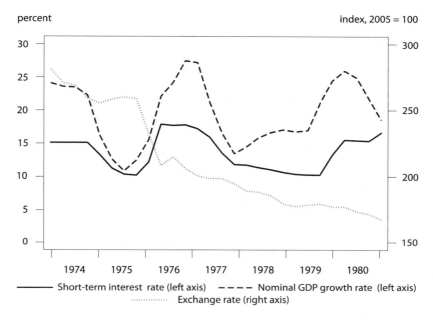

Short-term interest rate (left axis) — — — — Nominal GDP growth rate (left axis)
.... Exchange rate (right axis)

Sources: IMF *International Financial Statistics* database, Bank for International Settlements.

Figure 6.11   United States, 1981–85: Allowing the dollar to rise

percent   index, 2005 = 100

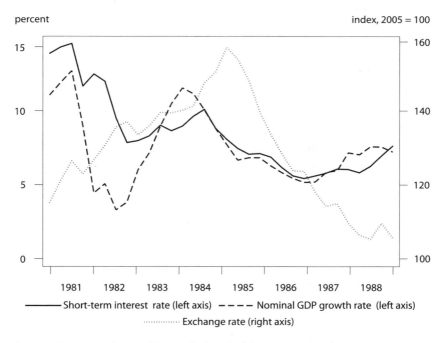

Short-term interest rate (left axis) — — — — Nominal GDP growth rate (left axis)
.... Exchange rate (right axis)

Sources: IMF *International Financial Statistics* database, Bank for International Settlements.

succeeded in taking underlying inflation down to 4 percent (not shown), a somewhat higher level than most central banks target now but widely viewed at the time as a remarkable accomplishment. In this environment, the Federal Reserve's objective was best characterized as a trend nominal GDP growth rate of 6 to 7 percent, with a modest additional increment in 1983–84 to allow for recovery from the deep recession.[22]

As inflation dropped, the Federal Reserve lowered the interest rate. A rapid recovery took hold, temporarily pushing nominal GDP growth above its long-run trend, and the Federal Reserve gradually tightened policy in 1983 and early 1984. In part, this rapid recovery and monetary tightening was a result of loose fiscal policy in these years. High US interest rates and growing optimism about the US economy pushed the dollar up fairly steadily from 1981 through early 1985. At first, the dollar appreciation was viewed as supportive of the Federal Reserve's drive to conquer inflation. By late 1984, however, as the recovery matured and the dollar continued to rise, the Federal Reserve began to lower the interest rate but only to a moderate degree. Nominal GDP growth was remarkably stable during the second half of the decade. The final spike and long descent of the dollar over this period did not destabilize the US economy. Overall, the Federal Reserve was successful in disinflating the US economy and returning it to moderate growth with stable inflation despite an enormous swing in the foreign exchange value of the dollar.

Japan, 1987–88: Resisting Yen Appreciation[23]

Figure 6.12 displays key macroeconomic variables during the 1980s financial bubble in Japan. The considerable appreciation of the yen in 1986 spooked Japanese policymakers, and in 1987 and 1988, they were determined to resist further yen appreciation. They sold massive amounts of yen for dollars to retard the yen's advance, and they reduced the short-term interest rate to a historically low level. Some policy easing was justified, as seen by the drop in nominal GDP growth through early 1987. However, nominal GDP growth bounced back rapidly in 1987, was very high in 1988, and remained well above a desirable 4 to 5 percent level through 1990. Yet, policymakers remained overly focused on the continuing strength of the yen and thus kept short-term interest rates too low—well below the growth rate of nominal GDP. Fiscal policy did tighten, but only by a modest amount. According to OECD (2001, annex table 31), Japan's structural budget balance rose 1.8 percent of GDP between 1985 and 1989.

The net effect of these policies was to overstimulate the Japanese economy

---

22. The Federal Reserve's forecast of nominal GDP growth at the longest available horizon may be taken as a rough guide to the Federal Reserve's objective for nominal GDP. According to the Federal Reserve Bank of Philadelphia's Greenbook Data Set, the furthest available Federal Reserve forecast (seven quarters ahead) of nominal GDP growth was 8 percent in 1982, declining to 7 percent by 1985.

23. An excellent summary of this episode is IMF (2011b, box 1.4).

Figure 6.12 Japan, 1987–88: Resisting yen appreciation

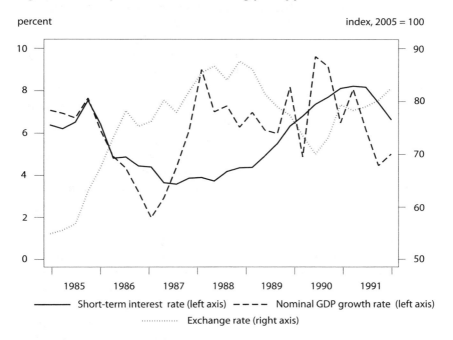

percent   index, 2005 = 100

Short-term interest rate (left axis) — — — Nominal GDP growth rate (left axis)
.... Exchange rate (right axis)

Note: Nominal GDP growth adjusted for value-added tax in April 1989.

Sources: IMF *International Financial Statistics* database, Bank for International Settlements.

and exacerbate massive bubbles in real estate and equity prices. If monetary policy had focused more on domestic price and output stabilization rather than exchange rate stabilization, interest rates would have been higher. Higher interest rates would have reduced the size of the asset bubbles and thus limited—to at least a small extent—the damage from the subsequent slow-down.[24]

Box 6.1 reviews the politics and economics of international attempts during the 1980s to stabilize exchange rates between the United States and Japan as well as between the United States and Germany.

Finland, 1990–92: Holding the Peg into Recession

Finland held on to its exchange rate peg against the Deutsche mark for nearly two years after the collapse of Finnish exports to the Soviet bloc and a banking crisis that began in 1990. The economy entered a deep recession in late 1990,

---

24. The continued yen appreciation in 1987 and 1988 despite low interest rates suggests that the bubble was driven mainly by excessive optimism about Japan's future growth prospects and only partially by loose monetary policy.

Box 6.1   International cooperation on floating exchange rates: The Plaza Agreement and Louvre Accord

In 1985 it was widely believed that the US dollar was extremely overvalued against other major currencies, notably the Deutsche mark and the Japanese yen. In September 1985, the finance ministers of the Group of 5 (G-5) industrial countries met at the Plaza Hotel in New York and agreed to conduct coordinated intervention in foreign exchange markets to put further downward pressure on the value of the dollar. As shown in figure B6.1.1, the dollar's exchange value in terms of the mark and the yen dropped sharply on the day of the Plaza Agreement, and the downward trend persisted for many months thereafter.

At their meeting in the Louvre Museum in February 1987, the G-5 finance ministers announced that the dollar had depreciated enough, and they agreed to cooperate on future policies, including exchange market intervention, to prevent further dollar depreciation. As shown in the figure, there was no notable movement in key dollar exchange rates on the day of the Louvre Accord. Roughly speaking, the dollar appears to have stabilized against the German mark for some time after February 1987, but it continued to fall against the Japanese yen both over the next few weeks and over the next year on balance, despite historically large purchases of dollar reserves by the Japanese and other governments.[1] The months following the Louvre Accord were marked by notable conflicts between US and German officials, which may have contributed to dollar weakness (Henning 1994).

Economists generally are skeptical of the potency of small or moderate interventions in the foreign exchange market, at least for the major advanced economies, where financial markets are deep and sophisticated (Truman 2003a). All agree that such intervention is more likely to be successful when it is conducted jointly by both governments involved. The apparent success of the Plaza Agreement supports the view that intervention can be effective, but the mixed results following the Louvre Accord suggest that the case for intervention potency remains rather weak.[2]

---

1. Global purchases of foreign exchange reserves (mainly US dollars) were nearly 2 percent of US GDP in 1987, the highest level since 1971 (IMF *International Financial Statistics* database).

2. See Henning (1994) and Meyer et al. (2004) for more detailed summaries of the events surrounding these agreements.

(box continues next page)

**Figure B6.1.1   Dollar-mark and dollar-yen exchange rates,
1984–88 (daily)**

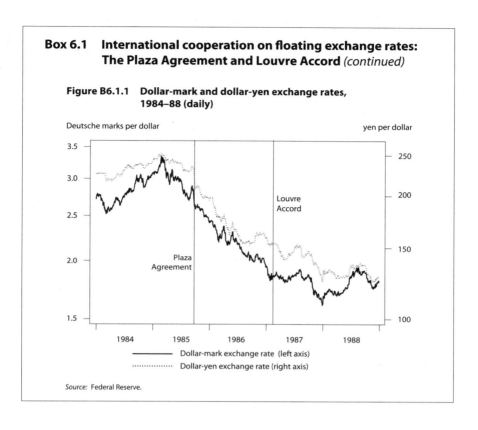

Source: Federal Reserve.

as indicated by the steep decline in nominal GDP growth (figure 6.13). In November 1991, the markka was devalued by 12 percent but monetary policy remained tight. In September 1992, Finland abandoned the markka peg and eased monetary policy to fight the massive recession. The economy quickly began to recover and inflation stayed low.

Sweden and the United Kingdom, 1990–92: Overvaluation during Crisis

Sweden and the United Kingdom also suffered banking crises and economic slowdowns beginning in 1990, as displayed in figures 6.14 and 6.15.[25] Their currencies were in the Exchange Rate Mechanism (ERM) of the European Monetary System, essentially pegged to the Deutsche mark. Sweden and the United Kingdom were forced to set high interest rates—far above the growth rate of nominal GDP—to match the high policy rate set by Germany in response to the unification boom. Sweden, in particular, had to set its policy

---

25. Nominal GDP growth was distorted by indirect tax increases in Sweden in 1990, 1991, and 1993, according to IMF (1993).

Figure 6.13   Finland, 1990–92: Holding the peg too long

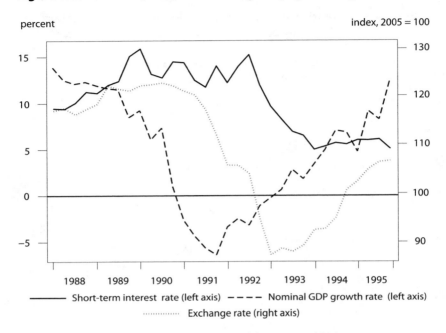

percent   index, 2005 = 100

——— Short-term interest rate (left axis)   – – – Nominal GDP growth rate (left axis)
.... Exchange rate (right axis)

Sources: IMF *International Financial Statistics* database, Bank for International Settlements.

rate significantly higher than Germany in 1992 to compensate for market worries that Sweden might decide to devalue the krona. The market seemed to be less worried about a UK devaluation, which allowed the policy rate to be lower in the United Kingdom, although policy remained tight in comparison to nominal GDP growth. Tight monetary policies exacerbated the economic slowdowns, forcing both Sweden and the United Kingdom into recession. Both countries abandoned the ERM in September 1992 and eased monetary policy. Recovery quickly followed and inflation remained low.

Australia and New Zealand, 1997–98: Different Strategies during the Asian Financial Crisis

As shown in figures 6.16 and 6.17, the currencies of both Australia and New Zealand appreciated strongly in 1995 and 1996. These appreciations caused a slowing in nominal GDP growth, and the central banks eased policy rates in response. With the onset of the Asian crisis in 1997, both countries' exchange rates began to fall. At the same time, demand for Australian and New Zealand exports from Asia dropped considerably.

Figure 6.14   Sweden, 1990–92: Overvaluation during crisis

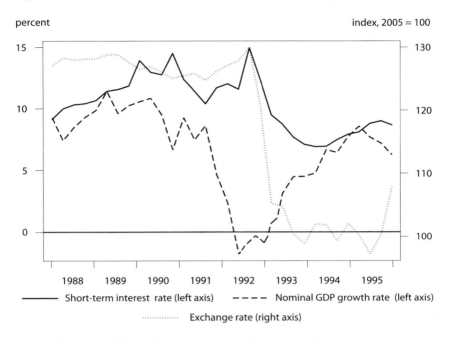

percent   index, 2005 = 100

Sources: IMF *International Financial Statistics* database, Bank for International Settlements.

Figure 6.15   United Kingdom, 1990–92: Overvaluation during crisis

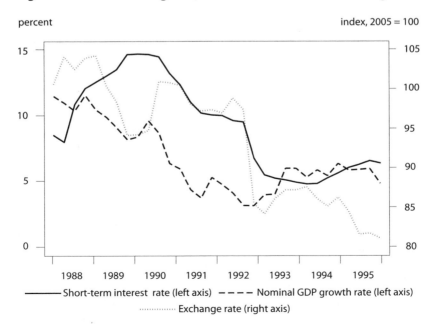

percent   index, 2005 = 100

Sources: IMF *International Financial Statistics* database, Bank for International Settlements.

Figure 6.16 Australia, 1997–98: Asian financial crisis

percent   index, 2005 = 100

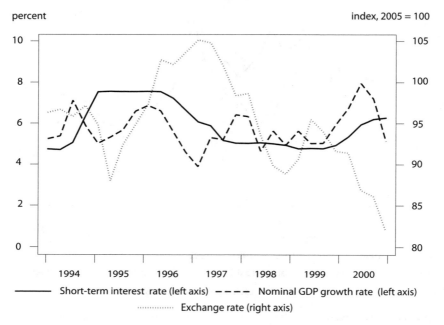

—————— Short-term interest rate (left axis)   – – – – Nominal GDP growth rate (left axis)

················· Exchange rate (right axis)

Note: Nominal GDP adjusted for value-added tax in July 2000.

Source: IMF *International Financial Statistics* database, Bank for International Settlements.

In response to the currency depreciation, the Reserve Bank of New Zealand raised its policy rate in 1997 and early 1998 to offset expected inflation pressure.[26] The Reserve Bank of Australia eased policy a bit further in 1997 because it feared the recessionary impact of lost Asian demand. In hindsight, it appears that Australia was right not to worry about its currency depreciation: The depreciation and relaxed policy stance helped to keep the Australian economy growing through the crisis, whereas New Zealand suffered an economic slowdown. The Reserve Bank of New Zealand reversed course and eased policy rapidly in mid-1998. Growth rebounded strongly in 1999. Inflation remained subdued in both countries.

---

26. At that time, the Reserve Bank of New Zealand viewed its policy stance primarily in terms of a monetary conditions index (MCI) that was a weighted average of the short-term interest rate and the trade-weighted exchange rate. The idea behind the MCI is that monetary policy operates through both interest rates and exchange rates. To stabilize the MCI when the exchange rate depreciates, a central bank must raise interest rates. However, during the Asian crisis, the collapse of Asian demand for New Zealand exports called for a sharp drop in the MCI (easier monetary policy) to offset the loss of external demand. The importance of the MCI in monetary policy deliberations is apparent in the regular *Monetary Policy Statements* issued by the Reserve Bank of New Zealand during 1997–98.

Figure 6.17   New Zealand, 1997–98: Asian financial crisis

percent   index, 2005 = 100

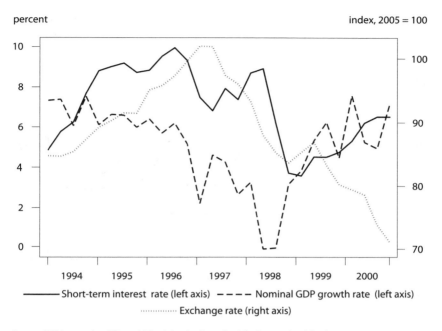

———— Short-term interest rate (left axis)   – – – – Nominal GDP growth rate (left axis)
·············· Exchange rate (right axis)

Source: IMF *International Financial Statistics* database, Bank for International Settlements.

Korea, 1997–98: Credibility after a Crisis

The experience of Korea in 1998 demonstrates that a sharp depreciation in an economy that has borrowed heavily in foreign currency need not lead to high inflation (figure 6.18). In 1997, as markets began to realize that Korean corporations would not be able to fully repay their bonds and loans, investors sold off Korean assets. At first, the government tried to stabilize the won by raising interest rates and selling foreign exchange reserves. By December 1997, the Korean government was in danger of running out of foreign exchange reserves and it abandoned the mostly fixed exchange rate in December 1997. The depreciation had three effects. First, it exacerbated the bankruptcies of Korean banks and corporations, which was depressing Korean economic output. Second, it boosted the export competitiveness of Korean manufacturers. Third, it allowed the central bank to lower interest rates in response to the economic slowdown.

The experience of Korea and other Asian economies in 1997–98 is a lesson in the dangers of foreign-currency debt. Korean nominal GDP growth continued to decline for three quarters after the crisis, whereas the return to growth was immediate for the United Kingdom and Sweden after their crises of late 1992. Because Korea quickly moved to an inflation targeting framework for monetary policy, it did not succumb to high inflation.

Figure 6.18   Korea, 1997–98: Asian financial crisis

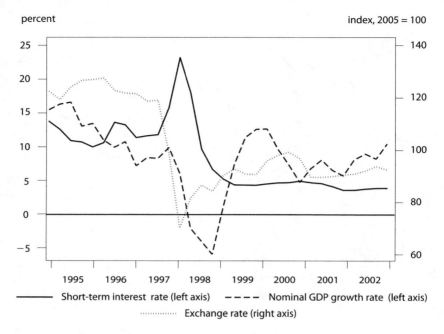

Sources: IMF *International Financial Statistics* database, Bank for International Settlements.

United Kingdom, 1997-98: Living with a Strong Currency

As shown in figure 6.19, the UK trade-weighted exchange rate appreciated roughly 25 percent between 1996 and 1998. Despite this substantial appreciation, the policy rate was tightened slightly in 1997. Policy was eased moderately in late 1998. Nominal GDP continued to grow at a steady rate during and after the appreciation.

United Kingdom, 2008: Depreciation during a Financial Crisis

The global financial crisis and UK housing slowdown steadily reduced nominal GDP growth in 2008. As shown in figure 6.20, market participants appeared to believe that the United Kingdom would be hurt more than other advanced economies by the gathering crisis, and the pound depreciated about 25 percent. Monetary policy also eased and effectively reached the lower bound of zero on nominal interest rates. To provide further policy ease in 2009, the Bank of England made large-scale purchases of long-term bonds designed to push down long-term interest rates. Nominal GDP made an impressive rebound in 2010, although recovery remained a bit slow in light of the depth of the recession.

Headline CPI inflation in the United Kingdom has been affected by the

Figure 6.19 United Kingdom, 1997–98: Living with a strong currency

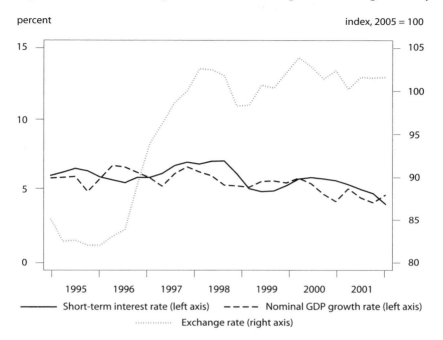

percent   index, 2005 = 100

——— Short-term interest rate (left axis)   – – – – Nominal GDP growth rate (left axis)
.... Exchange rate (right axis)

Sources: IMF *International Financial Statistics* database, Bank for International Settlements.

global volatility in commodity prices and by large temporary shifts in value-added tax rates. In terms of the GDP deflator (which is less influenced by these transient factors), inflation has remained close to or slightly above 2 in the United Kingdom, whereas it has been around 1 in the euro area and the United States. Thus, the sterling depreciation appears to have supported growth and prevented unwanted disinflation in the United Kingdom.

Lessons from the Case Studies

Policymakers should not focus obsessively on unusual strength or weakness in their currencies. In hindsight, Japanese policymakers were too concerned about the strength of the yen in the late 1980s and not sufficiently concerned about domestic excesses. In contrast, UK policymakers in the late 1990s correctly held policy steady when the pound rose dramatically, allowing the strong currency to siphon off excess domestic demand in order to stabilize output and inflation. The strong US dollar in the 1980s at least partly reflected excessively loose fiscal policy, but—taking fiscal policy as given—US monetary policy was right to allow the dollar to rise in order to divert excess demand away from US producers and thereby lock in the conquest of US inflation.

Currency weakness poses an equal challenge. Policymakers in Finland,

Figure 6.20　United Kingdom, 2008: Depreciation during the global financial crisis

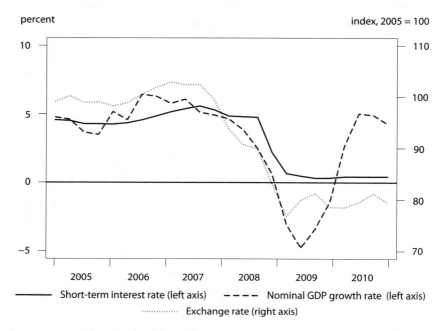

Sources: IMF *International Financial Statistics* database, Bank for International Settlements.

Sweden, and the United Kingdom all held on to exchange rate targets for too long in the early 1990s, despite the obvious need for macroeconomic stimulus. These countries obtained solid recoveries without rising inflation after they let go of their exchange rate pegs. During the Asian crisis, policymakers in New Zealand were overly concerned about the implications for inflation of a sharp exchange rate depreciation. Policymakers in Australia, hit by a similar set of shocks, correctly saw that a depreciated exchange rate was appropriate in light of the drop in export demand. In 1997, Korea had no choice but to let its currency depreciate. Despite the harmful effects on the burden of foreign-currency debt, Korea was able to benefit from an export boom without suffering high inflation. Finally, in the recent global financial crisis, the United Kingdom benefited from the growth-enhancing effects of a currency depreciation without any significant cost in terms of higher inflation.

Appendix 6A
A Modern Economic Model

This appendix describes a small macroeconomic model that is used to demonstrate how floating exchange rates allow policymakers to achieve better outcomes than can be obtained with fixed exchange rates. The model is a simplified dynamic stochastic general equilibrium (DSGE) model, patterned after the Federal Reserve Board's SIGMA model as described by Erceg, Guerrieri, and Gust (2006). It is also similar to the models of Bergin (2004), Smets and Wouters (2007), Corsetti, Dedola, and Leduc (2007, forthcoming), and Kumhof et al. (2010). This model is a bit smaller than SIGMA; it omits separate equations for investment, intermediate goods, wage adjustment, and fiscal policy.

A key difference between DSGE models and conventional macroeconomic models is that DSGE models have explicit microeconomic foundations, and agents in each sector take account of behavior in all sectors when calculating their expectations of future economic conditions (rational expectations). Using a model with rational expectations is particularly important when exchange rate behavior is central to the analysis. Nevertheless, the result that independent monetary policy can stabilize the economy better than a fixed exchange rate is also a property of more conventional, non-rational-expectations models.

To date, the different empirical DSGE models have had fairly similar properties, perhaps reflecting the relatively recent history of DSGE modeling. Some of the differences are along dimensions explored in this book. These include assumptions about pricing to market by exporters, the existence of nontradable goods, the elasticity of substitution across traded goods, and the stickiness of prices. These simulations consider the robustness of the results to all of the foregoing factors. Two major areas of difference that are not explored concern consumption and investment. The basic DSGE model assumes households have infinite lives and anticipate future taxes and transfers. Under this assumption, changes in tax rates have only minor effects on the economy. In order to build in more potent fiscal policy, some DSGE models assume that either a fraction of households are not forward-looking and simply consume their current income or households are not infinitely-lived and thus discount the future at a faster rate than the return on government bonds. (Kumhof et al. 2010 make both assumptions.) These simulations use the former approach in order to maintain a more plausible connection between output and consumption in our simulations. But differences along this dimension are not critical for the issues explored in this book. Similarly, DSGE models differ in their specifications of investment behavior and various financial frictions related to investment, but these are not of critical importance for the issues addressed here.

Features of the Model

The model has two countries: home and foreign. The sizes of the two countries are adjustable, which allows us to examine the cases of both small and large home economies. The simulations presented in figures 6.4 through 6.9 are for the small economy case. The model incorporates the features discussed in previous chapters. Details of the model are listed in table 6A.1.

Producers

There are two types of goods, tradable and nontradable.[27] Productivity (output per worker) in each sector is exogenous. Potential output in each sector is equal to labor supply in that sector times productivity in that sector.[28] Total labor supply is exogenous, but labor can move between sectors subject to an adjustment cost. When the ratio of the tradable goods price to the nontradable goods price exceeds the ratio of labor input required in tradables to labor input required in nontradables, labor flows from the nontradable sector to the tradable sector. Implicitly, both wages and profit margins are the same across the two sectors in equilibrium. The adjustment costs to changing labor in each sector are sufficiently high that the equilibration of relative prices in response to shocks takes many years.

In each sector, producers set domestic prices to keep output near potential while also responding to both past inflation and expected future inflation within the sector. The sensitivity of price adjustment is set to roughly match that displayed in Erceg, Guerrieri, and Gust (2006). Export prices are a weighted average of the domestic price of tradable goods and the foreign price of foreign-produced tradable goods. The weight on the foreign price is equivalent to the degree of pricing to market in exports; it is set to the median value of 0.5 reported by Goldberg and Knetter (1997). This estimate is also near the mid-point of subsequent estimates. All income earned by producers is turned over to the households in each country.

Households

Households are divided into two groups. One group consists of hand-to-mouth consumers who simply consume each year's income. The other group smoothes their consumption both by responding to changes in expected future income and by adjusting slowly from past levels. When current and expected future real interest rates rise, this group reduces consumption based on an intertemporal elasticity of substitution of 2. The share of income earned

---

27. For simplicity, the term goods is used as shorthand for goods and services.

28. For simplicity, there is no capital stock in the model, and issues related to economic growth are ignored because they are not relevant for the question of exchange rate regime and economic stabilization.

Table 6A.1   Model listing

Behavioral Equations

$C1_t = \gamma1\, C1_{t-1} + \gamma2\, {}_tC1_{t+1} + (1 - \gamma1 - \gamma2)\, ((1 - \omega1)Y_t + NFI_t - \omega0) \times (PY_t/PC_t) \times (\beta/RR_t)^{\gamma3} + UC_t$

$C2_t = \omega1\, Y_t$

$X_t = \alpha_X \Delta C^f_t + \lambda\, X_{t-1} + (1 - \lambda)\, \alpha_X\, [C^f_{t-1} \times (E_t \times PX_t/PT^f_t)^{-\eta}] + UX_t$

$M_t = \alpha_M \Delta C_t + \lambda\, M_{t-1} + (1 - \lambda)\, \alpha_M\, [C_{t-1} \times (PM_t/PT_t)^{-\eta}] + UM_t$

$PX_t = (PT^f_t/E_t)^\theta \times PT_t^{(1-\theta)} + UPX_t$

$PM_t = (PT_t)^\theta \times (PT^f_t/E_t)^{(1-\theta)} + UPM_t$

$DPT_t = \rho1\, {}_tDPT_{t+1} + (1 - \rho1)\, DPT_{t-1} + \rho2\, [(T_t + X_t)/TXPOT_t - 1] + UDPT_t$

$DPN_t = \delta1\, {}_tDPN_{t+1} + (1 - \delta1)\, DPN_{t-1} + \delta2\, (N_t/NPOT_t - 1) + UDPN_t$

$LN_t = \varphi1\, {}_tLN_{t+1} + (1 - \varphi1)\, LN_{t-1} + \varphi2\, (PN_t/PT_t - KTX_t/KN_t) + ULN_t$

$E_t/{}_tE_{t+1} = (1 + I_t)/(1 + I^f_t) + \varepsilon\, NFA_t/Y_t - UE_t$

$I_t = \mu0\, I_{t-1} + (1 - \mu0)\, [\sigma + DPC_t + \mu1\, (DPC_t - \pi) + \mu2\, (Y_t/YPOT_t - 1)] + UI_t$

$N_t = \alpha_N C_t \times (PN_t/PT_t)^{-\upsilon} + UN_t$

Identities

$C_t = C1_t + C2_t + \omega0$

$Y_t = C_t + X_t - M_t$

$PY_t \times Y_t = PC_t \times C_t + PX_t \times X_t - PM_t \times M_t$

$C_t = N_t + T_t + M_t$

$PC_t \times C_t = PN_t \times N_t + PT_t \times T_t + PM_t \times M_t$

$DPN_t = PN_t/PN_{t-1} - 1$

$DPT_t = PT_t/PT_{t-1} - 1$

$DPC_t = PC_t/PC_{t-1} - 1$

$1 + RR_t = (1 + I_t)/(1 + {}_tDPC_{t+1})$

$NFA_t = (1 + I_{t-1}) \times NFA_{t-1}/(1 + DPY_t) + (PX_t \times X_t - PM_t \times M_t)/PY_t$

$NFI_t = [(1 + I_{t-1})/(1 + DPY_t) - 1] \times NFA_{t-1}$

$RER_t = E_t \times PY_t/PY^f_t$

$NPOT_t = KN_t \times LN_t$

$TXPOT_t = KTX_t \times LTX_t$

$YPOT_t = NPOT_t + TXPOT_t$

$L_t = LN_t + LTX_t$

Variables and Parameters

Endogenous

C:	Total Consumption	PC:	Consumption Price
C1:	Optimizing Consumption	C2:	Hand-to-Mouth Consumption
Y:	Output	PY:	Output Price
X:	Exports	PX:	Export Price

(table continues next page)

Table 6A.1 Model listing (continued)

Variables and Parameters (continued)

M:	Imports	PM:	Import Price
N:	Nontradables	PN:	Nontradables Price
T:	Domestic Tradables	PT:	Domestic Tradables Price
DPC:	Consumer Inflation	YPOT:	Potential Output
DPN:	Nontradables Inflation	DPT:	Domestic Tradables Inflation
I:	Interest Rate	RR:	Real Interest Rate
NFA:	Net Foreign Asset (real)	NFI:	Net Factor Income (real)
E:	Exchange Rate	RER:	Real Exchange Rate
LN:	Labor in Nontradables	LTX:	Labor in Tradables
NPOT:	Nontradables Potential	TXPOT:	Tradables Potential

Note: Superscript f denotes foreign country variable. Foreign variables are exogenous in the small-country simulations and endogenous in the large-country simulations. The large-country simulations include a complete set of foreign variables. The small-country simulations include only those foreign variables that appear directly in the home-country equations.

Exogenous

UC:	Consumption Shock	ULN:	Labor Allocation Shock
UX:	Export Shock	UM:	Import Shock
UPX:	Export Price Shock	UPM:	Import Price Shock
UE:	Risk Premium Shock	UI:	Monetary Shock
UDPN:	Nontradables Price Shock	UDPT:	Tradables Price Shock
KN:	Nontradables Productivity	KTX:	Tradables Productivity
L:	Total Labor		

Initial Steady State Values (Same for Foreign)

$C = Y = YPOT = 1$

$C1 = C2 = 0.4$

$N = LN = LTX = NPOT = TXPOT = 0.5$

$T = M = X = 0.25$

$PY = PC = PN = PT = PX = PM = E = RER = 1$

$L = KN = KTX = 1$

$DPY = DPC = 0$

$UC = UDPN = UDPT = UX = UM = UPX = UPM = UE = UI = ULN = 0$

$I = RR = 0.03$

$NFA = NFI = 0$

Parameter Values (Alternate in Brackets)

$\gamma1 = \gamma2 = 0.45$

$\gamma3 = 0.5 [1]$

$\beta = 0.03$

$\omega0 = 0.2$

$\omega1 = 0.4$

$\alpha_X = \alpha_M = 0.25$

$\lambda = 0.6$

$\eta = 1.5 [1] [2]$

Table 6A.1   Model listing *(continued)*

$\theta = 0.5$ [0] [1]
$\upsilon = 0.5$
$\rho1 = \delta1 = \varphi1 = 0.5$
$\rho2 = \delta2 = 0.1$
$\varphi2 = 0.005$
$\varepsilon = 0.04$ [0.01] [0.1]
$\sigma = 0.03$
$\pi = 0$
$\mu0 = \mu1 = \mu2 = 0.5$ [1, $\mu1$ and $\mu2$ only]

by hand-to-mouth consumers is 40 percent. In addition, 20 percent of total consumption is given autonomously, mainly to ensure stable solution properties of the model.

There is a low elasticity of substitution (0.5) between tradable and nontradable goods. This low elasticity in part reflects that tradable and nontradable goods are more differentiated from each other than traded goods produced in different countries are. It also reflects that some nontradable goods (specifically, distribution and retail services) are required to deliver tradable goods to consumers, so that there is essentially a zero elasticity of substitution between these nontradable goods and tradable goods.[29] Consumers prefer goods produced at home, in part reflecting trade barriers and trade costs, but they are willing to substitute between home and foreign goods with a fixed elasticity of substitution equal to 1.5.[30] This elasticity is somewhat higher than typically estimated using aggregate data (see appendix 5A). None of the results would be qualitatively affected by trade elasticities between 1 and 2. However, as discussed in chapter 5, assuming a very high elasticity, such as 100, can have important effects. Exports and imports respond to exchange rates and prices with a lag. The half-life of the response to exchange rates and prices is two years. Exports and imports respond immediately to changes in consumption.

Investors

Investors respond to differences in expected returns on bonds in the two countries as in the uncovered interest rate parity (UIRP) model, but there is a risk premium with two components. The first component is exogenous and unexplained but set equal to zero except for the risk premium shocks. The second

---

29. Burstein, Neves, and Rebelo (2003), Goldberg and Hellerstein (2007), Campa and Goldberg (2006), Berger et al. (2009), and Nakamura and Zerom (2009) explore the role of distribution margins in consumer prices of imported goods.

30. In a world of differentiated products with no home bias and no transportation cost, nearly all the tradables produced in a small country would be exported and nearly all the tradables consumed would be imported.

component is a portfolio balance effect that helps to stabilize exchange rates and capital flows over time. The portfolio balance effect is relatively small: A risk premium of 100 basis points is sufficient to induce foreign investors to hold home-country assets equivalent to 25 percent of home-country output.[31] There is no cross-country trade in equity.

Central Banks

Under a floating exchange rate, central banks follow Taylor-style rules in each country. They raise interest rates when inflation is above target and when output is above potential. They lower interest rates when inflation is below target and when output is below potential. The coefficients are set at the original values reported by Taylor (1993). Under a fixed exchange rate, the foreign central bank follows a Taylor-style rule and the home central bank pegs the exchange rate.

Robustness of Results

The model responses to all shocks were checked in the large economy version of the model.[32] The results for the home country are very similar to the small economy results except for the consumption shock. (A consumption shock in a large home country raises the real rate of return for foreign consumers, who then save more, and this reaction enables the trade balance and all other variables to respond more strongly in the same direction as in the small economy shock.) The foreign country always reacts in the expected way. None of the conclusions regarding the exchange rate disconnect are different in the large economy version.

The exchange rate risk premium shock under a floating exchange rate was run using a sequence of alternative parameter values. These values are shown in brackets in the model listing of table 6A.1. None of the results concerning the exchange rate disconnect were sensitive to these alternative parameter values.

Welfare Analysis

A rigorous analysis of welfare-maximizing policies is beyond the scope of this book. The starting point for rigorous welfare analysis is a general equilibrium model with fully specified behavioral equations based on utility maximization. The model of this chapter is largely based on modern utility-maximizing DSGE models. But three features were introduced in an ad hoc manner: (1) tradable and nontradable goods with lagged adjustment across sectors in production, (2) lagged adjustment in trade, and (3) incomplete exchange rate pass-through

---

31. This effect is similar in magnitude to that used in Erceg, Guerrieri, and Gust (2006). It is larger than that used by Bergin (2004) or that estimated by Lane and Milesi-Ferretti (2002).

32. In this version, the home economy is equal in size to the rest of the world.

in exports. Grounding these features more rigorously is an important avenue for future research, but not one this book can pursue.

Woodford (2006, 1) states that for the

> familiar classes of sticky-price DSGE models...it is possible to show that the expected utility of the representative household varies inversely with the expected discounted value of a quadratic loss function, the arguments of which are measures of price and wage inflation on the one hand and measures of real activity relative to a (time-varying) target level of activity on the other.

In other words, to maximize social welfare, the central bank should stabilize a weighted average of inflation and the output gap. Chapter 2 showed that such an objective function is consistent with the explicit or implicit mandate of many central banks. Woodford (2006) shows that the exact form of the optimal stabilization depends on the economic model. One key principle is that central banks should stabilize prices and wages that are sticky but not those that are flexible. This principle supports the common practice of many central banks of focusing on measures of underlying, or core, inflation. Whether inflation should be stabilized around zero or some other value, such as a moving average of past inflation, depends on the nature of price adjustment. Some of the arguments for choosing a positive inflation target (see box 2.2) have not yet been incorporated into this class of models.

In a framework similar to Woodford's, Bergin, Shin, and Tchakarov (2006) show that the welfare gains from optimal monetary policy with a floating exchange rate (compared with a fixed exchange rate) are very small—less than one-tenth of a percent of economic output. Galí (2008, 177) reaches a similar conclusion.

Corsetti, Dedola, and Leduc (forthcoming) show that a number of other considerations make the analysis of optimal policy considerably more complicated. For example, the optimal price index to stabilize depends on whether import prices are sticky in local or foreign currency.[33] When sticky in the exporter's currency, central banks should stabilize the price of domestic output. When sticky in the importer's currency, central banks should stabilize the price of consumer goods. This result echoes the principle asserted by Woodford (2006) that central banks should stabilize sticky prices rather than flexible prices. Corsetti, Dedola, and Leduc raise many more interesting issues, including game theory elements between central banks. However, owing to the complexity introduced by the international setting, their analysis is limited to a relatively restrictive range of shocks and model specifications. This is clearly the new frontier for international policy research.

Engel (2009) takes the argument further and advocates that central banks should include exchange rate stabilization in their objective functions (not to the exclusion of output and inflation) because exchange rate fluctuations often

---

33. Engel (2002) also argues that stabilization policy should be related to the stickiness of traded goods prices in importer or exporter currency.

push relative prices away from the levels associated with efficient allocation of goods and capital across countries. Engel warns that there may be externalities in the effects of exchange rates that may tempt central banks to pursue policies that reduce global welfare. Thus, central bank efforts to control exchange rate fluctuations should be limited to cooperative actions. This conclusion may be theoretically justifiable, but the evidence in this book suggests that the actual cost of exchange rate fluctuations is not great. Moreover, the record of international macroeconomic policy dialogue suggests that it would be difficult to reach agreement on desired levels of exchange rates and on timely actions to achieve those levels.

As discussed earlier in this chapter, a major shortcoming of these studies of optimal monetary policy is that their welfare losses are limited entirely to the second-order effects of fluctuations in consumption and labor on average household utility. The representative agent formulations implicitly assume that agents are able to fully insure themselves against idiosyncratic shocks such as spells of unemployment. If measured at all, unemployment is viewed as a positive contribution to utility because time spent working reduces utility. Thus, this framework completely misses the high personal and social costs of unemployment. It also omits any direct disutility from variability in inflation.

7

Fiscal Policy and Exchange Rate Regimes

Anyone who lives within their means suffers from a lack of imagination.
—Oscar Wilde

Fiscal policy is not well-suited for stabilizing inflation and output in most circumstances, with the exception of automatic stabilizers such as unemployment benefits. Unsustainable fiscal deficits lead inexorably to fiscal crises under all exchange rate regimes. However, such crises tend to come earlier and more abruptly in currency unions or for governments that have borrowed in foreign currency.

Fiscal Policy for Economic Stabilization

This book focuses on monetary policy as the primary tool for domestic economic stabilization—that is, for the stabilization of inflation and output—both for simplicity and in concert with the widely held view that this is a reasonable prescription for economic policy in most circumstances. Nevertheless, there is a long tradition—dating back at least to Keynes (1936)—that accords fiscal policy a major role in economic stabilization. Fiscal policy operates through government spending, taxation, and transfer programs such as unemployment insurance and medical coverage. All these elements of fiscal policy can affect economic output and inflation.

The convention in economic textbooks is to assert that fiscal policy is more potent with a fixed exchange rate and monetary policy is more potent with a floating exchange rate (Krugman and Obstfeld 2000, Feenstra and Taylor 2008). But this assessment depends critically on the assumed behavior of monetary policy. With a fixed exchange rate and international capital mobility, the interest rate must remain fixed at the world level at all times, and so monetary policy is tautologically impotent.[1] With a floating exchange rate, there is no such constraint on monetary policy, and that is the sense in which monetary policy is more potent with a floating exchange rate. Whether fiscal policy is less potent with a floating exchange rate depends on how monetary policy responds. If the central bank does not raise interest rates in response to a fiscal expansion, then fiscal policy is equally potent with either a fixed or a floating exchange rate.

However, during most of the past two decades many economists have presumed—as described by Blanchard (2009)—that under normal circumstances monetary policy is, or should be, set continuously to stabilize inflation and output over the medium term, leaving no role for activist fiscal policy stabilization. Indeed, under this presumption, fiscal policy actions are inherently destabilizing and need to be counteracted by monetary policy, a conclusion that is supported by numerous episodes of harmful fiscal actions. The textbook conclusion that fiscal policy is less potent with floating exchange rates essentially reflects the view that monetary policy tools already have the situation well in hand and will offset any effects of fiscal policy on inflation and output.

The Great Recession of 2008–09 shocked this simple macroeconomic consensus. Even aggressive monetary actions were insufficient to adequately stabilize inflation and output. The impossibility of lowering nominal interest rates below zero posed a novel dilemma for central banks seeking to fight a collapse in aggregate demand.[2] The International Monetary Fund (IMF 2009) urged governments in many economies to adopt large fiscal stimulus programs in response to the crisis. Blanchard, Dell'Ariccia, and Mauro (2010, 9) acknowledge the helpful role played by fiscal policy, stating that the crisis had "returned fiscal policy to center stage as a macroeconomic tool." But they also argue that the crisis "further exposed some drawbacks of discretionary fiscal policy for more 'normal' fluctuations." Moreover, recent studies show that monetary policy may not necessarily be hobbled by the zero bound on nominal short-term interest rates when there is scope to reduce longer-term interest rates (Joyce et al. 2010, Gagnon et al. 2011, Hamilton and Wu 2011).

The presumption that monetary policy is the main stabilization tool is relevant mainly for floating exchange rate regimes. But for economies with pegged exchange rates, the textbook conclusion of fiscal policy potency and monetary policy impotence remains valid. These economies need to make countercyclical fiscal policy as automatic as possible, in order to avoid the legislative and managerial delays associated with discretionary fiscal policy. Examples of automatic fiscal stabilizers include unemployment benefits and progressive tax systems that increase spending and reduce revenues automatically when

---

1. As elsewhere in this book, the home economy is presumed insufficiently large to affect interest rates in the rest of the world.

2. Japan's experience at the so-called zero interest rate bound a decade earlier had been a warning call for new policy analysis that was not heeded by many outside, or even inside, Japan.

economic output slows. Automatic stabilizers can be greatly enhanced when a currency union has a unified fiscal system that provides for automatic transfers from regions that are performing well to those that are not.

Fiscal Crises under Fixed and Floating Exchange Rates

Economic stability ultimately requires fiscal stability. When a government borrows more than it is able to repay, the result is damaging under any exchange rate regime. However, the nature of any fiscal crisis, and the options for dealing with it, do differ under different regimes.

Domestic-Currency Debt and Flexible Exchange Rates

Fiscal crises under flexible exchange rate regimes are generally relatively slow-moving. As government debt rises, the central bank gradually raises interest rates to keep output close to potential levels and to keep inflation stable. Higher interest rates divert capital from productive projects to unproductive government debt, thereby slowing the potential growth rate of the economy. To pay interest on the debt, either the tax burden must continually rise or the government must force the central bank to abandon its inflation target in order to print money to service the debt. There is no clearly defined tipping point. Eventually, the public concludes that ever-slower growth with either ever-higher taxes or ever-higher inflation is unacceptable. Mild examples of this pattern occurred in Australia and Canada in the early 1990s. Extreme examples led to hyperinflation in Austria, Germany, Hungary, and Poland in the 1920s and Argentina and Brazil in the 1980s.[3]

Domestic-Currency Debt and Fixed Exchange Rates

The early stages of a profligate fiscal policy are especially expansionary under a fixed exchange rate regime because interest rates do not rise. Eventually, however, markets begin to push up domestic interest rates out of concern that the government will be forced to choose between defaulting on its debt and abandoning the exchange rate peg in order to print money. These concerns break the tight link between domestic and foreign interest rates. As interest rates rise, the government's debt service costs rise. When the government becomes unable to raise more taxes or cut enough spending to service the debt, it must choose between default and depreciation. Default imposes large immediate losses on domestic and foreign investors and shuts the government out of capital markets, thereafter forcing it to live within its means. Abandoning the fixed exchange rate is the more common choice. This starts a transition to the flexible exchange rate regime described in the previous section, with high and rising inflation.

---

3. Sargent (1982) provides a good account of the hyperinflations during the 1920s.

Domestic-Currency Debt and Currency Unions: The Euro-Area Debt Crisis

A currency union is distinct from a fixed exchange rate regime because government debt in a currency union is denominated in a currency beyond the government's control. This means that the government is not free to devalue its debt by abandoning the exchange rate peg. Any break with the currency union that involves a conversion of debt into the new local currency would be considered a default. Moreover, exiting a currency union is considerably more difficult than abandoning a fixed exchange rate because of the need to immediately establish a new currency. For these reasons, default—or restructuring, as it is more politely called—is a more likely policy choice for countries in a currency union.

A noteworthy feature of fiscal crises in a currency union is that they are more sudden and sharp than in countries that have the option of printing money to service their debts. As markets begin to fear default, investors demand higher interest rates on the debt to compensate for this increased risk. However, the higher interest burden makes it harder for the government to service its debt. This sets up a vicious cycle in which bond yields soar.[4] At some point, higher interest rates become meaningless because they raise the probability of default by more than they raise the expected future payoff for bondholders. At this point, the country is immediately shut out of the capital markets.[5]

This vicious cycle is readily apparent in the euro-area sovereign debt crisis that began in 2010. Greece, Ireland, and Portugal were effectively shut out of the capital markets. They were rescued from default by the European Union and the IMF, which provided large loan packages.

Foreign-Currency Debt

Many developing economies have experienced fiscal crises after their governments borrowed heavily in foreign currencies. Because these governments lack the option of printing money to service their foreign-currency debts, the dynamic pattern of fiscal crisis resembles that in the euro area beginning in 2010. Responding to foreign-currency debt crises has been the mainstay of IMF lending programs since the founding of the institution after World War II.

For economies with a floating exchange rate—and for those that are prepared to abandon their fixed exchange rate—easy monetary policy may provide some offset to the contractionary economic effects of the necessary fiscal tightening. But easy money causes the currency to depreciate, and currency depreciation increases the burden of the debt and the cost of interest payments in terms

---

4. De Grauwe (2011) describes this process in greater detail with a focus on the euro area.

5. When the government has the option of printing money to service its debt, higher interest rates do not have such a direct effect on the probability of default, and there is no sudden break in the ability to borrow.

of local currency. This increased debt burden further increases the needed fiscal adjustment, which can be especially harmful if the private sector also has borrowed in foreign currency (Allen et al. 2002, Arteta 2005).

Even in the absence of a fiscal crisis, the existence of a large stock of foreign-currency liabilities—issued either by the government or by the private sector—greatly reduces the stabilization benefits of a floating exchange rate (Bergin, Shin, and Tchakarov 2006; Acosta-Ormaechea and Coble 2011). The dangers of foreign-currency borrowing, and currency mismatches in general, have been more widely acknowledged in recent years (Goldstein 2002). The Committee on the Global Financial System (CGFS 2007) documented the significant growth of—and increased policy emphasis on—local-currency borrowing in developing economies as a superior alternative to borrowing in foreign currency.

Conclusions

Fiscal policy is more potent—and potentially more disruptive—in a currency union or a pegged exchange rate regime than in a floating regime. When the exchange rate cannot move, the burden of macroeconomic stabilization falls on fiscal policy, preferably through automatic stabilizers. But excessive fiscal deficits also precipitate crises that are more abrupt and severe under firmly fixed exchange rate regimes than under flexible regimes.

8

Exchange Rate Regimes in Developing Economies

Industry is the root of all ugliness.
—Oscar Wilde, *Phrases and Philosophies for the Use of the Young*

Pegging the exchange rate to conquer inflation is a strategy that has succeeded in some developing economies, but the exit from this strategy has proven difficult to manage smoothly.

In most developing economies, private capital is less mobile than in advanced economies. The speed with which developing economies should develop their financial markets and increase capital mobility is a matter of hot debate. As long as there are restrictions on private capital mobility, central banks in developing economies have some ability to stabilize both the exchange rate (through foreign exchange market intervention) and inflation and output (through monetary policy). Aggressive use of this enhanced policy freedom leads to large increases or decreases in a central bank's foreign exchange reserves. Many developing economies are testing the limits to foreign exchange reserve accumulation by deliberately holding down the value of their currencies in order to generate higher current account surpluses (or smaller deficits). In recent years, the combined current account surplus (and foreign exchange reserve accumulation) of the developing economies has reached an unprecedented level in relation to global output.

Floating exchange rates reduce the risk of financial crisis in developing economies because they avoid the sharp disruptions caused by unexpected changes in the level of an exchange rate peg. Even some very small and poor developing economies have had a largely satisfactory experience with floating exchange rates over the past decade.

Exchange-Rate-Based Inflation Stabilization

As mentioned in chapter 5, for developing economies, pegged exchange rate regimes tend to be associated with lower inflation than floating regimes. This is because central banks in some developing economies lack the institutional capacity to conduct a monetary policy oriented toward stabilization of inflation and output. Pegging the exchange rate to the currency of a country with low inflation is a simple strategy that may deliver acceptable results provided that the central bank and the government are able to take the actions necessary to maintain the exchange rate peg.

It may seem odd that central banks and governments are sometimes able to maintain an exchange rate peg but not to stabilize inflation and output directly. However, stabilizing inflation and output poses technical challenges greater than those associated with stabilizing the exchange rate. In addition, exchange rate stabilization is more immediately and publicly visible, whereas the effects of monetary and fiscal policy on inflation and output are known only after a long lag and are subject to statistical errors and even deliberate distortions. The difficulty of monitoring inflation and output makes central banks subject to political forces that may skew monetary decisions away from pursuit of what is socially optimal. In contrast, the exchange rate is a price that is readily and continuously observed, enabling all members of society to easily monitor monetary policy. If the authorities seek to mask profligate monetary policy by placing direct controls on the exchange rate, a black market rapidly develops. Even those who are compelled to trade on the official market quickly become aware of any substantial discrepancy between the controlled rate and the black-market rate. It is the simplicity and verifiability of an exchange rate peg that matters in economies where institutions are weak and where more complicated policy strategies are prone to fail.

Developing economies that have set out to conquer very high inflation generally peg their exchange rates simultaneously with announced cuts in the fiscal deficit. Such a strategy often proves successful, but continued fiscal discipline is essential for a durable disinflation (Mussa et al. 2000; Ghosh, Gulde, and Wolf 2002). When fiscal policy is not brought under control, inflation creeps up and the real exchange rate (RER) becomes progressively more overvalued. The current account deficit grows larger than net private capital inflows, foreign exchange reserves run out, and the government can no longer defend the peg and is forced to abandon it. Often, such a forced exit has traumatic economic consequences because many households and firms base their plans on a continuation of the peg and are not prepared for a sharp change in the exchange rate. Also, there are fiscal costs involved in attempts to defend a peg that ultimately is abandoned because the government's foreign exchange reserves are sold off at prices lower than the cost to replenish them. The Russian stabilization of 1995, which ended with a sovereign default and a currency crash in 1998, is a prominent failure of exchange-rate-based stabilization.

On the other hand, a successful long-lasting exchange-rate-based stabilization of inflation builds the reputations of the central bank and the government. Over time, it is natural for the public to ask whether even better outcomes are possible under other, less restrictive policy regimes. But handling the transition to a new regime can be tricky. Poland enjoyed one of the smoother transitions. In 1990, Poland launched an exchange-rate-based stabilization with a pegged exchanged rate. Over time, the regime was moved to a crawling peg, then to a crawling band, and finally to a free float. Inflation declined relatively smoothly from around 600 percent in 1989 to 3 percent in 2010.[1] Other countries, including Bulgaria and the Baltic countries of Estonia, Latvia, and Lithuania, chose to use an exchange rate peg as a transition to eventual entry into the euro area.[2] Despite intense pressures on some of these countries to devalue in the wake of the financial crisis of 2008–09, they were able to maintain their pegs and keep inflation relatively stable.

In some cases of otherwise successful stabilizations, later events gave rise to market pressures that governments proved unable or unwilling to defy, and the subsequent transition to a new regime was abrupt. In the wake of the Asian and Russian financial crises, Brazil was forced to devalue in January 1999, and many feared that high inflation would be the likely result. The government moved quickly to adopt an inflation targeting regime with a floating exchange rate, and the country managed to avoid a financial crash or a spike in inflation, as described in chapter 5. Argentina, on the other hand, had a far more costly transition (Ghosh, Gulde, and Wolf 2002, chapter 7). After a successful stabilization under a currency board linked to the US dollar in the 1990s, the Argentine economy took sharp hits both from the Brazilian depreciation in 1999 and from the strength of the US dollar in 2000–2001, which forced Argentina's exchange rate to rise on a trade-weighted basis. The cost of being unable to use monetary policy for domestic stabilization was dear. The Argentine government defaulted on its foreign debt in December 2001 and floated the currency days later. The transition was anything but smooth, however, and inflation soared while the economy stagnated for the next two years.

Policy Options with Immobile Private Capital

The analysis in most of this book assumes few restrictions on the flow of capital across borders. The standard model of exchange rates, in particular, is based on the assumption that private capital is free to seek the highest return across countries. This section explores how things change when capital is not free (or not fully free) to cross borders.

Sources of Capital Immobility

Restrictions on the mobility of capital across borders are endemic in the poorer developing economies, which do not have sophisticated financial markets. Because these economies typically lack modern and efficient supervisory, regu-

---

1. Inflation data are from the International Monetary Fund's *International Financial Statistics* database.

2. See Mussa et al. (2000, appendix III) for a discussion of these and other exchange-rate-based stabilizations.

latory, and legal institutions, they can be risky places to invest. They therefore are unattractive to most forms of outside capital, and they have little inside capital except for relatively fixed land and domestic enterprises. As a consequence, there is little basis for arbitrage between rates of return on assets in these economies and in the rest of the world.

In addition to these endemic sources of capital immobility, governments in some developing economies have imposed regulatory restrictions or taxes on capital inflows and/or outflows. Some of these controls take the form of outright prohibitions on certain classes of transactions. But they also include more flexible forms, such as taxes on foreign exchange transactions or other financial transactions between domestic and foreign residents, taxes on domestic dividends or interest earned by foreign residents, taxes on foreign dividends or interest earned by domestic residents, and requirements that foreign investors post a non-interest-bearing deposit with the central bank for certain classes of inflows. In recent episodes of the imposition of capital controls, there is evidence of a moderate increase in the ability of the central bank to manage both the short-term interest rate (monetary policy) and the exchange rate independently (Magud, Reinhart, and Rogoff 2011).

Some direct evidence of lower capital mobility in developing economies is the failure of covered interest rate parity (CIRP). As discussed in chapter 3, CIRP holds very closely for the advanced economies, with spreads in rates of return well under 1 percentage point and often under 0.1 percentage point. For some developing economies, however, the spread is much higher. In China, for example, the rate on one-year domestic bank deposits in Chinese renminbi was 3.25 percent in June 2011, while the corresponding rate in the United States on US dollar deposits was 0.5 percent. According to CIRP, the renminbi-dollar forward exchange rate should have priced in a renminbi depreciation of 2.75 percent, but the nondeliverable futures rates on the Chicago Mercantile Exchange called for a 2 percent *appreciation* of the renminbi against the dollar. The implied CIRP spread was nearly 5 percentage points! US residents seeking to take advantage of this spread would have found it difficult to obtain renminbi for deposit in China, and Chinese residents would have found it difficult to borrow dollars to fund additional renminbi deposits, because both of these transactions are strictly controlled by the Chinese government.

A common element of capital controls is that they discriminate between internal and external transactions. Other policies may reduce capital flows without making such distinctions. These include, for example, prudential restrictions on loan-to-value ratios, minimum capital ratios for financial institutions, and reserve requirements for banks.

New Perspectives on Capital Controls

For many years, the standard prescription of most academics and international financial institutions, such as the IMF and the World Bank, was that capital flows to less developed economies are both important and beneficial for their development. Indeed, the raison d'être of international development institutions such as the World Bank and the regional development banks was to channel capital to developing economies. The policy recommendations that naturally followed were for countries to build up their legal, supervisory, and regulatory systems in order to make themselves attractive to outside capital and to use that capital efficiently (Dell'Ariccia et al. 2008).

The insight behind this standard prescription was a powerful one: Poor economies are almost universally characterized by low levels of capital and abundant levels of unskilled labor. The standard model of economic production states that increasing either of these two fundamental factors of production increases total output.[3] However, the extra output from a given unit of capital is higher in an economy that has a lot of workers and little capital. As a result, investors achieve higher rates of return—and the world as a whole generates higher output—when more capital goes to poorer economies. Later refinements of this basic model include acknowledgment of the importance of human capital, such as education and training, and the role of institutions and governance in determining the efficiency with which capital and labor can be used to produce economic output.

The occurrence of financial crises in developing economies, especially during the 1990s, increasingly led to questions about the benefits of capital inflows to these economies. Joseph Stiglitz is one of the first prominent economists to call for an assessment of the costs and benefits of official controls on capital flows (Stiglitz 1998). He points in particular at short-term debt flows as potentially destabilizing and distortionary. Around the same time, Calvo (1998) documents the existence and harmful consequences of sudden stops in capital inflows to developing economies.[4] A subsequent survey of economic research on capital flows emphasizes the risks they pose to financial systems in developing economies (Aizenman 2004). A recent paper proposes using tax-based controls to reduce the volatility of such flows and thus mitigate the harm to financial systems (Jeanne and Korinek 2010).

Another challenge to the presumed benefits of capital inflows arises from the fact that they do not appear to raise an economy's productivity growth, contrary to the predictions of the basic model (Gourinchas and Jeanne 2009; Prasad, Rajan, and Subramanian 2007). One explanation for these results is that capital inflows tend to push up a country's exchange rate and thus stifle its trad-

---

3. For more on the standard economic model of capital and growth, see the essays edited by Stiglitz and Uzawa (1969). The standard model focuses on physical capital—that is, factories, offices, and infrastructure. Financial capital, such as bonds, bank deposits, and equity, ultimately reflects claims on underlying physical capital. Financial capital provides the instruments through which international capital flows can increase a country's physical capital.

4. The harm from sudden stops arises because depreciation of the domestic currency raises the burden of debts denominated in foreign currencies. For countries that have not borrowed in foreign currencies, the depreciation caused by an incipient sudden stop actually boosts economic activity, as demonstrated in the case studies in chapter 6.

ables sector, which is the sector most important to productivity growth. Rodrik and Subramanian (2009) review the subsequent debate on these findings and suggest that the institutional framework in many developing economies may constrain productive investment opportunities to a level that may be close to or lower than available domestic savings. In such circumstances, capital inflows may boost consumption at the expense of long-run growth because they cause the currency to appreciate and harm the competitiveness of the tradables sector.

These results do not mean that capital inflows are always harmful for developing economies. They do suggest that governments in developing economies should seek ways to improve investment opportunities and should adopt relatively tight fiscal policies and loose monetary policies to offset some of the impact on their currencies of capital inflows. Also, inward foreign direct investment in business operations generally is helpful in raising productivity to world standards. Moreover, all advanced economies have embraced capital mobility and seem unwilling—many would even say unable—to go back to pervasive use of capital controls. Many of the more advanced developing economies also have moved in this direction. Therefore, it seems likely that increasing capital mobility and declining use of discriminatory capital controls will continue to be an important characteristic of the more successful developing economies.

In 2010, the IMF attracted considerable attention when it published a Staff Position Note (Ostry et al. 2010) endorsing narrowly targeted capital controls under limited circumstances. This publication was followed by a Staff Discussion Note (Ostry et al. 2011) that examines country experiences with capital controls and provides further guidance on when such controls might be helpful. The recommendations included in these IMF staff notes received the explicit backing of the managing director of the IMF at a conference on the international monetary system (Strauss-Kahn 2011). The new IMF guidelines state that the first response to capital inflows should be adoption of appropriate monetary and fiscal policies. The second response should be use of appropriate financial prudential (nondiscriminatory) regulations. Only if these first two lines of defense prove insufficient should a country consider direct controls on capital inflows, and the design of any controls should depend on the nature of the inflows. In general, the focus of controls should be on directing inflows into longer-term and less risky forms, such as foreign direct investment, and away from debt flows, especially short-term and/or foreign-currency-denominated debt. With a number of countries having imposed new capital controls since the global financial crisis of 2008, there is a risk that some may go further than justified in the circumstances and end up distorting capital in ways that are harmful rather than beneficial.

Sustainable Policy Regimes with Capital Immobility

Incomplete mobility of capital violates a key assumption of the standard model of exchange rates and opens up the possibility that central banks can independently control both the exchange rate and the interest rate. Recall the impossible trinity discussed in chapter 2, which states that a central bank can achieve only two of the following three objectives: independent monetary (interest rate) policy; independent exchange rate policy (including a fixed exchange rate); and free private capital markets. Subsequent chapters considered free private capital markets as given and examined the tradeoff between the first and second objectives.

This section now considers the alternative extreme assumption, in which there is no private capital mobility. In this case, the central bank can set the short-term interest rate directly and can use foreign exchange intervention to set the exchange rate. In principle, the central bank is able to stabilize domestic spending (and hence inflation and output) as well as the exchange rate. There are some limits to this policy independence, however, which are based on the maximum and minimum levels of foreign exchange reserves the central bank is willing or able to tolerate. In particular, over the long run, foreign exchange reserves cannot continually increase or decrease relative to GDP.

When the current account is in deficit, the central bank must run down its foreign exchange reserves, and when the current account is in surplus, the central bank must augment its foreign exchange reserves. A current account deficit is not sustainable in the long run because the central bank will run out of reserves.[5] A current account surplus has a less obvious limit, but ever-rising foreign exchange reserves require ever-increasing borrowing in domestic currency to sterilize the effects on domestic interest rates.[6] In most cases, the earnings on reserves are lower than the borrowing cost in domestic currency. A central bank with ever-increasing foreign exchange reserves will incur ever-increasing losses on the costs of financing those reserves. In addition, the central bank is exposed to the potential for large capital losses in the event that the currency appreciates in the future, because this would reduce the value of its reserves relative to its domestic-currency liabilities.

The bottom line is that immobile private capital enables the central bank to stabilize both the domestic economy and the exchange rate, but it is free to stabilize the exchange rate only within a range of values that do not result in an unsustainable accumulation or decumulation of foreign exchange reserves. At some point, a misaligned exchange rate causes a current account deficit or surplus that the central bank will be unwilling or unable to support.

Deliberate Undervaluation and the Global Saving Glut

Since 1999, many developing economies have kept their currencies undervalued, generating large current account surpluses and growing stocks of foreign exchange reserves and other official assets. Figure 8.1 displays net

---

5. In principle, a central bank can have negative foreign exchange reserves—that is, foreign-currency debts. But this has rarely happened.

6. Technically speaking, a small current account surplus is sustainable if it does not increase reserves relative to GDP.

Figure 8.1   Net official capital outflows and current account balances for developing economies

billions of US dollars

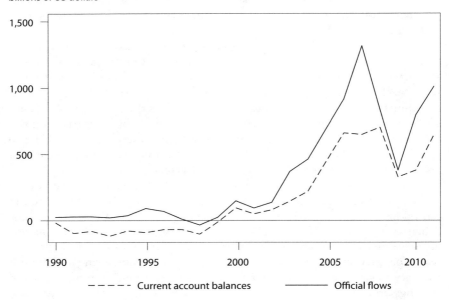

— — — — Current account balances   ———— Official flows

Note: 2011 data are IMF projections.

Source: IMF *World Economic Outlook* database.

official capital outflows (including purchases of foreign exchange reserves) for all developing economies, along with their aggregate current account balances.[7] For 2011, the IMF projects that net official flows from these economies (not including outflows from most sovereign wealth funds) will equal 1.5 percent of world GDP. In addition, a group of newly industrialized economies that are no longer classified as developing economies by the IMF has been pursuing a similar strategy, with an aggregate current account surplus of $99 billion and an increase in foreign exchange reserves of $83 billion in 2010.[8] This level of official capital flows from developing economies to the advanced economies is unprecedented. According to the IMF's *International Financial Statistics* database, reserve accumulation by developing economies

7. Net official flows are increases in official assets, including reserve assets, minus increases in official liabilities. The data do not include capital outflows from most sovereign wealth funds in these economies. Data cover all but the advanced economies.

8. These economies are Israel, Hong Kong, Korea, and Singapore. Taiwan Province of China also is classified as a newly industrialized economy, but data for Taiwan are not available. Projections for 2011 are not available for these economies. Data on official flows for these economies in 2010 were not available when this book went to press, and so the change in reserves is used as a proxy.

Figure 8.2   Foreign exchange reserves of selected economies in 2010

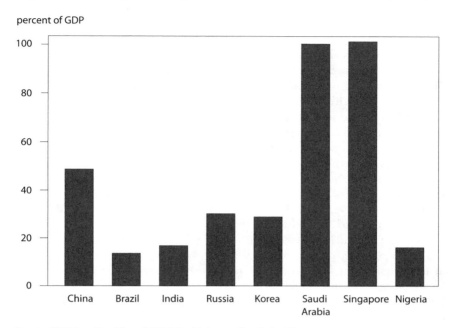

percent of GDP

Sources: IMF *International Financial Statistics* database, authors' calculations.

exceeded 1 percent of US GDP in only one year between 1948 and 2002. Since 2003 it has averaged roughly 3 percent of US GDP—a number that understates the growth in total flows because it excludes most sovereign wealth funds, which emerged from obscurity only in the past decade (Truman 2010). Official capital outflows of this magnitude are not sustainable indefinitely, but they have persisted for quite a while and it is not clear when or how they will eventually subside.

Figure 8.2 displays foreign exchange reserves as a share of GDP for eight important developing and newly industrialized economies. According to the IMF, as of December 2010, total foreign exchange reserves of developing economies were $4 trillion, and reserves of the newly industrialized economies were $0.5 trillion. According to Truman (2010, 12), foreign assets held by developing-economy sovereign wealth funds, which are not included in foreign exchange reserve data, were estimated to be roughly $1.5 trillion as of mid-2009. These investments surely continued to grow in 2010. The vast majority of these foreign exchange reserves and wealth fund assets were invested in advanced economies, equaling roughly 15 percent of GDP in the recipient economies and 25 percent of GDP in the source economies in 2010.

The motivations for this sustained outflow of official capital and consequent currency undervaluation are various and complex. After the Asian financial crisis of 1997–98, many Asian governments decided to build up a war chest of foreign exchange reserves to counteract capital outflows during any future crisis.[9] Meanwhile, China combined a policy of pegging the renmimbi to the US dollar with an interest rate policy aimed at containing domestic inflation. This policy combination stymied the natural tendency of the RER to increase over time, as it usually does in fast-growing developing economies because of the Harrod-Balassa-Samuelson (HBS) effect, which was discussed in appendix 3B. The increasing undervaluation of China's currency led to its rising current account surplus. Other Asian economies did not want to lose competitiveness against China, and so they continued to accumulate reserves longer than they might have done otherwise (Katada and Henning 2010). Businesses in the tradables sector have a powerful political voice throughout the developing world, and they have fought to maintain undervalued currencies in many economies to protect their competitiveness in export markets. Finally, several major oil-exporting countries have chosen to save the windfall from high oil revenues during the past decade, rather than to spend it quickly as they had during previous periods of high oil prices.

Overall, there is a widespread feeling in developing economies that sustained currency undervaluation has "worked" as a development strategy—at least that it has led to better outcomes than previous strategies. Indeed, this strategy does appear to have avoided the trap identified by Rodrik and Subramanian (2009), namely, when developing economies allow their currencies to become overvalued by capital inflows and then suffer stagnation in critical tradable industries. In addition, through direct government saving in the form of foreign assets, sovereign wealth funds in resource-exporting economies alleviate upward pressure on their currencies and thus provide a cure for the so-called Dutch disease.[10] But, has this strategy gone too far?

The net effect of these policies has been called the "global saving glut" by Federal Reserve Chairman Ben Bernanke (2005, 2011). The undervalued exchange rates of the developing economies have siphoned demand away from the advanced economies, and the vast outflow of official capital from the developing economies has held down market interest rates in the advanced economies. In an effort to keep their economies growing, central banks in the advanced economies have kept policy interest rates low (near zero in many cases). Although the global saving glut did not create the deficiencies in financial supervision and regulation that ultimately caused the global financial crisis of 2008–09, the resulting low interest rates and large financial flows did feed housing bubbles around the world and made the ultimate crash much larger than it otherwise would have been.

A collapse of domestic spending in the major advanced economies narrowed their current account deficits and the corresponding current account surpluses

---

9. As discussed in chapter 7 and in the next section, a better defense is to avoid borrowing in foreign currency and to place prudential controls on other forms of risky capital.

10. Dutch disease is the tendency for increasing exports of natural resources to drive up the value of the currency and cause the rest of the tradables sector of the economy to shrink.

of the developing economies in 2008 and 2009. But in 2010, the imbalances began to rebound. How long can these massive imbalances persist?

The rise of inflation pressures in many developing economies suggests that a limit to this policy configuration may be near. Central banks in the developing economies have been reluctant to raise interest rates as much as needed to prevent inflation. In part, this may reflect the fact that higher domestic interest rates increase the losses to central banks from financing their foreign exchange reserves. In addition, to the extent that capital is at least partially mobile, higher domestic interest rates may encourage greater private capital inflows that the central bank will have to purchase in order to prevent appreciation of the currency. In this way, central banks in many developing economies already may be facing an unpleasant tradeoff between achieving their inflation and their exchange rate objectives. If they allow higher inflation, they face an increase in their RERs that ultimately will undo the real undervaluation of their currencies and narrow their current account surpluses. If they fight inflation, they face the prospect of either buying ever-larger quantities of foreign exchange reserves at an increasing fiscal cost or abandoning their exchange rate targets.

Tighter fiscal policy is one way for these economies to maintain undervalued currencies without high inflation, but tighter fiscal policy can be a difficult political choice. Nevertheless, tight fiscal policy and massive government or central bank purchases of foreign assets is the policy mix adopted by some of the major oil exporters. If other developing economies also make this choice, the global saving glut will persist and the advanced economies will continue to struggle with negative net external demand.

With developing economies becoming an increasingly large part of the world economy, the deliberate undervaluation strategy and the policy response in the advanced economies has created growing tensions. Brazilian Finance Minister Guido Mantega dubbed the situation a "currency war".[11] C. Fred Bergsten warns of a "new mercantilism" as some advanced economies (such as Switzerland) began to emulate the undervaluation strategy of much of the developing world.[12] Goldstein (2010, 5) argues that a policy of deliberate currency undervaluation through massive purchases of foreign exchange reserves violates Article IV of the IMF *Articles of Agreement*, which states that

> each member shall ... avoid manipulating exchange rates or the international monetary system in order to prevent effective balance of payments adjustment or to gain an unfair competitive advantage over other members.

In the April 2011 issue of its *World Economic Outlook* (p. 25), the IMF agrees that the "accumulation of official foreign exchange reserves in the

---

11. See Jonathan Wheatley and Peter Garnham, "Brazil in 'Currency War' Alert," *Financial Times*, September 27, 2010.

12. C. Fred Bergsten, "New Imbalances Will Threaten Global Recovery," Op-ed, *Financial Times*, June 10, 2010.

major surplus economies presents an important obstacle to global demand rebalancing." As this book goes to press, it remains unclear how much longer the deliberate undervaluation strategy would persist and what might be the outcome of the global tensions it has engendered.

Financial Stability and Exchange Rate Regimes

The benchmarks considered until now, either complete capital mobility or complete immobility, are obviously stylized extremes. Capital is highly— though not perfectly—mobile in the advanced economies, is increasingly mobile in some of the more advanced developing economies, and may be close to completely immobile in some of the poorest economies. But many developing economies lie in between, with partial mobility of private capital. As discussed in chapter 2, advanced economies with highly mobile capital have moved out of the intermediate exchange rate regimes because of the risk of costly exchange rate crises that can arise when markets begin to doubt the durability of a peg. Less than complete capital mobility reduces this risk for many developing economies, but it does not eliminate it. Given that many developing economies have chosen to retain intermediate exchange rate regimes, are such regimes a source of financial instability?

Currency and financial crises occur more often in developing economies that have pegged or intermediate exchange rate regimes than in floating regimes (Rogoff et al. 2003; Ghosh, Ostry, and Tsangarides 2010).[13] These results correspond with the casual observation that the most serious developing economy crises in recent decades occurred in countries that had a de jure or a de facto exchange rate peg. An inflexible exchange rate makes the financial system more unstable because it encourages domestic households, firms, and the government to borrow in foreign currency. Foreign banks generally offer lower interest rates on lending in foreign currency, and domestic residents are more willing to borrow in foreign currency when they expect that the domestic currency will remain fixed in value relative to the foreign currency.

A typical crisis unfolds either because the central bank has allowed inflation to erode the economy's competitiveness or because of an adverse shock to a country's export market. In either case, the current account turns negative, and the central bank starts to run out of reserves to defend the exchange rate peg. The authorities have two options: (1) jack up interest rates to push down inflation and defend the currency—which causes a recession and causes banks to lose money both from falling bond prices and from bankrupt borrowers;

---

13. By definition, a country with a floating exchange rate cannot have a currency crisis because it is not trying to defend any specific value of the currency, but it can have a large and sudden depreciation. There is little difference in the frequency of large currency depreciations across exchange rate regimes in developing economies, but the damage from such depreciations is greater in less flexible regimes for reasons discussed below. Kuttner and Posen (2001) show that large depreciations are less common in floating exchange rate regimes in which the central bank is independent from the government (and typically assigned responsibility for domestic economic stabilization.)

or (2) abandon the exchange rate peg—which causes banks (or corporations or households) to lose money on their borrowing in foreign currencies or may force the government to default on its foreign-currency debt. Either of these options can precipitate a financial crisis. Note that neither of these unpleasant choices is forced on policymakers in an economy with a floating exchange rate and no foreign-currency debt.

In recognition of these adverse dynamics, the IMF (2011a) recommends that a developing economy with a fixed exchange rate should hold twice the level of foreign exchange reserves as a comparable economy with a floating exchange rate. This recommendation begs the question of why an economy with a floating exchange rate and little foreign-currency debt should hold any foreign exchange reserves at all.

Externally transmitted financial bubbles are another source of risk to financial stability.[14] When global investors become bullish about an economy, they push up the value of its financial assets until these assets become expensive in terms of foreign currency. For an economy with a fixed exchange rate, that means that asset prices also rise in terms of domestic currency, which in turn can lead to unsustainable investment and an eventual crash of asset prices. For an economy with a floating exchange rate, the main effect of these bullish sentiments is to appreciate the exchange rate. There is no bubble in terms of domestic prices and so no subsequent crash.

Successful Floats in Developing Economies

One of the striking developments of the past 20 years is the increase in the number of developing economies with floating exchange rates. For most of the 1980s, the IMF de facto exchange rate classification listed fewer than 10 developing economies with either a managed float or a free float. By 1999 there were 53 developing economies with a floating exchange rate; as of 2010, in the wake of the financial crisis, there were still 45.[15]

The experiences of developing economies with floating exchange rates are varied, reflecting the varied institutional frameworks for monetary policy. One policy framework that has received much approbation in recent years is that of inflation targeting. For the six developing economies that have had an inflation targeting framework and a floating exchange rate continuously over the past 10 years, the outcomes have been favorable. Figure 8.3 displays the output growth rates of these economies since 1980, and figure 8.4 displays their inflation rates since 1980. In each panel, a vertical line denotes the beginning of the inflation targeting regime (Truman 2003b, 29). In Brazil, Chile, Colombia, and Mexico, the switch from a fixed or intermediate regime to a floating exchange rate occurred in the same year as the start of inflation targeting. In South

---

14. The authors thank Tamim Bayoumi for suggesting this point.

15. Included are Israel and Korea, which used to be in the developing economy group but were later reclassified as newly industrialized advanced economies.

Figure 8.3   GDP growth in developing economies with at least 10 years of inflation targeting

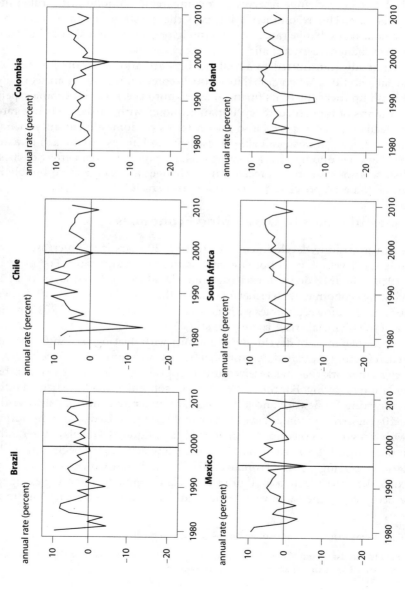

Note: Vertical line denotes start of inflation targeting.

Sources: IMF *World Economic Outlook* database, Truman (2003b, table 2.3).

Figure 8.4   CPI inflation in developing economies with at least 10 years of inflation targeting

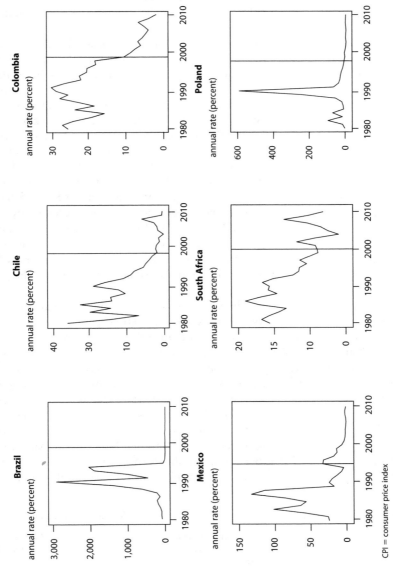

CPI = consumer price index

Note: Vertical line denotes start of inflation targeting.

Sources: IMF *World Economic Outlook* database, Truman (2003b, table 2.3).

Africa, the switch to a floating exchange rate occurred four years before inflation targeting. In Poland, the switch to a floating exchange rate occurred two years after inflation targeting.

Output growth rates have been somewhat higher on average with inflation targeting, although the increase is not statistically significant. There has been little change in the variability of the rate of growth after the switch to inflation targeting. Inflation, however, either declined further or remained at 30-year low levels after the switch to inflation targeting, and the difference is striking. The volatility of inflation also declined, except in South Africa, which already had the lowest inflation rate of these economies before it switched to a floating exchange rate.

On balance, the economic performance of these economies under inflation targeting with a floating exchange rate has been better than that under the previous, less flexible exchange rate regimes. But how flexible have these exchange rate regimes actually been? Have central banks in these economies been managing their currencies within tight ranges? According to table 4.4, all these economies had exchange rate variability (standard deviations) above the global median value for 2000–09. Except for Brazil, they also have increased their foreign exchange reserves to a much lower extent than other developing economies. Between 2000 and 2010, foreign exchange reserves of all developing economies increased by a factor of 7.[16] Brazil's reserves also increased by a factor of 7, and South Africa's reserves increased by a factor of 5, but foreign exchange reserves in Chile, Colombia, Mexico, and Poland increased by less than a factor of 3 over this period. Moreover, as shown in figure 8.2, Brazil has the lowest reserve-to-GDP ratio of the four largest developing economies. By and large, it seems reasonable to assert that these six developing economies did have truly flexible exchange rates and good economic outcomes over the past 10 years.

The developing economies displayed in figures 8.3 and 8.4 are all medium to large economies. What about small economies? There is no objective way to separate the smallest developing economies into those with a good monetary framework and those with irresponsible monetary policies. Nevertheless, even if all the smallest developing economies are lumped together, the evidence suggests that those with a floating exchange rate had outcomes at least as good as the rest. Defining small economies to be those with purchasing power parity (PPP) GDP in 2009 of less than $50 billion[17] and using available data, there are 70 in this group. Eight of these had floating exchange rates every year from 2000 through 2010: Albania, Armenia, The Gambia, Madagascar, Mauritius, Moldova, Uganda, and Zambia. Table 8.1 shows that, over the past ten years, the eight floaters had somewhat higher and slightly more variable inflation,

---

16. Foreign exchange reserve data are from the IMF *International Financial Statistics* database.

17. For comparison, the smallest economy in figures 8.3 and 8.4, Chile, had a 2009 PPP GDP of $243 billion. The three smallest advanced economies, Iceland, Luxembourg, and New Zealand, had 2009 PPP GDPs of $12 billion, $42 billion, and $125 billion, respectively.

Table 8.1   Inflation and output in the smallest developing economies, 2000–2009

Inflation/output	Consistent floaters	All others
Average inflation rate (percent)	7.7	5.8
Standard deviation of inflation	4.1	3.7
Growth rate of GDP per capita (percent)	3.7	2.5
Standard deviation of growth rate	3.7	4.0

Note: Includes economies with 2009 purchasing power parity GDP less than $50 billion.

Sources: IMF World Economic Outlook database, April 2011; various issues of IMF Annual Report on Exchange Rate Arrangements and Exchange Restrictions; and authors' calculations.

but that they also had somewhat higher and slightly less variable growth rates of per capita PPP GDP. To get 1.2 percentage points more growth with only 1.9 percentage points more inflation and little difference in volatility seems like a good bargain. At a minimum, floating exchange rates cannot be said to be an obviously mistaken policy choice for even the smallest developing economies.

9

Policy Conclusions

> *But the past is of no importance. The present is of no importance.*
> *It is with the future that we have to deal.*
> —Oscar Wilde, *The Soul of Man under Socialism*

This book examines a number of issues related to exchange rate volatility and the implications of large swings in currency values in a globalized economy. The analysis points to the following conclusions:

- Floating exchange rates appear to be excessively volatile, but the harm from this volatility is less than the potential harm of moving to fixed exchange rates.

- Many economies would benefit from greater exchange rate flexibility and few, if any, would benefit from reduced exchange rate flexibility.

- Exchange rate flexibility has no measurable effect on economic output in the long run, but—when combined with sound monetary policy—flexible exchange rates help to effectively stabilize inflation and output.

- An internationally coordinated strategy to set "reference rates" for verbal and actual foreign exchange intervention might lead to a gradual and modest reduction in excess exchange rate volatility, but such a strategy should not involve the defense of any specific levels for exchange rates nor should it detract in any way from the use of monetary policy to stabilize inflation and output.

Volatility of Exchange Rates

The standard model of exchange rates does not explain much of the actual behavior of floating exchange rates. The two main explanations proposed for this failure are that there is a systematic error in market expectations of the future exchange rate and that there is a factor missing from the standard model, commonly called a risk premium. Chapter 3 developed new evidence that the risk premium is indeed the main reason for the poor performance of the standard model, reinforcing the findings of a preponderance of studies of this issue.

Attempts to explain the risk premium raise as many questions as they answer, and no single explanation has garnered convincing support. There is a general presumption that the risk premium may be excessive and harmful, although that is far from certain. Not surprisingly, risk premiums are much smaller and less volatile in long-lasting fixed exchange rate regimes, which effectively reduce the risk arising from future exchange rate movements.

Costs and Benefits of Floating

The costs and benefits of floating exchange rates can be grouped into two categories: (1) the effects on the long-run level of economic output and/or growth; and (2) the effects on the stability of inflation and economic output.

Effects on Long-Run Economic Output

Floating exchange rates influence long-run economic output through a variety of channels. They increase the costs of international transactions, and they appear to reduce the volume of international trade. Floating rates may cause wasteful shifts of resources across sectors of the economy, and they increase uncertainty about the future levels of exchange rates, which may deter productive investment. On the other hand, floating exchange rates free central banks to adopt monetary policies aimed at stabilizing inflation and output. This enhanced economic stability may encourage productive investment and raise the long-run level of economic output.

It is not possible to detect any reliable effect of exchange rate volatility or the type of exchange rate regime on the level of economic output or the long-run growth rate. The data show that long-run economic output is influenced by many other more important factors than the exchange rate regime.

Effects on the Stability of Inflation and Output

A floating exchange rate, by itself, does not guarantee economic stability. But, by allowing policymakers the freedom to take actions to stabilize the economy, a floating exchange rate can foster greater stability of inflation and output. Chapter 6 demonstrated this interrelationship using a small theoretical model under a wide range of parameter values. Existing research broadly confirms the results of this theoretical model. In addition, chapter 6 presented new statistical and case-study evidence of the benefits of a floating exchange rate in terms of stabilizing inflation around a target and stabilizing output around its potential.

Overall, the benefits of floating exchange rates are difficult to measure and surely vary across economies. One particular difficulty is that countries with floating exchange rates often fail to pursue sound monetary policy, which dilutes or even reverses the benefits of exchange rate flexibility. For a country with sound monetary policy, however, a switch from a fixed to a floating exchange rate may help stabilize inflation and output, potentially reducing the standard deviation of both by as much as 1 percentage point or even more. Potential improvements in economic stability of such magnitudes clearly could be very advantageous in improving social well-being, particularly compared with other options available to policymakers.

Exchange Rate Regime Recommendations

Economies with Highly Mobile Capital

Economies with a high degree of capital mobility, which includes all the advanced economies, have been forced out of the middle of the spectrum of exchange rate regimes (adjustable pegs and soft pegs) by the damaging crises that are associated with these regimes. These crises typically result from speculative attacks launched when exchange rate targets appear to conflict with other policy objectives, such as stable inflation and output. As developing economies progress to advanced levels of per capita economic output, their capital markets will become increasingly open and they will become increasingly subject to such speculative attacks. As a result, they too likely will be forced out of the middle of the spectrum, notwithstanding the recent consensus about the potential value of using capital controls in limited circumstances.

For economies with at least a moderate degree of capital mobility, the pairing between economies and optimal exchange rate regimes can be described as follows:

- *Free float.* On purely economic terms, and assuming that the central bank is capable of conducting sound monetary policy aimed at stabilizing inflation and output, a free float is the most desirable regime.

- *Currency union.* If there is a strong desire to unite economically and politically with neighboring countries and if economic policies are established to integrate the national economies, currency union may be a reasonable option. As the euro-area sovereign debt crisis of 2010–11 demonstrates, putting the necessary policies in place can be difficult. Dollarization is a less attractive version of currency union because it means forgoing a voice in setting monetary policy and forfeiting seigniorage revenues, but it may be the least bad option for economies seeking a hard peg that they cannot otherwise attain. About 50 countries are currently members of a currency union or are dollarized. Few other countries are likely candidates to join this group.

- *Hard peg.* For countries that lack the necessary institutional ability to conduct sound independent monetary policy and that have no strong desire for greater economic and political union with their neighbors, a hard peg may be the best option. This group comprises mainly small economies.

Economies with Limited Capital Mobility

For the relatively poorer developing economies with limited capital mobility, a wider range of regimes is feasible. But even for these countries, there is a presumption that floating exchange rates will deliver better outcomes if the central bank has the capacity to stabilize inflation and output. A number of developing economies have successfully managed floating exchange rates during the past 10 years or so.

Improving the Current System

The most important improvement to be made to the current system is for developing economies that already have some flexibility in their exchange rate to make stabilization of inflation and economic output the only goals of monetary (interest rate) policy. These economies should not attempt to use monetary policy to stabilize their exchange rates; this should be accomplished solely by foreign exchange intervention within reasonable limits. When the two goals are in conflict, inflation and output stabilization should take priority over exchange rate stabilization. In most respects, these recommendations follow closely those spelled out by Morris Goldstein (2002).

Reference Rates as an Incremental Improvement?

For the most part, this book has ignored foreign exchange intervention as a policy tool, arguing that such intervention has little effect when capital is highly mobile across economies. However, for developing economies with reduced capital mobility, foreign exchange intervention can have significant effects. Given that the extreme of perfect capital mobility does not exist in the real world, is there a role for foreign exchange intervention even in economies with relatively high capital mobility, including the advanced economies? In particular, might central banks be able to damp exchange rate volatility without sacrificing their primary objectives of stabilizing inflation and output?

The "reference rate" proposal by John Williamson (2007) provides a framework for foreign exchange intervention that may be helpful in reducing and stabilizing volatile risk premiums. Under the "monitoring zone" version of this proposal, the International Monetary Fund (IMF)—in consultation with member countries—would establish relatively wide zones around estimated equilibrium values of each economy's effective exchange rate. When the exchange rate is within this zone, the central bank would not be allowed to intervene in the foreign exchange market. When the exchange rate is above the zone, the central bank would be encouraged to sell domestic currency for foreign currency to put downward pressure on the exchange rate. Similarly, when the exchange rate is below the zone, the central bank would be encouraged to sell foreign currency for domestic currency to put upward pressure on the exchange rate. These operations would be aimed at damping wide swings in exchange rates and would not prevent central banks from setting their interest rate instrument as needed to achieve inflation and output stability. Most important, central banks would not try to limit the value of the exchange rate; the monitoring zone would be considered a guide for when the central bank should start and stop intervening, not as a limit to exchange rate movements.

Estimating Equilibrium Exchange Rates

The IMF has a long history of assessing equilibrium exchange rates for its members. The IMF's Consultative Group on Exchange Rate Issues (CGER) uses three different approaches for estimating medium-term (roughly five-year-ahead) equilibrium exchange rates (Lee et al. 2008). All three may be interpreted as producing estimates of the exchange rate consistent with long-run purchasing power parity (PPP), after factoring in influences from net foreign assets, the Harrod-Balassa-Samuelson (HBS) effect, and other structural conditions. The first approach compares current account balances to norms based on a country's fundamental conditions, such as demographics, net exports of primary commodities, and fiscal balance. The equilibrium exchange rate is determined by the change relative to the current exchange rate that would be needed to move the current account to its norm. The second approach relates exchange rates directly to fundamental factors in a cross-country setting, and predicts the equilibrium exchange rate by those fundamentals. The third approach simply asks what change in the exchange rate would be needed to stabilize net foreign assets assuming output grows at potential in all countries. All of these approaches focus on predicted values over the next five years or so.

For purposes of setting reference rates, it would be useful to augment the CGER medium-term estimates with an adjustment for the effect on the exchange rate of near-term macroeconomic conditions. Effectively, these would be based on interest rate differentials and prospects for inflation, as in the standard model of exchange rates. A country experiencing an economic boom with high interest rates would be expected to have a near-term exchange rate higher than its medium-term equilibrium, and conversely, a country in an economic slowdown would be expected to have a lower near-term rate.

Because of the uncertainties involved in estimating equilibrium exchange rates—for example, the three CGER approaches often give somewhat different results—it would be essential to establish a wide monitoring zone around the reference rate, at least ±10 percent and possibly as much as ±20 percent. Notably, one set of estimates of the disequilibrium among exchange rates of the G-20 countries in early 2011 ranged from −22 percent to +30 percent, with most estimates under 10 percent in absolute percentage points (Cline and Williamson 2011).

Reference Rates in Practice

The proposed reference rate system would not commit central banks to any specific level of intervention. In order to have a significant immediate effect on its exchange rate, an advanced-economy central bank would need to make very large purchases or sales of foreign currencies, but this would not be required under this proposed system. Instead, the aim would be for a central bank to make small to moderate interventions to provide a useful signal to the foreign exchange market that the central bank and the IMF believe the exchange rate has deviated significantly from its fundamental value—in other words, that there is an excessive risk premium.

Indeed, it is possible that central banks and the IMF have a better view of long-run exchange rate fundamentals than market participants, who can get caught up in short-run fads.[1] A recent study by Christopher Kubelec (2004) builds on this insight, finding evidence that central bank intervention is more effective when the exchange rate is far from its equilibrium rate and the intervention is aimed at returning the exchange rate toward that equilibrium. If central banks apply a strategy of buying low and selling high consistently over time, they should be able to make extra profits, which would gradually increase the credibility of their exchange rate pronouncements among market participants.

One central bank that appears to have embraced this approach is the Reserve Bank of Australia (RBA). Its view, clearly expressed on its website (www.rba.gov.au, accessed April 14, 2011), is that it may indeed know better than the financial markets. The RBA characterizes the foreign exchange market as subject to

> speculative bubbles, herding, fads, and other behavior which can drive market prices away from their equilibrium values, even in a market which is deep and liquid. When such overshooting occurs, intervention may help in limiting the move or returning the exchange rate toward its equilibrium level, thus obviating the need for costly adjustment by the real economy to the incorrect signals which the exchange rate would otherwise give.

The RBA notes that, over time, its intervention has shifted away from attempts to smooth short-term fluctuations and has moved toward less frequent operations aimed at large and relatively long-lasting misalignments. The acid test of such a strategy is profitability. The RBA has made excess profits on foreign exchange intervention during 1983–2003 as a whole as well as during each of three subperiods (Becker and Sinclair 2004).[2] The US Federal

---

1. Appendix 3A to chapter 3 noted that chartist trading strategies may be an important factor underlying exchange rate risk premiums.

2. Excess profits are defined as the difference between actual profits and profits on a hypothetical portfolio entirely invested in Australian dollars.

Reserve also has been profitable in its interventions on average during the floating rate period (Leahy 1995).[3]

A widespread and sustained reference rate strategy along these lines, with official support from the IMF, might have a gradual but transformative effect on financial markets. Such a strategy could be combined with verbal intervention—that is, communicating to markets when they appear to have things wrong. It also would be beneficial if central banks were to publicize their strategies, explain the long-run nature of their objectives, and stress the primacy of domestic objectives and the lack of any commitment to a specific value for their exchange rates. For economies with a high degree of capital mobility, the benefits of the reference rate strategy likely would be small at first, but they might build over time as financial markets came to more highly respect the track record of central bankers. The reference rate strategy would help to reduce harmful long-term swings in exchange rates, even if it had little effect on less damaging short-term ups and downs.

Reference Rates and the Global Saving Glut

The element of international cooperation inherent in the proposed reference rate system makes it a natural vehicle with which to counter the recent tendency of many developing economies to deliberately hold down the value of their currencies through massive purchases of foreign exchange. The reference rate rules would forbid these purchases of foreign exchange by central banks whose currencies were not judged by the IMF to be overvalued. In such cases, central banks seeking to put downward pressure on their currencies would have to lower their interest rates and accept any inflationary consequences. In other words, the reference rate system would put tighter restrictions on the policy freedom of central banks operating under conditions of imperfect capital mobility. Goldstein (2010) and Mattoo and Subramanian (2010) propose specific changes to international institutions to enforce such rules for all economies.

---

3. However, Humpage (2000) asserts that fewer than half of US interventions have been successful at changing market expectations of future exchange rate movements in the desired direction.

References

Abraham, Katharine. 1997. Testimony before the Senate Finance Committee, February 11. Available at at http://data.bls.gov/cgi-bin/print.pl/news.release/cpi.br21197.brief.htm (accessed on March 15, 2011).

Abraham, Katharine. 1998. Testimony before the Subcommittee on Human Resources of the House Committee on Government Reform and Oversight, April 29. Available at www.bls.gov/news.release/cpi.br042998.brief.htm (accessed on March 15, 2011).

Acosta-Ormaechea, Santiago, and David Coble. 2011. *Monetary Transmission in Dollarized and Non-Dollarized Economies: The Cases of Chile, New Zealand, Peru, and Uruguay.* IMF Working Paper WP/11/87. Washington: International Monetary Fund.

Adler, Matthew, and Gary Hufbauer. 2009. *Policy Liberalization and U.S. Merchandise Trade Growth, 1980–2006.* PIIE Working Paper 09-2. Washington: Peterson Institute for International Economics.

Aizenman, Joshua. 2004. Financial Opening: Evidence and Policy Options. In *Challenges to Globalization: Analyzing the Economics,* eds. Robert E. Baldwin and L. Alan Winters. Chicago: University of Chicago Press.

Aizenman, Joshua, Menzie Chinn, and Hito Ito. 2008. *Assessing the Emerging Global Financial Architecture: Measuring the Trilemma's Configuration over Time.* NBER Working Paper 14533. Cambridge, MA: National Bureau of Economic Research.

Akerlof, George, William Dickens, and George Perry. 1996. The Macroeconomics of Low Inflation. *Brookings Papers on Economic Activity,* no. 1: 1–76.

Allen, Mark, Christopher Rosenberg, Christian Keller, Brad Setser, and Nouriel Roubini. 2002. *A Balance Sheet Approach to Financial Crisis.* IMF Working Paper WP/02/210. Washington: International Monetary Fund.

Alvarez, Fernando, Andrew Atkeson, and Patrick Kehoe. 2007. *Time-Varying Risk, Interest Rates, and Exchange Rates in General Equilibrium.* Research Department Staff Report 371. Minneapolis, MN: Federal Reserve Bank of Minneapolis.

Alexius, Annika, and Anders Vredin. 1999. Pricing-to-Market in Swedish Exports. *Scandinavian Journal of Economics* 101, no. 2 (June): 223–39.

Andersen, Torben, Tim Bollerslev, Francis Diebold, and Clara Vega. 2007. Real-Time Price Discovery in Global Stock, Bond, and Foreign Exchange Markets. *Journal of International Economics* 73, no. 2: 251–77.

Armington, Paul. 1969. A Theory of Demand for Products Distinguished by Place of Production. *International Monetary Fund Staff Papers* 16: 159–78.Washington: International Monetary Fund.

Arteta, Carlos. 2005. Exchange Rate Regimes and Financial Dollarization: Does Flexibility Reduce Currency Mismatches in Bank Intermediation? *Berkeley Electronic Journals in Macroeconomics* 5, no. 1, article 10.

Auer, Raphael, and Thomas Chaney. 2009. Exchange Rate Pass-Through in a Competitive Model of Pricing-to-Market. *Journal of Money, Credit and Banking* 41: 151–75.

Bacchetta, Philippe, and Eric van Wincoop. 2006. Can Information Heterogeneity Explain the Exchange Rate Determination Puzzle? *American Economic Review* 96, no. 3: 552–76.

Bacchetta, Philippe, and Eric van Wincoop. 2007. Random Walk Expectations and the Forward Discount Puzzle. *American Economic Review* 97, no. 2: 346–50.

Backus, David, Federico Gavazzoni, Christopher Telmer, and Stanley Zin. 2010. *Monetary Policy and the Uncovered Interest Parity Puzzle.* NBER Working Paper 16218. Cambridge, MA: National Bureau of Economic Research.

Balassa, Bela. 1964. The Purchasing Power Parity Doctrine: A Reappraisal. *Journal of Political Economy* 72 (December): 584–96.

Baldwin, Richard. 2006. *The Euro's Trade Effects.* ECB Working Paper 594. Frankfurt: European Central Bank.

Bansal, Ravi, and Magnus Dahlquist. 2000. The Forward Premium Puzzle: Different Tales from Developed and Emerging Economies. *Journal of International Economics* 51: 115–44.

Barhoumi, Karim. 2006. Differences in Long-Run Exchange Rate Pass-Through into Import Prices in Developing Countries: An Empirical Investigation. *Economic Modelling* 23, no. 6 (December): 926–51.

Baxter, Marianne, and Alan Stockman. 1988. *Business Cycles and the Exchange Rate System: Some International Evidence.* NBER Working Paper 2689. Cambridge, MA: National Bureau of Economic Research.

Becker, Chris, and Michael Sinclair. 2004. *Profitability of Reserve Bank Foreign Exchange Operations: Twenty Years after the Float.* Research Discussion Paper 2004-06. Sydney: Reserve Bank of Australia.

Bekaert, Geert, Min Wei, and Yuhang Xing. 2007. Uncovered Interest Rate Parity and the Term Structure. *Journal of International Money and Finance* 26: 1038–69.

Berger, David, Jon Faust, John Rogers, and Kai Steverson. 2009. *Border Prices and Retail Prices.* International Finance Discussion Paper 972. Washington: Board of Governors of the Federal Reserve System.

Bergin, Paul. 2004. *How Well Can the New Open Economy Macroeconomics Explain the Exchange Rate and Current Account?* NBER Working Paper 10356. Cambridge, MA: National Bureau of Economic Research.

Bergin, Paul, and Robert Feenstra. 2007. *Pass-Through of Exchange Rates and Competition between Floaters and Fixers.* NBER Working Paper 13620. Cambridge, MA: National Bureau of Economic Research.

Bergin, Paul, Reuven Glick, and Jyh-Lin Wu. 2009. *The Micro-Macro Disconnect of Purchasing Power Parity.* NBER Working Paper 15624. Cambridge, MA: National Bureau of Economic Research.

Bergin, Paul, Hyung-Cheol Shin, and Ivan Tchakarov. 2006. Does Exchange Rate Variability Matter for Welfare? A Quantitative Investigation of Stabilization Policies. Unpublished manuscript, University of California, Davis.

Berman, Nicolas, Philippe Martin, and Thierry Mayer. 2010. How Do Different Exporters React to Exchange Rate Changes? Theory, Empirics, and Aggregate Implications. *European Summer Symposium in International Macroeconomics*: 1–38. Tarragona, Spain.

Bernanke, Ben. 2005. The Global Saving Glut and the US Current Account Deficit. The Sandridge Lecture, Virginia Association of Economics, March 10. Available at www.federalreserve.gov.

Bernanke, Ben. 2006. The Benefits of Price Stability. Speech at the Center for Economic Policy Studies and on the occasion of the Seventy-Fifth Anniversary of the Woodrow Wilson School of Public and International Affairs, Princeton University, February 24. Available at www.federalreserve.gov.

Bernanke, Ben. 2011. Global Imbalances: Links to Economic and Financial Stability. Speech at the Banque de France *Financial Stability Review* Launch Event (February 18). Available at www.federalreserve.gov.

Bernard, Andrew, J. Bradford Jensen, Stephen Redding, and Peter Schott. 2007. *Firms in International Trade*. NBER Working Paper 13054. Cambridge, MA: National Bureau of Economic Research.

Bernhofen, Daniel M. and Peng Xu. 2000. Exchange Rates and Market Power: Evidence from the Petrochemical Industry. *Journal of International Economics* 52: 283–97.

Bils, Mark, and Peter Klenow. 2004. Some Evidence on the Importance of Sticky Prices. *Journal of Political Economy* 112, no. 5: 947–85.

BIS (Bank for International Settlements). 2009. *79th Annual Report*. Basel.

BIS (Bank for International Settlements). 2010. *Triennial Central Bank Survey of Foreign Exchange and Derivatives Market Activity in 2010*. Basel.

Blanchard, Olivier. 2009. *The State of Macro*. NBER Working Paper 14259. Cambridge, MA: National Bureau of Economic Research.

Blanchard, Olivier, Giovanni Dell'Ariccia, and Paulo Mauro. 2010. *Rethinking Macroeconomic Policy*. IMF Staff Position Note SPN/10/03. Washington: International Monetary Fund.

Blanchard, Olivier, Francesco Giavazzi, and Filipa Sa. 2005. International Investors, the US Current Account, and the Dollar. *Brookings Papers on Economic Activity* 1: 1-49.

Bordo, Michael. 2003. *Exchange Rate Regime Choice in Historical Perspective*. NBER Working Paper 9654. Cambridge, MA: National Bureau of Economic Research.

Borio, Claudio, and William White. 2003. Whither Monetary and Financial Stability? The Implications of Evolving Policy Regimes. In *Monetary Policy and Uncertainty: Adapting to a Changing Economy*. Kansas City, MO: Federal Reserve Bank of Kansas City.

The Boskin Commission. 1996. Toward a More Accurate Measure of the Cost of Living. Final Report to the Senate Finance Committee from the Advisory Commission to Study the Consumer Price Index. Available at www.ssa.gov (accessed on March 8, 2011).

Branson, William, and Dale Henderson. 1985. The Specification and Influence of Asset Markets. In *Handbook of International Economics* II, eds. Ronald Jones and Peter Kenen. Amsterdam: Elsevier Science Publishers.

Brissimis, Sophocles N., and Theodora S. Kosma. 2007. Market Power and Exchange Rate Pass-Through. *International Review of Economics and Finance* 16: 202–22.

Broda, Christian, and David E. Weinstein. 2006. Globalization and the Gains from Variety. *Quarterly Journal of Economics* 121, no. 2: 541–85.

Broda, Christian, and David E. Weinstein. 2008. *Understanding International Price Differences Using Barcode Data*. NBER Working Paper 14017. Cambridge, MA: National Bureau of Economic Research.

Burnside, Craig, Martin Eichenbaum, Isaac Kleshchelski, and Sergio Rebelo. 2008. *Do Peso Problems Explain the Returns to the Carry Trade?* NBER Working Paper 14054. Cambridge, MA: National Bureau of Economic Research.

Burnside, Craig, Bing Han, David Hirshleifer, and Tracy Wang. 2011. Investor Overconfidence and the Forward Premium Puzzle. *Review of Economic Studies* 78, no. 2: 523–58.

Burstein, Ariel, Joao Neves, and Sergio Rebelo. 2003. Distribution Costs and Real Exchange Rate Dynamics during Exchange-Rate-Based Stabilizations. *Journal of Monetary Economics* 50, no. 6: 1189–214.

Bussiere, Matthieu, and Tuomas Peltonen. 2008. Exchange Rate Pass-Through in the Global Economy: The Role of Emerging Market Economies. Unpublished manuscript, Banque de France, Paris.

Calvo, Guillermo. 1998. Capital Flows and Capital-Market Crises: The Simple Economics of Sudden Stops. *Journal of Applied Economics* 1, no. 1: 35–54.

Calvo, Guillermo, and Carmen Reinhart. 2002. Fear of Floating. *Quarterly Journal of Economics* 117, no. 2: 379–408.

Campa, Jose, and Linda Goldberg. 2005. Exchange Rate Pass-Through into Import Prices. *Review of Economics and Statistics* 87, no. 4 (November): 679–90.

Campa, Jose, and Linda Goldberg. 2006. *Pass-Through of Exchange Rates to Consumption Prices: What Has Changed and Why?* NBER Working Paper 12547. Cambridge, MA: National Bureau of Economic Research.

Campa, Jose, and Jose Minguez. 2006. Differences in Exchange Rate Pass-Through in the Euro Area. *European Economic Review* 50, no. 1 (January): 121–45.

Caporale, Guglielmo, and Michael Chui. 1999. Estimating Income and Price Elasticities of Trade in a Cointegration Framework. *Review of International Economics* 7, no. 2: 254–64.

Caves, Richard, Jeffrey Frankel, and Ronald Jones. 2007. *World Trade and Payments: An Introduction,* 10th ed. Boston: Pearson Addison Wesley.

CGFS (Committee on the Global Financial System). 2007. *Financial Stability and Local Currency Bond Markets.* CGFS Papers 28. Basel.

Chaboud, Alain, and Jonathan Wright. 2005. Uncovered Interest Parity: It Works, but Not for Long. *Journal of International Economics* 66, no. 2: 349–62.

Cheung, Yin-Wong, Menzie Chinn, and Eiji Fujii. 2008. Pitfalls in Measuring Exchange Rate Misalignment: The Yuan and Other Currencies. *Open Economies Review* 20, no. 2: 183-206.

Cheung, Yin-Wong, Menzie Chinn, and Antonio Pascual. 2005. Empirical Exchange Rate Models of the Nineties: Are Any Fit to Survive? *Journal of International Money and Finance* 24: 1150–75.

Cheung, Yin-Wong, Kon Lai, and Michael Bergman. 2004. Dissecting the PPP Puzzle: The Unconventional Roles of Nominal Exchange Rate and Price Adjustments. *Journal of International Economics* 64: 135–50.

Chinn, Menzie. 2006. The (Partial) Rehabilitation of Interest Rate Parity in the Floating Rate Era: Longer Horizons, Alternative Expectations, and Emerging Markets. *Journal of International Money and Finance* 25: 7–21.

Chinn, Menzie, and Jeffrey Frankel. 1994. Patterns in Exchange Rate Forecasts for Twenty-Five Currencies. *Journal of Money, Credit and Banking* 26, no. 4: 759–70.

Chinn, Menzie, and Guy Meredith. 2004. Monetary Policy and Long-Horizon Uncovered Interest Parity. *IMF Staff Papers* 51, no. 3: 409–30.

Chong, Yanping, Oscar Jorda, and Alan Taylor. 2010. *The Harrod-Balassa-Samuelson Hypothesis: Real Exchange Rates and their Long-Run Equilibrium.* NBER Working Paper 15868. Cambridge, MA: National Bureau of Economic Research.

Choudhri, Ehsan, and Dalia Hakura. 2006. Exchange Rate Pass-Through to Domestic Prices: Does the Inflationary Environment Matter? *Journal of International Money and Finance* 25: 614–39.

Choudhri, Ehsan, Hamid Faruqee, and Dalia Hakura. 2005. Explaining the Exchange Rate Pass-Through in Different Prices. *Journal of International Economics* 65, no. 2: 349–74.

Chung, Hess, Jean-Philippe Laforte, David Reifschneider, and John Williams. 2011. *Have We Underestimated the Likelihood and Severity of Zero Lower Bound Events?* Working Paper 2011-01. San Francisco, CA: Federal Reserve Bank of San Francisco.

Clarida, Richard, Jordi Galí, and Mark Gertler. 1998. Monetary Policy Rules in Practice: Some International Evidence. *European Economic Review* 42: 1033–67.

Clarida, Richard, and Daniel Waldman. 2008. Is Bad News about Inflation Good News for the Exchange Rate? And, If So, Can That Tell Us Anything about the Conduct of Monetary Policy? In *Asset Prices and Monetary Policy,* ed. John Campbell. Chicago: University of Chicago Press.

Cline, William. 1989. *United States External Adjustment and the World Economy.* Washington: Institute for International Economics.

Cline, William, and John Williamson. 2011. *Estimates of Fundamental Equilibrium Exchange Rates, May 2011.* Policy Briefs in International Economics 11-5. Washington: Peterson Institute for International Economics.

Cogley, Timothy, and Thomas Sargent. 2005. Drifts and Volatilities: Monetary Policies and Outcomes in the Post WWII US. *Review of Economic Dynamics* 8: 262–302.

Corsetti, Giancarlo, Luca Dedola, and Sylvain Leduc. 2007. *Optimal Monetary Policy and the Sources of Local-Currency Price Stability.* NBER Working Paper 13544. Cambridge, MA: National Bureau of Economic Research.

Corsetti, Giancarlo, Luca Dedola, and Sylvain Leduc. Forthcoming. Optimal Monetary Policy in Open Economies. In *Handbook of Monetary Economics,* vol. III, eds. Benjamin Friedman and Michael Woodford. Available at www.eui.eu/personal/corsetti (accessed on January 25, 2011).

Das, Sanghamitra, Mark Roberts, and James Tybout. 2007. Market Entry Costs, Producer Heterogeneity, and Export Dynamics. *Econometrica* 75, no. 3: 837–73.

Dell'Ariccia, Giovanni, Julian di Giovanni, Andre Faria, M. Ayhan Kose, Paolo Mauro, Martin Schindler, Marco Terrones, and Jonathan Ostry. 2008. *Reaping the Benefits of Financial Globalization.* IMF Occasional Paper 264. Washington: International Monetary Fund.

Dellas, Harris, and George Tavlas. 2009. An Optimum-Currency-Area Odyssey. *Journal of International Money and Finance* 28: 1117–37.

De Grauwe, Paul. 2011. *The Governance of a Fragile Eurozone.* CEPS Working Document 346. Brussels: Centre for European Policy Studies.

De Grauwe, Paul, and Marianna Grimaldi. 2006. *The Exchange Rate in a Behavioral Finance Framework.* Princeton, NJ: Princeton University Press.

Di Mauro, Filippo, Sara Formai, Jaime Marquez, and Chiara Osbat. 2011. Pricing to Market by European Automobile Exporters. Chap. 17 in *Recovery and Beyond: Lessons for Trade Adjustment and Competitiveness,* eds. Filippo Di Mauro and Benjamin Mandel. Frankfurt: European Central Bank.

Dornbusch, Rudiger. 1976. Expectations and Exchange Rate Dynamics. *Journal of Political Economy* 84, no. 6 (December): 1161–76.

Dutoit, Laure, Karla Hernandez-Villafuerte, and Cristobal Urrutia. 2009. Price Transmission in Latin American Maize and Rice Markets. Unpublished manuscript, Economic Commission for Latin America and the Caribbean, Santiago. Available at www.cepal.org.

Eaton, Jonathan, and Samuel Kortum. 2002. Technology, Geography, and Trade. *Econometrica* 70, no. 5: 1741–79.

Edison, Hali. 1987. Purchasing Power Parity in the Long Run: A Test of the Dollar/Pound Exchange Rate (1890–1978). *Journal of Money, Credit and Banking* 19, no. 3: 376–87.

Edison, Hali, Joseph Gagnon, and William Melick. 1997. Understanding the Empirical Literature on Purchasing Power Parity: The Post-Bretton Woods Era. *Journal of International Money and Finance* 16, no. 1: 1–17.

Edison, Hali, and B. Dianne Pauls. 1993. A Re-assessment of the Relationship between Real Exchange Rates and Real Interest Rates: 1974–1990. *Journal of Monetary Economics* 31, no. 2: 165–87.

Emerson, Michael, Daniel Gros, and Alexander Italianer. 1990. One Market, One Money: An Evaluation of the Potential Benefits and Costs of Forming an Economic and Monetary Union. *European Economy* 44. Brussels: Commission of the European Communities.

Engel, Charles. 1996. The Forward Discount Anomaly and the Risk Premium: A Survey of Recent Evidence. *Journal of Empirical Finance* 3: 123–92.

Engel, Charles. 1999. Accounting for US Real Exchange Rate Changes. *Journal of Political Economy* 107, no. 3: 507–38.

Engel, Charles. 2002. *The Responsiveness of Consumer Prices to Exchange Rates and the Implications for Exchange-Rate Policy: A Survey of a Few Recent New Open-Economy Macro Models.* NBER Working Paper 8725. Cambridge, MA: National Bureau of Economic Research.

Engel, Charles. 2009. *Exchange Rate Policies.* Federal Reserve Bank of Dallas Staff Papers 8 (November). Dallas, TX: Federal Reserve Bank of Dallas.

Engel, Charles. 2010. The Real Exchange Rate, Real Interest Rates, and the Risk Premium. Unpublished manuscript, University of Wisconsin, Madison. Available at www.ssc.wisc.edu/~cengel/working_papers.htm.

Engel, Charles, Nelson Mark, and Kenneth West. 2008. Exchange Rate Models Are Not as Bad as You Think. *NBER Macroeconomics Annual 2008*: 381–441. Cambridge, MA: National Bureau of Economic Research.

Engel, Charles, and John Rogers. 1996. How Wide Is the Border? *American Economic Review* 86, no. 5: 1112–25.

Engel, Charles, and Kenneth West. 2006. Taylor Rules and the Deutschemark-Dollar Real Exchange Rate. *Journal of Money, Credit and Banking* 38, no. 5: 1175–94.

Erceg, Christopher, Luca Guerrieri, and Christopher Gust. 2006. SIGMA: A New Open Economy Model for Policy Analysis. *International Journal of Central Banking* 2, no. 1: 1–50.

Fair, Ray. 2003. Shock Effects on Stocks, Bonds, and Exchange Rates. *Journal of International Money and Finance* 22: 307–41.

Farhi, Emmanuel, Samuel Fraiberger, Xavier Gabaix, Romain Ranciere, and Adrien Verdelhan. 2009. *Crash Risk in Currency Markets.* NBER Working Paper 15062. Cambridge, MA: National Bureau of Economic Research.

Faruqee, Hamid. 1995. Long-Run Determinants of the Real Exchange Rate: A Stock-Flow Perspective. *IMF Staff Papers* 42, no. 1.

Faust, Jon, John Rogers, Shing-Yi Wang, and Jonathan Wright. 2007. The High-Frequency Response of Exchange Rates and Interest Rates to Macroeconomic Announcements. *Journal of Monetary Economics* 54, no. 4: 1051–68.

Feenstra, Robert. 1994. New Product Varieties and the Measurement of International Prices. *American Economic Review* 84, no. 1: 157–77.

Feenstra, Robert, Joseph Gagnon, and Michael Knetter. 1996. Market Share and Exchange Rate Pass-Through in World Automobile Trade. *Journal of International Economics* 40: 187–207.

Feenstra, Robert, Maurice Obstfeld, and Katheryn Russ. 2010. In Search of the Armington Elasticity. Unpublished manuscript, University of California, Davis.

Feenstra, Robert, and Alan Taylor. 2008. *International Macroeconomics.* New York: Worth Publishers.

Feinberg, Robert M. 1996. A Simultaneous Analysis of Exchange-Rate Passthrough into Prices of Imperfectly Substitutable Domestic and Import Goods. *International Review of Economics and Finance* 5, no.4: 407–16.

Flood, Robert, and Andrew Rose. 1995. Fixing Exchange Rates: A Virtual Quest for Fundamentals, *Journal of Monetary Economics* 36, no. 1: 3–37.

Frankel, Jeffrey. 1986. *International Capital Mobility and Crowding Out in the US Economy: Imperfect Integration of Financial Markets or of Goods Markets?* NBER Working Paper 1773. Cambridge, MA: National Bureau of Economic Research.

Frankel, Jeffrey. 1999. *No Single Currency Regime Is Right for All Countries or at All Times.* NBER Working Paper 7338. Cambridge, MA: National Bureau of Economic Research.

Frankel, Jeffrey, David Parsley, and Shang-Jin Wei. 2005. *Slow Pass-Through around the World: A New Import for Developing Countries?* NBER Working Paper 11199. Cambridge, MA: National Bureau of Economic Research.

Froot, Kenneth, and Jeffrey Frankel. 1989. Forward Discount Bias: Is It an Exchange Rate Risk Premium? *Quarterly Journal of Economics* 104, no. 1: 139–61.

Gagnon, Etienne, Benjamin Mandel, and Robert Vigfusson. 2011. Don't Panic: The Hitchhiker's Guide to Missing Import Price Changes. Unpublished manuscript, Board of Governors of the Federal Reserve System.

Gagnon, Joseph. 1989. Adjustment Costs and International Trade Dynamics. *Journal of International Economics* 26: 327–44.

Gagnon, Joseph. 1996. *Net Foreign Assets and Equilibrium Exchange Rates: Panel Evidence.* International Finance Discussion Paper 574. Washington: Board of Governors of the Federal Reserve System.

Gagnon, Joseph. 2006. The Effect of Exchange Rates on Prices, Wages, and Profits: A Case Study of the United Kingdom in the 1990s. *International Economic Journal* 20, no. 2: 149–60.

Gagnon, Joseph. 2008. Growth-Led Exports: Implications for the Cross-Country Effects of Shocks to Potential Output. *The Berkeley Electronic Journal of Macroeconomics* 8, no. 1: Article 2.

Gagnon, Joseph. 2009a. *Currency Crashes in Industrial Countries: Much Ado about Nothing?* International Finance Discussion Papers 966. Board of Governors of the Federal Reserve System.

Gagnon, Joseph. 2009b. Currency Crashes and Bond Yields in Industrial Countries. *Journal of International Money and Finance* 28: 161–81.

Gagnon, Joseph. 2010. Currency Crashes in Industrial Countries: What Determines Good and Bad Outcomes? *International Finance* 13, no. 2: 165–94.

Gagnon, Joseph, and Jane Ihrig. 2004. Monetary Policy and Exchange Rate Pass-Through. *International Journal of Finance and Economics* 9: 315–38.

Gagnon, Joseph, and Michael Knetter. 1995. Markup Adjustment and Exchange Rate Fluctuations: Evidence from Panel Data on Automobile Exports. *Journal of International Money and Finance* 14, no. 2: 289–310.

Gagnon, Joseph, Matthew Raskin, Julie Remache, and Brian Sack. 2011. The Financial Market Effects of the Federal Reserve's Large-Scale Asset Purchases. *International Journal of Central Banking* 7, no. 1: 3–44.

Galí, Jordi. 2008. *Monetary Policy, Inflation, and the Business Cycle: An Introduction to the New Keynesian Framework.* Princeton, NJ: Princeton University Press.

Ghosh, Atish, Anne-Marie Gulde, and Holger Wolf. 2002. *Exchange Rate Regimes: Choices and Consequences.* Cambridge, MA: MIT Press.

Ghosh, Atish, Jonathan Ostry, and Charalambos Tsangarides. 2010. *Exchange Rate Regimes and the Stability of the International Monetary System.* IMF Occasional Paper 270. Washington: International Monetary Fund.

Gil-Pareja, Salvador. 2003. Pricing to Market Behaviour in European Car Markets. *European Economic Review* 47: 945–962.

Goldberg, Pinelopi, and Rebecca Hellerstein. 2007. *A Framework for Identifying the Sources of Local-Currency Price Stability with an Empirical Application.* NBER Working Paper 13183. Cambridge, MA: National Bureau of Economic Research.

Goldberg, Pinelopi, and Michael Knetter. 1997. Goods Prices and Exchange Rates: What Have We Learned? *Journal of Economic Literature* 35 (September): 1243–72.

Goldberg, Pinelopi, and Frank Verboven. 1998. *The Evolution of Price Dispersion in the European Car Market*. NBER Working Paper 6818. Cambridge, MA: National Bureau of Economic Research.

Goldfajn, Ilan, and Sergio Werlang. 2000. *The Pass-Through from Depreciation to Inflation: A Panel Study*. Banco Central do Brasil Working Paper 5. Brasilia: Banco Central do Brasil.

Goldstein, Morris. 2002. *Managed Floating Plus*. Washington: Institute for International Economics.

Goldstein, Morris. 2010. *Confronting Asset Bubbles, Too Big to Fail, and Beggar-thy-Neighbor Exchange Rate Policies*. Policy Briefs in International Economics 10-3. Washington: Peterson Institute for International Economics.

Goldstein, Morris, and Mohsin Khan. 1985. Income and Price Effects in Foreign Trade. In *Handbook of International Economics*, vol. 2, eds. Ronald Jones and Peter Kenen. Amsterdam: North-Holland.

Gopinath, Gita, Oleg Itskhoki, and Roberto Rigobon. 2007. *Currency Choice and Exchange Rate Pass-Through*. NBER Working Paper 13432. Cambridge, MA: National Bureau of Economic Research.

Gopinath, Gita and Oleg Itskhoki. 2008. *Frequency of Price Adjustment and Pass-Through*. NBER Working Paper 14200. Cambridge, MA: National Bureau of Economic Research.

Gottfries, Nils. 2002. Market Shares, Financial Constraints and Pricing Behaviour in the Export Market. *Economica* 69, no. 276 (November): 583–607.

Gourinchas, Pierre-Olivier, and Olivier Jeanne. 2009. *Capital Flows to Developing Countries: The Allocation Puzzle*. PIIE Working Paper 09-12. Washington: Peterson Institute for International Economics.

Gourinchas, Pierre-Olivier, and Aaron Tornell. 2002. *Exchange Rate Dynamics, Learning and Misperceptions*. NBER Working Paper 9391. Cambridge, MA: National Bureau of Economic Research.

Gron, Anne, and Deborah L. Swenson. 1996. Incomplete Exchange-Rate Pass-Through and Imperfect Competition: The Effect of Local Production. *American Economic Review* 86, no. 2, (May): 71–76.

Gross, Dominique M., and Nicolas Schmitt. 2000. Exchange Rate Pass-Through and Dynamic Oligopoly: An Empirical Investigation. *Journal of International Economics* 52: 89–112.

Gust, Christopher, Sylvain Leduc, and Robert Vigfusson. 2010a. Trade Integration, Competition, and the Decline in Exchange Rate Pass-Through. *Journal of Monetary Economics* 57: 309–24.

Gust, Christopher, Sylvain Leduc, and Robert Vigfusson. 2010b. *Entry Dynamics and the Decline in Exchange Rate Pass-Through*. International Finance Discussion Papers 1008. Washington: Board of Governors of the Federal Reserve System.

Gust, Christopher, and David Lopez-Salido. 2009. *Portfolio Inertia and the Equity Premium*. International Finance Discussion Paper 984. Washington: Board of Governors of the Federal Reserve System.

Hamilton, James, and Cynthia Wu. 2011. The Effectiveness of Alternative Monetary Policy Tools in a Zero Lower Bound Environment. *Journal of Money, Credit, and Banking* forthcoming.

Harrigan, James. 1993. OECD Imports and Trade Barriers in 1983. *Journal of International Economics* 35: 91–111.

Harrod, Roy. 1933. *International Economics*. Cambridge, UK: Cambridge University Press.

Henning, C. Randall. 1994. *Currencies and Politics in the United States, Germany, and Japan*. Washington: Institute for International Economics.

Holden, Steiner, and Fredrik Wulfsberg. 2008. Downward Nominal Wage Rigidity in the OECD. *The Berkeley Electronic Journal of Macroeconomics* 8, no. 1, article 15.

Hooper, Peter, Karen Johnson, and Jaime Marquez. 2000. *Trade Elasticities for the G-7 Countries.* Princeton Studies in International Economics 87. Princeton, NJ: Princeton University.

Horvath, Michael, and Mark Watson. 1995. Testing for Cointegration When Some of the Cointegrating Vectors Are Prespecified. *Econometric Theory* 11, no. 5: 984–1014.

Hummels, David. 2007. Transportation Costs and International Trade in the Second Era of Globalization. *Journal of Economic Perspectives* 21, no. 3: 131–54.

Humpage, Owen. 2000. The United States as an Informed Foreign-Exchange Speculator. *Journal of International Financial Markets, Institutions, and Money* 10: 287–302.

Ihrig, Jane, Mario Marazzi, and Alexander Rothenberg. 2006. *Exchange-Rate Pass-Through in the G-7 Countries.* International Finance Discussion Papers 851. Washington: Board of Governors of the Federal Reserve System.

Imbs, Jean, Haroon Mumtaz, and Helene Rey. 2003. *PPP Strikes Back: Aggregation and the Real Exchange Rate.* IMF Working Paper WP/03/68. Washington: International Monetary Fund.

IMF (International Monetary Fund). 1993. Sweden—Recent Economic Developments. Staff Memorandum SM/93/169 (August 3). Washington.

IMF (International Monetary Fund). 2009. *World Economic Outlook* (April). Washington

IMF (International Monetary Fund). 2010. *Annual Report on Exchange Arrangements and Exchange Restrictions.* Washington.

IMF (International Monetary Fund). 2011a. *Assessing Reserve Adequacy.* Document prepared by Monetary and Capital Markets, Research, and Strategy, Policy, and Review Departments. Washington.

IMF (International Monetary Fund). 2011b. *World Economic Outlook* (April). Washington

Ito, Hiro, and Menzie Chinn. 2007. Price-Based Measurement of Financial Globalization: A Cross-Country Study of Interest Rate Parity. *Pacific Economic Review* 12, no. 4: 419–44.

Ito, Takatoshi, and Kiyotaka Sato. 2006. *Exchange Rate Changes and Inflation in Post-Crisis Asian Economies: VAR Analysis of the Exchange Rate Pass-Through.* NBER Working Paper 12395. Cambridge, MA: National Bureau of Economic Research.

Jeanne, Olivier, and Andrew Rose. 2002. Noise Trading and Exchange Rate Regimes. *Quarterly Journal of Economics* 117, no. 2: 537–69.

Jeanne, Olivier, and Anton Korinek. 2010. *Excessive Volatility in Capital Flows: A Pigouvian Taxation Approach.* NBER Working Paper 15927. Cambridge, MA: National Bureau of Economic Research.

Jensen, J. Bradford, and Lori Kletzer. 2005. *Tradable Services: Understanding the Scope and Impact of Services Outsourcing.* PIIE Working Paper 05-9. Washington: Peterson Institute for International Economics.

Jevons, William. 1875. *Money and the Mechanism of Exchange.* New York: D. Appleton and Company.

Johnson, Simon, William Larson, Chris Papageorgiou, and Arvind Subramanian. 2009. *Is Newer Better? Penn World Table Revisions and Their Impact on Growth Estimates.* CGD Working Paper 191. Washington: Center for Global Development.

Jorda, Oscar, and Alan Taylor. 2009. *The Carry Trade and Fundamentals: Nothing to Fear but FEER Itself.* NBER Working Paper 15518. Cambridge, MA: National Bureau of Economic Research.

Joyce, Michael, Ana Lasaosa, Ibrahim Stevens, and Matthew Tong. 2010. *The Financial Market Impact of Quantitative Easing.* Working Paper 393. London: Bank of England.

Kadiyali, Vrinda. 1997. Exchange Rate Pass-Through for Strategic Pricing and Advertising: An Empirical Analysis of the U.S. Photographic Film Industry. *Journal of International Economics* 43: 437–61.

Katada, Saori, and C. Randall Henning. 2010. Too Nested to Hatch? East Asian and European Currency Arrangements under Dollar Dependence. Manuscript presented at the workshop on Institutionalizing Asia: Theory, Practice, and Power in Time, University of Washington, Seattle, September 29.

Kenen, Peter. 1969. The Theory of Optimum Currency Areas: An Eclectic View. In *Monetary Problems of the International Economy,* eds. Robert Mundell and Alexander Swoboda. Chicago: University of Chicago Press.

Keynes, J. Maynard. 1936. *The General Theory of Employment, Interest and Money.* London: Palgrave Macmillan.

Khan, Mohsin, and Abdelhak Senhadji. 2001. Threshold Effects in the Relationship between Inflation and Growth. *IMF Staff Papers* 48, no. 1: 1–25.

Killeen, William, Richard Lyons, and Michael Moore. 2006. Fixed versus Flexible: Lessons from EMS Order Flow. *Journal of International Money and Finance* 25: 551–79.

Klein, Michael, and Jay Shambaugh. 2010. *Exchange Rate Regimes in the Modern Era.* Cambridge, MA: MIT Press.

Knetter, Michael. 1989. Price Discrimination by US and German Exporters. *American Economic Review* 79, no. 1: 198–210.

Kohn, Donald. 2008. Monetary Policy and Asset Prices Revisited. Speech at Cato Institute, Washington, DC, November 19. Available at www.federalreserve.gov.

Krugman, Paul. 1989a. Differences in Income Elasticities and Trends in Real Exchange Rates. *European Economic Review* 33, no. 5: 1031–46.

Krugman, Paul. 1989b. *Exchange-Rate Instability.* Cambridge, MA: The MIT Press.

Krugman, Paul, and Maurice Obstfeld. 2000. *International Economics: Theory and Policy,* 5th ed. Reading, MA: Addison-Wesley.

Kubelec, Christopher. 2004. Intervention When Exchange Rate Misalignments Are Large. In *Dollar Adjustment: How Far? Against What?* eds. C. Fred Bergsten and John Williamson. Washington: Peterson Institute for International Economics.

Kumhof, Michael, Douglas Laxton, Dirk Muir, and Susanna Mursula. 2010. *The Global Integrated Monetary and Fiscal Model (GIMF): Theoretical Structure.* IMF Working Paper WP/10/34. Washington: International Monetary Fund.

Kuttner, Kenneth, and Adam Posen. 2001. Beyond Bipolar: A Three-Dimensional Assessment of Monetary Frameworks. *International Journal of Finance and Economics* 6, no. 4: 369–87.

Lai, Huiwen, and Daniel Trefler. 2002. *The Gains from Trade with Monopolistic Competition: Specification, Estimation, and Mis-specification.* NBER Working Paper 9169. Cambridge, MA: National Bureau of Economic Research.

Lane, Philip. 2006. The Real Effects of European Monetary Union. *Journal of Economic Perspectives* 20, no. 4: 47–66.

Lane, Philip, and Gian-Maria Milesi-Ferretti. 2002. Long-Term Capital Movements. In *NBER Macroeconomics Annual 2001,* eds. Ben Bernanke and Kenneth Rogoff. Cambridge, MA: National Bureau of Economic Research. 73–116.

Leahy, Michael. 1995. The Profitability of US Intervention in the Foreign Exchange Markets. *Journal of International Money and Finance* 14, no. 6: 823–44.

Lee, Jaewoo. 1997. The Response of Exchange Rate Pass-Through to Market Concentration in a Small Economy: The Evidence from Korea. *Review of Economics and Statistics* 79, no. 1 (February): pp. 142–45.

Lee, Jaewoo, Gian Maria Milesi-Ferretti, Jonathan Ostry, Alessandro Prati, and Luca Ricci. 2008. *Exchange Rate Assessments: CGER Methodologies.* IMF Occasional Paper 261. Washington: International Monetary Fund.

Lee, Jaewoo, and Man-Keung Tang. 2007. Does Productivity Growth Appreciate the Real Exchange Rate? *Review of International Economics* 15, no. 1: 164–87.

Levy-Yeyati, Eduardo, and Federico Sturzenegger. 2003. To Float or to Fix: Evidence on the Impact of Exchange Rate Regimes on Growth. *American Economic Review* 93, no. 4: 1173–93.

Lothian, James, and Mark Taylor. 2008. Real Exchange Rates over the Past Two Centuries: How Important Is the Harrod-Balassa-Samuelson Effect? *Economic Journal* 118 (October): 1742–63.

Lustig, Hanno, and Adrien Verdelhan. 2007. The Cross-Section of Foreign Currency Risk Premia and Consumption Growth Risk. *American Economic Review* 97, no. 1: 89–117.

Lutz, Matthias. 2000. *Pricing in Segmented Markets, Arbitrage and the Law of One Price: Evidence from the European Car Market.* CSGR Working Paper 53/00. Warwick, UK: Centre for the Study of Globalisation and Regionalisation.

Magud, Nicolas, Carmen Reinhart, and Kenneth Rogoff. 2011. *Capital Controls: Myth and Reality—A Portfolio Balance Approach.* Working Paper 11-7. Washington: Peterson Institute for International Economics.

Marazzi, Mario, and Nathan Sheets. 2007. Declining Exchange Rate Pass-Through to US Import Prices: The Potential Role of Global Factors. *Journal of International Money and Finance* 26, no. 6 (October): 924–47.

Maria-Dolores, Ramon. 2010. Exchange Rate Pass-Through in New Member States and Candidate Countries of the EU. *International Review of Economics and Finance* 19, no. 1 (January): 23–35.

Mark, Nelson. 2009. Changing Monetary Policy Rules, Learning, and Real Exchange Rate Dynamics. *Journal of Money, Credit and Banking* 41 no. 6: 1047–70.

Marquez, Jaime. 2002. *Estimating Trade Elasticities.* Boston: Kluwer Academic Publishers.

Mattoo, Aaditya, and Arvind Subramanian. 2010. *Currency Undervaluation and Sovereign Wealth Funds: A New Role for the World Trade Organization.* Working Paper 08-2. Washington: Peterson Institute for International Economics.

McCarthy, Jonathan. 2000. Pass-Through of Exchange Rates and Import Prices to Domestic Inflation in Some Industrialized Economies. Federal Reserve Bank of New York Staff Report 111. New York: Federal Reserve Bank of New York.

McKinnon, Ronald. 1963. Optimum Currency Areas. *American Economic Review* 53: 717–24.

McKinnon, Ronald. 2010. Rehabilitating the Unloved Dollar Standard. *Asian-Pacific Economic Literature.* Canberra: Crawford School of Economics and Government, Australian National University.

Meese, Richard, and Kenneth Rogoff. 1983. Empirical Exchange Rate Models of the Seventies: Do They Fit Out of Sample? *Journal of International Economics* 14: 3–24.

Meyer, Laurence, Brian Doyle, Joseph Gagnon, and Dale Henderson. 2004. International Coordination of Macroeconomic Policies: Still Alive in the New Millennium? In *The IMF and Its Critics: Reform of Global Financial Architecture,* eds. David Vines and Christopher Gilbert. Cambridge, UK: Cambridge University Press.

Mundell, Robert. 1961. A Theory of Optimum Currency Areas. *American Economic Review* 51: 509–17.

Mundell, Robert. 2011. International Monetary Reform 2011. Presentation at the G-20 Seminar in Nanjing, China, March 31. Available at http://robertmundell.net.

Mussa, Michael. 1986. Nominal Exchange Rate Regimes and the Behavior of Real Exchange Rates: Evidence and Implications. *Carnegie-Rochester Conference Series on Public Policy* 25: 117–214.

Mussa, Michael, Paul Masson, Alexander Swoboda, Esteban Jadresic, Paolo Mauro, and Andrew Berg. 2000. *Exchange Rate Regimes in an Increasingly Integrated World Economy.* IMF Occasional Paper 193. Washington: International Monetary Fund.

Nakamura, Emi, and Dawit Zerom. 2009. *Accounting for Incomplete Pass-Through.* NBER Working Paper 15255. Cambridge, MA: National Bureau of Economic Research.

Nakamura, Emi, and Jón Steinsson. 2009. *Lost in Transit: Product Replacement Bias and Pricing to Market.* NBER Working Paper 15359. Cambridge, MA: National Bureau of Economic Research.

Obstfeld, Maurice, and Kenneth Rogoff. 1995. The Mirage of Fixed Exchange Rates. *Journal of Economic Perspectives* 9, no. 4: 73–96.

Obstfeld, Maurice, and Kenneth Rogoff. 2000. *The Six Major Puzzles in International Macroeconomics: Is There a Common Cause?* NBER Working Paper 7777. Cambridge, MA: National Bureau of Economic Research.

Obstfeld, Maurice, Jay Shambaugh, and Alan Taylor. 2004. *The Trilemma in History: Tradeoffs among Exchange Rates, Monetary Policies, and Capital Mobility.* NBER Working Paper 10396. Cambridge, MA: National Bureau of Economic Research.

O'Connell, Paul. 1998. The Overvaluation of Purchasing Power Parity. *Journal of International Economics* 44, no. 1: 1–19.

OECD (Organization for Economic Cooperation and Development). 2001. *Economic Outlook 2001/2.* Paris.

Olivei, Giovanni. 2002. Exchange Rates and the Prices of Manufacturing Products Imported into the United States. *New England Economic Review* (First Quarter): 3–18.

Ostry, Jonathan, Atish Ghosh, Karl Habermeier, Marcos Chamon, Mahvash Qureshi, and Dennis Reinhardt. 2010. *Capital Inflows: The Role of Controls.* IMF Staff Position Note SPN/10/04. Washington: International Monetary Fund.

Ostry, Jonathan, Atish Ghosh, Karl Habermeier, Luc Laeven, Marcos Chamon, Mahvash Qureshi, and Annamaria Kokenyne. 2011. *Managing Capital Inflows: What Tools to Use?* IMF Staff Discussion Note SDN/11/06. Washington: International Monetary Fund.

Palais-Royal Initiative. 2011. Reform of the International Monetary System: A Cooperative Approach for the Twenty First Century. Paris. Available at www.elysee.fr.

Papell, David, and Ruxandra Prodan. 2003. Long-Run Purchasing Power Parity: Cassel or Balassa-Samuelson? Unpublished manuscript, University of Houston, Texas.

Parsley, David, and Helen Popper. 2010. Understanding Real Exchange Rate Movements with Trade in Intermediate Products. *Pacific Economic Review* 15, no. 2: 171–88.

Parsley, David, and Shang-Jin Wei. 2001. Explaining the Border Effect: The Role of Exchange Rate Variability, Shipping Costs, and Geography. *Journal of International Economics* 55, no. 1: 87–105.

Plantin, Guillaume, and Hyun Shin. 2006. Carry Trades and Speculative Dynamics. Unpublished manuscript, Princeton University, Princeton, NJ. Available at http://ssrn.com/abstract=898412.

Pollard, Patricia, and Cletus Coughlin. 2003. *Size Matters: Asymmetric Exchange Rate Pass-Through at the Industry Level.* Working Paper 2003-029C. St. Louis, MO: Federal Reserve Bank of St. Louis.

Posen, Adam. 2009. Finding the Right Tool for Dealing with Asset Price Booms. Speech at the MPR Monetary Policy and Markets Conference, London, December 1. Available at www.bankofengland.co.uk/publications/news/2009/131.htm.

Prasad, Eswar, Raghuram Rajan, and Arvind Subramanian. 2007. Foreign Capital and Economic Growth. *Brookings Papers on Economic Activity* 1: 153–209.

Qureshi, Mahvash, and Charalambos Tsangarides. 2010. *The Empirics of Exchange Rate Regimes and Trade: Words vs. Deeds.* IMF Working Paper WP/10/48. Washington: International Monetary Fund.

Reinhart, Carmen, and Kenneth Rogoff. 2004. The Modern History of Exchange Rate Arrangements: A Reinterpretation. *Quarterly Journal of Economics.* 119, no. 1: 1–48.

Reinhart, Carmen, Kenneth Rogoff, and Miguel Savastano. 2003. *Addicted to Dollars.* NBER Working Paper 10015. Cambridge, MA: National Bureau of Economic Research.

Ricci, Luca, and Federico Trionfetti. 2011. *Evidence on Productivity, Comparative Advantage, and Networks in the Export Performance of Firms.* IMF Working Paper WP/11/77. Washington: International Monetary Fund.

Rodrik, Dani, and Arvind Subramanian. 2009. Why Did Financial Globalization Disappoint? *IMF Staff Papers* 56: 112–38.

Rogoff, Kenneth. 1996. The Purchasing Power Parity Puzzle. *Journal of Economic Literature* 34, no. 2: 647–68.

Rogoff, Kenneth, Aasim Husain, Ashoka Mody, Robin Brooks, and Nienke Oomes. 2003. *Evolution and Performance of Exchange Rate Regimes*. IMF Working Paper WP/03/243. Washington: International Monetary Fund.

Rose, Andrew. 2000. One Money, One Market: Estimating the Effect of Common Currencies on Trade. *Economic Policy: A European Forum* 30 (April): 7–33.

Rose, Andrew. 2008. Is EMU Becoming an Optimum Currency Area? The Evidence on Trade and Business Cycle Synchronization. Unpublished manuscript. University of California, Berkeley.

Rose, Andrew. 2010. Exchange Rate Regimes in the Modern Era: Fixed, Floating, and Flaky. Unpublished manuscript, University of California, Berkeley, September 12. Available at http://faculty.haas.berkeley.edu/arose.

Rose, Andrew, and Eric van Wincoop. 2001. National Money as a Barrier to International Trade: The Real Case for Currency Union. *American Economic Review* 91, no. 2: 386–90.

Ruhl, Kim. 2008. The International Elasticity Puzzle. Unpublished manuscript, University of Texas, Austin.

Samuelson, Paul. 1964. Theoretical Notes on Trade Problems. *Review of Economics and Statistics* 46 (March): 145–54.

Sargent, Thomas. 1982. The Ends of Four Big Inflations. In *Inflation: Causes and Effects*, ed. Robert Hall. Chicago: University of Chicago Press.

Senhadji, Abdelhak. 1998. Time-Series Estimation of Structural Import Demand Equations: A Cross-Country Analysis. *International Monetary Fund Staff Papers* 45, no. 2: 236–66.

Senhadji, Abdelhak, and Claudio Montenegro. 1999. Time-Series Analysis of Export Demand Equations: A Cross-Country Analysis. *International Monetary Fund Staff Papers* 46, no. 3: 259–73.

Shambaugh, Jay. 2004. The Effect of Fixed Exchange Rates on Monetary Policy. *Quarterly Journal of Economics* 119, no. 1: 301–52.

Shintani, Mototsugu, Akiko Terada-Hagiwara, and Tomoyoshi Yabu. 2009. *Exchange Rate Pass-Through and Inflation: A Nonlinear Time Series Analysis*. Working Paper 09-W20. Nashville, TN: Department of Economics, Vanderbilt University.

Simonovska, Ina, and Michael Waugh. 2011. *The Elasticity of Trade: Estimates and Evidence*. NBER Working Paper 16796. Cambridge, MA: National Bureau of Economic Research.

Smets, Frank, and Rafael Wouters. 2007. Shocks and Frictions in US Business Cycles: A Bayesian DSGE Approach. *American Economic Review* 97, no. 3: 586–606.

Sprinkel, Beryl. 1991. Why Central Bank Intervention Can't Control Exchange Rates. *Futures* (Cedar Falls, IA), March 1.

Stiglitz, Joseph. 1998. Sound Finance and Sustainable Development in Asia. Keynote Address to the Asia Development Forum, Manila, March 12. Available at http://web.worldbank.org.

Stiglitz, Joseph, and Hirofumi Uzawa, eds. 1969. *Readings in the Modern Theory of Economic Growth*. Cambridge, MA: MIT Press.

Stock, James, and Mark Watson. 2003. Has the Business Cycle Changed? Evidence and Explanations. In *Monetary Policy and Uncertainty: Adapting to a Changing Economy*. Symposium sponsored by the Federal Reserve Bank of Kansas City, MO. Available at www.kc.frb.org.

Strauss-Kahn, Dominique. 2011. Nanjing and the New International Monetary System. iMFDirect—The IMF Blog. March 31.

Sveriges Riksbank. 1993. Inflation and Inflation Expectations in Sweden. Stockholm: Economics Department,Sveriges Riksbank (October).

Taylor, Alan. 2002. A Century of Purchasing-Power Parity. *Review of Economics and Statistics* 84, no. 1: 139–50.

Taylor, Alan, and Mark Taylor. 2004. The Purchasing Power Parity Debate. *Journal of Economic Perspectives* 18, no. 4: 135–58.

Taylor, John. 1993. Discretion versus Policy Rules in Practice. *Carnegie-Rochester Conference on Public Policy* 39: 195–214.

Taylor, John. 2000. Low Inflation, Pass-Through, and the Pricing Power of Firms. *European Economic Review* 44: 1389–1408.

Taylor, Mark, David Peel, and Lucio Sarno. 2001. Nonlinear Mean-Reversion in Real Exchange Rates: Toward a Solution to the Purchasing Power Parity Puzzles. *International Economic Review* 42, no. 4: 1015–42.

Tobin, James. 1977. How Dead Is Keynes? *Economic Inquiry* 15: 459–68.

Towbin, Pascal, and Sebastian Weber. 2011. *Limits of Floating Exchange Rates: The Role of Foreign Currency Debt and Import Structure.* IMF Working Paper WP/11/42. Washington: International Monetary Fund.

Truman, Edwin. 2003a. The Limits of Exchange Market Intervention. In *Dollar Overvaluation and the World Economy,* eds. C. Fred Bergsten and John Williamson. Washington: Institute for International Economics.

Truman, Edwin. 2003b. *Inflation Targeting in the World Economy.* Washington: Institute for International Economics.

Truman, Edwin. 2010. *Sovereign Wealth Funds: Threat or Salvation?* Washington: Peterson Institute for International Economics.

Verboven, Frank. 1996. International Price Discrimination in the European Car Market. *RAND Journal of Economics* 27, no. 2 (Summer): 240–268.

Vigfusson, Robert, Nathan Sheets, and Joseph Gagnon. 2009. Exchange Rate Pass-Through to Export Prices: Assessing Some Cross-Country Evidence. *Review of International Economics* 17, no. 1 (February): 17–33.

Volcker, Paul. 1995. The Quest for Exchange Rate Stability: Realistic or Quixotic? Speech at Senate House, University of London, November 29.

Volcker, Paul. 2000. The Exchange Rate System Needs a New Look. *The 2000 Annual Essay.* New York: Conference Board.

Welteke, Ernst. 2001. Russian-German Relations Facing New Monetary Challenges. Speech at the Finance Academy of the Russian Federation, Moscow, March 27. Available at http://cbr.ru/eng.

Williamson, John. 2007. *Reference Rates and the International Monetary System.* Policy Analyses in International Economics 82. Washington: Peterson Institute for International Economics.

Woodford, Michael. 2003. *Interest and Prices: Foundations of a Theory of Monetary Policy.* Princeton, NJ: Princeton University Press.

Woodford, Michael. 2006. Rules for Monetary Policy. *NBER Reporter: Research Summary* (Spring). Cambridge, MA: National Bureau of Economic Research.

Working, Holbrook. 1960. Note on the Correlation of First Differences of Averages in a Random Chain. *Econometrica* 28, no. 4: 916–18.

Yang, Jiawen. 1998. Pricing-to-Market in US Imports and Exports: A Time Series and Cross-Sectional Study. *Quarterly Review of Economics and Finance* 38, no. 4 (Winter): 843–61.

Yellen, Janet. 2011. The Federal Reserve's Asset Purchase Program. Speech at the Brimmer Policy Forum, Allied Social Science Associations Meeting, Denver, CO, January 8. Available at www.federalreserve.gov.

About the Authors

Joseph E. Gagnon, senior fellow since September 2009, was visiting associate director, Division of Monetary Affairs (2008–09) at the US Federal Reserve Board. Previously he served at the US Federal Reserve Board as associate director, Division of International Finance (1999–2008), and senior economist (1987–97). He has also served at the US Treasury Department (1994–95 and 1997–99) and has taught at the University of California's Haas School of Business (1990–91). He has published numerous articles in economics journals, including the *Journal of International Economics*, the *Journal of Monetary Economics*, the *Quarterly Journal of Economics*, and the *Journal of International Money and Finance*, and has contributed to several edited volumes. He received a BA from Harvard University in 1981 and a PhD in economics from Stanford University in 1987.

Marc Hinterschweiger has been a research analyst with the Peterson Institute since 2008. He is also a PhD candidate in economics at Ludwig-Maximilians University (LMU) in Munich, Germany. His research focuses on the transmission mechanism of monetary policy, asset prices, and financial crises. He previously worked at the Rhenish-Westfalian Institute for Economic Research (RWI) in Essen, Germany. He holds a BA in economics (2005) and a BA in international affairs (2006) from the University of St. Gallen, Switzerland. He earned a master's degree in public policy from Harvard University's Kennedy School of Government (2008), where he was a McCloy scholar, specializing in international trade and finance. He has been a member of the German National Academic Foundation (Studienstiftung des deutschen Volkes) since 2002.

Index

Other Publications from the Peterson Institute for International Economics

WORKING PAPERS

79 Trade Relations Between Colombia and the United States Jeffrey J. Schott, ed.
August 2006 ISBN 978-0-88132-389-4

80 Sustaining Reform with a US-Pakistan Free Trade Agreement
Gary Clyde Hufbauer and Shahid Javed Burki
November 2006 ISBN 978-0-88132-395-5

81 A US–Middle East Trade Agreement: A Circle of Opportunity?
Robert Z. Lawrence
November 2006 ISBN 978-0-88132-396-2

82 Reference Rates and the International Monetary System John Williamson
January 2007 ISBN 978-0-88132-401-3

83 Toward a US-Indonesia Free Trade Agreement Gary Clyde Hufbauer and Sjamsu Rahardja
June 2007 ISBN 978-0-88132-402-0

84 The Accelerating Decline in America's High-Skilled Workforce
Jacob Funk Kirkegaard
December 2007 ISBN 978-0-88132-413-6

85 Blue-Collar Blues: Is Trade to Blame for Rising US Income Inequality?
Robert Z. Lawrence
January 2008 ISBN 978-0-88132-414-3

86 Maghreb Regional and Global Integration: A Dream to Be Fulfilled
Gary Clyde Hufbauer and Claire Brunel, eds.
October 2008 ISBN 978-0-88132-426-6

87 The Future of China's Exchange Rate Policy Morris Goldstein and Nicholas R. Lardy
July 2009 ISBN 978-0-88132-416-7

88 Capitalizing on the Morocco-US Free Trade Agreement: A Road Map for Success
Gary Clyde Hufbauer and Claire Brunel, eds
September 2009 ISBN 978-0-88132-433-4

89 Three Threats: An Analytical Framework for the CFIUS Process Theodore H. Moran
August 2009 ISBN 978-0-88132-429-7

90 Reengaging Egypt: Options for US-Egypt Economic Relations Barbara Kotschwar and Jeffrey J. Schott
January 2010 ISBN 978-088132-439-6

91 Figuring Out the Doha Round
Gary Clyde Hufbauer, Jeffrey J. Schott, and Woan Foong Wong
June 2010 ISBN 978-088132-503-4

92 China's Strategy to Secure Natural Resources: Risks, Dangers, and Opportunities Theodore H. Moran
June 2010 ISBN 978-088132-512-6

93 The Implications of China-Taiwan Economic Liberalization
Daniel H. Rosen and Zhi Wang
January 2011 ISBN 978-0-88132-501-0

94 The Global Outlook for Government Debt over the Next 25 Years: Implications for the Economy and Public Policy
Joseph E. Gagnon with Marc Hinterschweiger
June 2011 ISBN 978-0-88132-621-5

95 A Decade of Debt
Carmen M. Reinhart and Kenneth S. Rogoff
September 2011 ISBN 978-0-88132-622-2

96 Carbon Abatement Costs and Climate Change Finance William R. Cline
July 2011 ISBN 978-0-88132-607-9

BOOKS

IMF Conditionality* John Williamson, ed.
1983 ISBN 0-88132-006-4

Trade Policy in the 1980s* William R. Cline, ed.
1983 ISBN 0-88132-031-5

Subsidies in International Trade*
Gary Clyde Hufbauer and Joanna Shelton Erb
1984 ISBN 0-88132-004-8

International Debt: Systemic Risk and Policy Response* William R. Cline
1984 ISBN 0-88132-015-3

Trade Protection in the United States: 31 Case Studies* Gary Clyde Hufbauer, Diane E. Berliner, and Kimberly Ann Elliott
1986 ISBN 0-88132-040-4

Toward Renewed Economic Growth in Latin America* Bela Balassa, Gerardo M. Bueno, Pedro Pablo Kuczynski, and Mario Henrique Simonsen
1986 ISBN 0-88132-045-5

Capital Flight and Third World Debt*
Donald R. Lessard and John Williamson, eds.
1987 ISBN 0-88132-053-6

The Canada-United States Free Trade Agreement: The Global Impact*
Jeffrey J. Schott and Murray G. Smith, eds.
1988 ISBN 0-88132-073-0

World Agricultural Trade: Building a Consensus* William M. Miner and Dale E. Hathaway, eds.
1988 ISBN 0-88132-071-3

Japan in the World Economy* Bela Balassa and Marcus Noland
1988 ISBN 0-88132-041-2

America in the World Economy: A Strategy for the 1990s* C. Fred Bergsten
1988 ISBN 0-88132-089-7

Managing the Dollar: From the Plaza to the Louvre* Yoichi Funabashi
1988, 2d ed. 1989 ISBN 0-88132-097-8

United States External Adjustment and the World Economy* William R. Cline
May 1989 ISBN 0-88132-048-X

Free Trade Areas and U.S. Trade Policy*
Jeffrey J. Schott, ed.
May 1989 ISBN 0-88132-094-3

Dollar Politics: Exchange Rate Policymaking in the United States* I. M. Destler and C. Randall Henning
September 1989 ISBN 0-88132-079-X

Latin American Adjustment: How Much Has Happened?* John Williamson, ed.
April 1990 ISBN 0-88132-125-7

The Future of World Trade in Textiles and Apparel* William R. Cline
1987, 2d ed. June 1999 ISBN 0-88132-110-9

Completing the Uruguay Round: A Results-Oriented Approach to the GATT Trade Negotiations*   Jeffrey J. Schott, ed.
September 1990   ISBN 0-88132-130-3
Economic Sanctions Reconsidered (2 volumes)
Economic Sanctions Reconsidered:
Supplemental Case Histories
Gary Clyde Hufbauer, Jeffrey J. Schott, and
Kimberly Ann Elliott
1985, 2d ed. Dec. 1990   ISBN cloth 0-88132-115-X
                          ISBN paper 0-88132-105-2
Economic Sanctions Reconsidered: History
and Current Policy   Gary Clyde Hufbauer,
Jeffrey J. Schott, and Kimberly Ann Elliott
December 1990   ISBN cloth 0-88132-140-0
                          ISBN paper 0-88132-136-2
Pacific Basin Developing Countries: Prospects
for the Future*   Marcus Noland
January 1991   ISBN cloth 0-88132-141-9
                          ISBN paper 0-88132-081-1
Currency Convertibility in Eastern Europe*
John Williamson, ed.
October 1991   ISBN 0-88132-128-1
International Adjustment and Financing: The
Lessons of 1985-1991*   C. Fred Bergsten, ed.
January 1992   ISBN 0-88132-112-5
North American Free Trade: Issues and
Recommendations*   Gary Clyde Hufbauer and
Jeffrey J. Schott
April 1992   ISBN 0-88132-120-6
Narrowing the U.S. Current Account Deficit*
Alan J. Lenz
June 1992   ISBN 0-88132-103-6
The Economics of Global Warming
William R. Cline
June 1992   ISBN 0-88132-132-X
US Taxation of International Income:
Blueprint for Reform   Gary Clyde Hufbauer,
assisted by Joanna M. van Rooij
October 1992   ISBN 0-88132-134-6
Who's Bashing Whom? Trade Conflict in High-
Technology Industries   Laura D'Andrea Tyson
November 1992   ISBN 0-88132-106-0
Korea in the World Economy*   Il SaKong
January 1993   ISBN 0-88132-183-4
Pacific Dynamism and the International
Economic System*   C. Fred Bergsten and
Marcus Noland, eds.
May 1993   ISBN 0-88132-196-6
Economic Consequences of Soviet
Disintegration*   John Williamson, ed.
May 1993   ISBN 0-88132-190-7
Reconcilable Differences? United States-Japan
Economic Conflict*   C. Fred Bergsten and
Marcus Noland
June 1993   ISBN 0-88132-129-X
Does Foreign Exchange Intervention Work?
Kathryn M. Dominguez and Jeffrey A. Frankel
September 1993   ISBN 0-88132-104-4
Sizing Up U.S. Export Disincentives*
J. David Richardson
September 1993   ISBN 0-88132-107-9

NAFTA: An Assessment
Gary Clyde Hufbauer and Jeffrey J. Schott, rev. ed.
October 1993   ISBN 0-88132-199-0
Adjusting to Volatile Energy Prices
Philip K. Verleger, Jr.
November 1993   ISBN 0-88132-069-2
The Political Economy of Policy Reform
John Williamson, ed.
January 1994   ISBN 0-88132-195-8
Measuring the Costs of Protection in the
United States   Gary Clyde Hufbauer and
Kimberly Ann Elliott
January 1994   ISBN 0-88132-108-7
The Dynamics of Korean Economic
Development*   Cho Soon
March 1994   ISBN 0-88132-162-1
Reviving the European Union*
C. Randall Henning, Eduard Hochreiter, and
Gary Clyde Hufbauer, eds.
April 1994   ISBN 0-88132-208-3
China in the World Economy
Nicholas R. Lardy
April 1994   ISBN 0-88132-200-8
Greening the GATT: Trade, Environment,
and the Future   Daniel C. Esty
July 1994   ISBN 0-88132-205-9
Western Hemisphere Economic Integration*
Gary Clyde Hufbauer and Jeffrey J. Schott
July 1994   ISBN 0-88132-159-1
Currencies and Politics in the United States,
Germany, and Japan   C. Randall Henning
September 1994   ISBN 0-88132-127-3
Estimating Equilibrium Exchange Rates
John Williamson, ed.
September 1994   ISBN 0-88132-076-5
Managing the World Economy: Fifty Years
after Bretton Woods   Peter B. Kenen, ed.
September 1994   ISBN 0-88132-212-1
Reciprocity and Retaliation in U.S. Trade
Policy   Thomas O. Bayard and
Kimberly Ann Elliott
September 1994   ISBN 0-88132-084-6
The Uruguay Round: An Assessment*
Jeffrey J. Schott, assisted by Johanna Buurman
November 1994   ISBN 0-88132-206-7
Measuring the Costs of Protection in Japan*
Yoko Sazanami, Shujiro Urata, and Hiroki Kawai
January 1995   ISBN 0-88132-211-3
Foreign Direct Investment in the United States,
3d ed.   Edward M. Graham and
Paul R. Krugman
January 1995   ISBN 0-88132-204-0
The Political Economy of Korea-United States
Cooperation*   C. Fred Bergsten and
Il SaKong, eds.
February 1995   ISBN 0-88132-213-X
International Debt Reexamined*
William R. Cline
February 1995   ISBN 0-88132-083-8
American Trade Politics, 3d ed.   I. M. Destler
April 1995   ISBN 0-88132-215-6

Global Trade in Services: Fear, Facts, and
Offshoring   J. Bradford Jensen
August 2011   ISBN 978-0-88132-601-7
NAFTA and Climate Change
Meera Fickling and Jeffrey J. Schott
September 2011   ISBN 978-0-88132-436-5
Eclipse: Living in the Shadow of China's
Economic Dominance   Arvind Subramanian
September 2011   ISBN 978-0-88132-606-2
Flexible Exchange Rates for a Stable World
Economy   Joseph E. Gagnon with
Marc Hinterschweiger
September 2011   ISBN 978-0-88132-627-7

SPECIAL REPORTS

1   Promoting World Recovery: A Statement
    on Global Economic Strategy*
    by 26 Economists from Fourteen Countries
    December 1982   ISBN 0-88132-013-7
2   Prospects for Adjustment in Argentina,
    Brazil, and Mexico: Responding to the
    Debt Crisis*   John Williamson, ed.
    June 1983   ISBN 0-88132-016-1
3   Inflation and Indexation: Argentina, Brazil,
    and Israel*   John Williamson, ed.
    March 1985   ISBN 0-88132-037-4
4   Global Economic Imbalances*
    C. Fred Bergsten, ed.
    March 1986   ISBN 0-88132-042-0
5   African Debt and Financing*
    Carol Lancaster and John Williamson, eds.
    May 1986   ISBN 0-88132-044-7
6   Resolving the Global Economic Crisis:
    After Wall Street*   by Thirty-three
    Economists from Thirteen Countries
    December 1987   ISBN 0-88132-070-6
7   World Economic Problems*
    Kimberly Ann Elliott and John Williamson,
    eds.
    April 1988   ISBN 0-88132-055-2
    Reforming World Agricultural Trade*
    by Twenty-nine Professionals from
    Seventeen Countries
    1988   ISBN 0-88132-088-9
8   Economic Relations Between the United
    States and Korea: Conflict or Cooperation?*
    Thomas O. Bayard and Soogil Young, eds.
    January 1989   ISBN 0-88132-068-4
9   Whither APEC? The Progress to Date and
    Agenda for the Future*
    C. Fred Bergsten, ed.
    October 1997   ISBN 0-88132-248-2
10 Economic Integration of the Korean
    Peninsula   Marcus Noland, ed.
    January 1998   ISBN 0-88132-255-5
11 Restarting Fast Track*   Jeffrey J. Schott, ed.
    April 1998   ISBN 0-88132-259-8
12 Launching New Global Trade Talks: An
    Action Agenda   Jeffrey J. Schott, ed.
    September 1998   ISBN 0-88132-266-0

13 Japan's Financial Crisis and Its Parallels to
    US Experience   Ryoichi Mikitani and
    Adam S. Posen, eds.
    September 2000   ISBN 0-88132-289-X
14 The Ex-Im Bank in the 21st Century: A
    New Approach   Gary Clyde Hufbauer and
    Rita M. Rodriguez, eds.
    January 2001   ISBN 0-88132-300-4
15 The Korean Diaspora in the World
    Economy   C. Fred Bergsten and
    Inbom Choi, eds.
    January 2003   ISBN 0-88132-358-6
16 Dollar Overvaluation and the World
    Economy   C. Fred Bergsten and
    John Williamson, eds.
    February 2003   ISBN 0-88132-351-9
17 Dollar Adjustment: How Far? Against
    What?   C. Fred Bergsten and
    John Williamson, eds.
    November 2004   ISBN 0-88132-378-0
18 The Euro at Five: Ready for a Global Role?
    Adam S. Posen, ed.
    April 2005   ISBN 0-88132-380-2
19 Reforming the IMF for the 21st Century
    Edwin M. Truman, ed.
    April 2006   ISBN 978-0-88132-387-0
20 The Long-Term International Economic
    Position of the United States
    C. Fred Bergsten, ed.
    May 2009   ISBN 978-0-88132-432-7

WORKS IN PROGRESS

Global Identity Theft: Economic and Policy
Implications   Catherine L. Mann
Globalized Venture Capital: Implications
for US Entrepreneurship and Innovation
Catherine L. Mann
Why Reform a Rich Country? Germany and the
Future of Capitalism   Adam S. Posen
Global Forces, American Faces: US Economic
Globalization at the Grass Roots
J. David Richardson
Banking System Fragility in Emerging
Economies   Morris Goldstein and Philip Turner
Private Rights and Public Problems: The
Global Economics of Intellectual Property in
the 21st Century   Keith Maskus
Inflation, Debt, and Exchange Rate Issues
Carmen M. Reinhart and Kenneth Rogoff
Launching a Comprehensive US Export
Strategy   Howard F. Rosen and
C. Fred Bergsten, editors
Sustaining China's Economic Growth after the
Global Financial Crisis   Nicholas Lardy
The Future of the World Trade Organization
Gary Clyde Hufbauer and Jeffrey J. Schott

**Australia, New Zealand,
and Papua New Guinea**
D. A. Information Services
648 Whitehorse Road
Mitcham, Victoria 3132, Australia
Tel: 61-3-9210-7777
Fax: 61-3-9210-7788
Email: service@dadirect.com.au
www.dadirect.com.au

India, Bangladesh, Nepal, and Sri Lanka
Viva Books Private Limited
Mr. Vinod Vasishtha
4737/23 Ansari Road
Daryaganj, New Delhi 110002
India
Tel: 91-11-4224-2200
Fax: 91-11-4224-2240
Email: viva@vivagroupindia.net
www.vivagroupindia.com

**Mexico, Central America, South America,
and Puerto Rico**
US PubRep, Inc.
311 Dean Drive
Rockville, MD 20851
Tel: 301-838-9276
Fax: 301-838-9278
Email: c.falk@ieee.org

Asia *(Brunei, Burma, Cambodia, China,
Hong Kong, Indonesia, Korea, Laos, Malaysia,
Philippines, Singapore, Taiwan, Thailand,
and Vietnam)*
East-West Export Books (EWEB)
University of Hawaii Press
2840 Kolowalu Street
Honolulu, Hawaii 96822-1888
Tel: 808-956-8830
Fax: 808-988-6052
Email: eweb@hawaii.edu

Canada
Renouf Bookstore
5369 Canotek Road, Unit 1
Ottawa, Ontario KlJ 9J3, Canada
Tel: 613-745-2665
Fax: 613-745-7660
www.renoufbooks.com

Japan
United Publishers Services Ltd.
1-32-5, Higashi-shinagawa
Shinagawa-ku, Tokyo 140-0002
Japan
Tel: 81-3-5479-7251
Fax: 81-3-5479-7307
Email: purchasing@ups.co.jp
*For trade accounts only. Individuals will find
Institute books in leading Tokyo bookstores.*

Middle East
MERIC
2 Bahgat Ali Street, El Masry Towers
Tower D, Apt. 24
Zamalek, Cairo
Egypt
Tel. 20-2-7633824
Fax: 20-2-7369355
Email: mahmoud_fouda@mericonline.com
www.mericonline.com

United Kingdom, Europe
*(including Russia and Turkey)***, Africa,
and Israel**
The Eurospan Group
c/o Turpin Distribution
Pegasus Drive
Stratton Business Park
Biggleswade, Bedfordshire
SG18 8TQ
United Kingdom
Tel: 44 (0) 1767-604972
Fax: 44 (0) 1767-601640
Email: eurospan@turpin-distribution.com
www.eurospangroup.com/bookstore

**Visit our website at:
www.piie.com
E-mail orders to:
petersonmail@presswarehouse.com**